KING ALFRED'S COLLEGE

Approaches to Sir Thomas Browne

Sir Thomas Browne (circa 1641–1650), by an unknown artist (detail). Courtesy National Portrait Gallery, London.

Approaches to Sir Thomas Browne

The Ann Arbor Tercentenary Lectures and Essays

Edited by C. A. Patrides

University of Missouri Press
Columbia & London, 1982

Library of Congress Cataloging in Publication Data
Main entry under title:

Approaches to Sir Thomas Browne.

Includes index.
Contents: Browne and Milton, the divided and the
distinguished / Balachandra Rajan—Sir Thomas
Browne and the ethics of knowledge / Leonard
Nathanson—Sir Thomas Browne and the labyrinth of
truth / John R. Knott, Jr.—[etc.]
    1. Browne, Thomas, Sir, 1605–1682—Criticism and
interpretation—Addresses, essays, lectures.
I. Brockbank, Philip.   II. Patrides, C. A.
PR3327.A9   1982   828'.409   81–13017
ISBN 0–8262–0357–4   AACR2

Passages from *Self-Consuming Artifacts: The Experience of
Seventeenth-Century Literature,* by Stanley Fish,
copyright © 1972 by the University of California Press,
reprinted by permission of the University of California Press.
The drawings by Paul Nash for *"Urne Buriall"* and
"The Garden of Cyrus" have been reproduced with
the permission of Cassell and Company, Ltd.

Preface

The ensuing fifteen essays have been collected to mark the occasion of the three hundredth anniversary of the death of Sir Thomas Browne in 1682. Six of these essays were also delivered as lectures at the University of Michigan in Ann Arbor, the entire effort made possible by a generous grant from the Horace H. Rackham School of Graduate Studies.

The pattern of the present work is not unlike that of the two series on Milton and Marvell.[1] Now, as before, the contributors were simply invited to address themselves to Sir Thomas Browne, their particular approach subject only to their interests. In consequence, the essays are here arranged not in the light of any communal theme but according to an order that coincidentally advances from general studies to particular ones. Only Dr. Hall's special contribution, commissioned expressly for this collection, is published last, in line with the parallel endeavors in the series on Milton and Marvell.

Acknowledgment is gratefully made to the University of California Press for permission to quote Stanley Fish's *Self-Consuming Artifacts* in the essay by Professor Warnke; to The National Gallery, London, and The Prado, Madrid, for permission to reproduce the two plates accompanying the contribution by Professor Roston; and to Cassell and Company, Ltd., of London for permission to reproduce the Paul Nash drawings accompanying the contribution by Professor Brockbank. But I should also like to express my gratitude to Eugene Feingold, Associate Dean of the University of Michigan's Horace H. Rackham School of Graduate Studies, for his enthusiastic commitment to the present enterprise; to my colleagues Professors William Ingram, Ejner Jensen, and Jay Robinson for their indispensable support and encouragement; to Professors William B. Hunter of the University of Houston and John R. Mulder of Drew University for their decisive vote of confidence at a crucial moment in our preparations for the press; and to Mr. Paul Thompson for the essential loan of his copy of the elegant volume illustrated by Paul Nash.

A more general acknowledgment must additionally be made to the custodians of the University of Michigan's Taubman Medical Library for advancing our knowledge of Browne through the Crummer Collection. The collection consists of over 1,000 medical books that, including 39 early editions and translations of *Religio Medici* in their original bindings, were bequeathed by Dr. Leroy Crummer (1872–1934). It has been sup-

---

1. *Approaches to "Paradise Lost": The York Tercentenary Lectures* (London: Edward Arnold, Ltd., and Toronto: University of Toronto Press, 1968), and *Approaches to Marvell: The York Tercentenary Lectures* (London and Boston: Routledge & Kegan Paul, Ltd., 1978), both edited by the present editor.

plemented by more than 250 secondary sources on Browne given to the
library by Professor Frank L. Huntley.

Abbreviations

Quotations from *Religio Medici, Hydriotaphia, The Garden of Cyrus, A
Letter to a Friend,* and *Christian Morals* are from C. A. Patrides's edition of
The Major Works (Penguin Books, 1977), hereafter abbreviated as *P.*
Quotations from Browne's other works, notably *Pseudodoxia Epidemica* and
the letters, are from Sir Geoffrey Keynes's edition of *The Works* (London:
Faber and Faber, Ltd., and Chicago: The University of Chicago Press,
1964), 4 vols., hereafter abbreviated as *K.*

C. A. P.
Ann Arbor, Mich.
October 1981

The Contributors

PHILIP BROCKBANK, Director, The Shakespeare Institute of The University of Birmingham

MARIE BOAS HALL, formerly Reader in the History of Science and Technology, Imperial College, London

FRANK L. HUNTLEY, Professor Emeritus of English Literature, The University of Michigan at Ann Arbor

D. W. JEFFERSON, Professor Emeritus of the School of English, The University of Leeds

JOHN R. KNOTT, JR., Professor and Chairman, Department of English, The University of Michigan at Ann Arbor

J. R. MULRYNE, Professor of English and Comparative Literary Studies, The University of Warwick

LEONARD NATHANSON, Professor of English Literature, Vanderbilt University

C. A. PATRIDES, G. B. Harrison Professor of English Literature, The University of Michigan at Ann Arbor

TED-LARRY PEBWORTH, Professor of English Literature, The University of Michigan at Dearborn

BALACHANDRA RAJAN, Senior Professor of English Literature, The University of Western Ontario

ROBIN ROBBINS, University Lecturer in English Literature and Tutorial Fellow, Wadham College, Oxford

MURRAY ROSTON, Professor of English Literature, Bar-Ilan University

RAYMOND B. WADDINGTON, Professor of English Literature, The University of Wisconsin–Madison

FRANK J. WARNKE, Professor and Head, Department of Comparative Literature, The University of Georgia

MICHAEL WILDING, Reader in English Literature, The University of Sydney

Contents

Browne and Milton:
The Divided and the Distinguished

Balachandra Rajan

In 1639 an eager and angry scholar-poet returned to England from a Continental journey to enlist vehemently in the wars of truth. He had foretold "the ruine of our corrupted Clergy then in their height."[1] Elated by this success, he hoped to become one of the mediating voices through which God spoke to his Englishmen. In three years he produced five pamphlets in which the false institutions of a delinquent clergy were held up to scorn against the dazzling clarity of appropriate biblical texts. The bishopry were by now in disarray, and the scholar-poet turned his energies to another chamber in the mansion of liberty. In 1643 he published a highly advanced pamphlet on divorce, the only one of his works so far to be immediately reprinted.

In the same year, 1643, a Norfolk doctor published the official edition of a work that had already appeared in two unauthorized editions. The English Civil War had begun the year before, but the doctor's book-lined study, which seemed the natural environment of the new publication, was well insulated from the sounds of gunfire. The doctor was only three years older than the scholar-poet, but he had already discarded a heresy (*P,* 66–67) that the younger man would be espousing twenty years later. Heresy for one was part of the exuberance of youth; for the other it was one of the gifts reserved for age, the lonely truth attained by the informed and tested understanding. The older man had already sown his intellectual wild oats, which he described, typically, as his "junior endeavors." He had tasted and dismissed the relish of being "a Peripatetick, a Stoick and an Academick." He now preferred, in Donne's phrase, to "doubt wisely" and to "stand like Janus in the field of knowledge" (*P,* 148).

The two identities will be obvious by now, and in the years to come they were to pursue their characteristic courses of embattled involvement and urbane withdrawal. In 1649 Milton published *The Tenure of Kings and Magistrates,* a heavily documented, tightly reasoned statement that might well serve as a model contribution to the *Quarterly Journal of Regicide.* In the

1. Headnote to *Lycidas.*

1

same year, Browne was preparing an enlarged and revised edition of *Pseudo-doxia Epidemica*. The existence of griffins, the varying descriptions of the horn of the unicorn, and the possibility of Adam and Eve having navels were among the matters discussed (*P*, 208, 214, 236). Regicide was not among the errors. In 1660, faced with the collapse of the Good Old Cause, Milton was frantically writing pamphlets aimed at delaying or deflecting the inevitable restoration of the monarchy. In 1658, Browne published *Hydriotaphia*, which fervently considers funeral rites but not those of a collapsing Puritanism. The postscript came in 1671. In that year Browne was knighted. Milton belligerently published a poem attacking the establishment that knighted Browne.

The careers of these two prose writers (one writing admittedly with his left hand) are both comprised within the same two decades but span them in entirely different ways. It would seem that the divided and distinguished worlds that the two men inhabited are incapable of being related. Yet the critic, that great amphibium, is invited to bridge these worlds. He can best do so by charting the different tenancies by the two writers of the common ground that they not infrequently share.

Religio Medici is not as distant from the wars of truth as it superficially seems to be. Its studied disengagements are a comment on the futility of those wars. Browne sees the church of his time as "decaied, impaired and fallen from its native beauty" but also as felicitously restored to its "primitive integrity" by "the careful and charitable hand of these times" (*P*, 65). It is therefore a voice to be trusted. In making this commitment, Browne is not so subservient to authority as to think that the truth needs to be certified by a Cranmer, a Latimer, or a Ridley.[2] In this he approaches Milton, but unlike Milton he restricts discretionary interpretation to "points indifferent." When Scripture speaks, the Church is Browne's "comment." When Scripture is silent and only the Church speaks, it does so with additional authority, providing not merely a guideline but a "Text" (*P*, 64). Milton would have found in this conformity some of the "peaceful sloth" that he later embodied in Belial (*Paradise Lost*, II, 227–28), but Browne has his warning to address to the future author of *Areopagitica*:

> Where we desire to be informed, 'tis good to contest with men above ourselves; but to confirme and establish our opinions, 'tis best to argue with judgements below our own. . . . Every man is not a proper Champion for Truth, nor fit to take up the Gantlet in the cause of Veritie; Many from the ignorance of these Maxims, and an inconsiderate zeale unto Truth, have too rashly charged the troopes, and remain as Trophees unto the enemies of Truth. (*P*, 65–66)

2. Donne, *Satyre* III, 93–98; Milton's "Custome Without Truth is but agednesse of Error" (*Complete Prose*, ed. Don M. Wolfe et al. [New Haven, 1953 ff.], 1:561) and his reference to the double tyranny of custom from without and blind affections within (ibid., 3:190) are not statements that Browne would have rejected, though he would of course have rejected their religious and political consequences for Milton.

For Browne the cause can be undermined by the fallibility of its champions. For Milton it is the nature of the cause itself that carries its champions to victory. Truth is strong next to the Almighty. It welcomes the encounter with the enemy. Indeed it is not fully itself as truth until it authenticates itself in combat. The structure of righteous understanding is built by the cumulative victories of truth, by its progressive disentanglement from the cunning resemblance of error. *Areopagitica* is fervent in its joining of the gathered truth and the gathered church, in its militant belief that an enlightened consensus can and must evolve from the ferment of religious debate. Browne, on the other hand, sees that "heads that are disposed unto Schisme and complexionally propense to innovation, are naturally indisposed for a community" (*P,* 69). The supremacy of individual judgment is likely to lead to fission rather than fusion. Sectarians will not be contented "with a general breach or dichotomie with their church." The dissidence of dissent[3] will continue till they "subdivide and mince themselves almost into Atomes" (ibid.). History is on Browne's side, even if one's heart is with Milton.

These different attitudes toward the defense and discernment of truth arise from different perceptions of the accessibility of truth to reason. For Browne the core of religious understanding is beyond and may be contrary to reason. He finds some pleasure in this prospect of contrariety: "me thinkes there be not impossibilities enough in Religion for an active faith" (*P,* 69). The wisdom of God re-creates human understanding, while the eternity of God confounds it (*P,* 72). To "beleave onely possibilities is not faith, but meere Philosophy" (*P,* 120). Browne may have described Tertullian's "Certum est quia impossibile est" as an "odde resolution" (*P,* 70), but he manifestly approved of it. He might also have endorsed Pomponazzi's statement, "I believe as a Christian what I cannot believe as a philosopher," though he may not have subscribed to the "double truth" implied in that proposition. Given a world that reason cannot organize and whose characteristics cannot be verified by the evidence of the senses, it is best to "follow the great wheele of the Church" rather than to insist on accommodating those celestial motions to the "epicycle" of one's "own braine" (*P,* 66). Milton, too, is prepared to admit that there is a boundary to reason, but his imagination is not excited by the corollary that logic-defying relationships must exist beyond that boundary. He suggests rather that the sacred places of the unknowable are to be approached with filial fear. "Solicit not thy thoughts with matters hid" is Raphael's counsel to Adam (*P. L.,* VIII, 167), and the language recognizes the dangerous fascination of what beckons beyond the allowed, of the hybris implicit in Aristotle's calm statement that the nature of man is to know (*Metaphysics,* 980a). Nevertheless, what lies beyond reason can and does make itself accessible to reason in all that appertains to man's relationship with his creator. It does so through a text that reason cannot originate but that reason is adequately equipped to

3. The phrase is used as a chapter heading in William Haller's *Liberty and Reformation in the Puritan Revolution* (New York, 1955), p. 216.

comprehend. Human understanding, Milton asserts, was created "fit and proportionable to Truth, the object and end of it, as the eye to the thing visible."[4] The later Milton would have been prepared to admit that original sin had somewhat impaired this intellectual eye, but he would also have maintained that the assistance of a grace to which all were free to turn could still enable that eye to perform its native function. The book of God was for Milton that "universall and publik Manuscript" that the book of nature was for Browne (*P,* 78). All that remained to be settled was the hermeneutics of the manuscript. To Milton in 1642 the text was unambiguously clear and luminously self-evident. When it became apparent that the text was armed with some of the obstinacies of literature, it remained possible to retreat to a position in which the structures of interpretation were to emerge authentically through debate among the devout. This is the position taken in *Areopagitica.* History, in stopping short at the confusion of sects rather than advancing to the emergence of structure, was not necessarily demonstrating the superior wisdom of institutional judgments. It was merely showing that the desirable, because of its nature, had to be difficult and that conformity promised the relief of stability. The great wheel follows a smoother course than do those organic gatherings that are exposed to subversion by the very forces that have caused them to cohere.

In their views of the relative status of the two books, that of God and that of nature, Browne and Milton at first seem to approach each other. Milton's statement that our understanding while in "this body" must found itself on "sensible things" and must arrive at a "knowledge of God and things invisible" by "orderly conning over the visible and inferior creature"[5] is one that we can think of Browne as endorsing. To the poet of Book III of *Paradise Lost,* blindness replaces the "book of knowledge" with a "universal blank" (lines 47–48). Browne would have understood the language of deprivation and the intensifying of that language in the next two lines with "Wisdom at one entrance quite shut out." Both Milton and Browne maintain the existence of what Browne calls "a Staire, or manifest Scale of creatures, rising not disorderly, or in confusion, but with a comely method and proportion" (*P,* 101). The phrase *comely method and proportion* refers to Browne's concept of a series of increasing intervals between the links in the chain, culminating presumably in the infinite interval between God and the highest of his creatures. Browne, like several Platonists, including Plato, is poised between continuity and discontinuity.[6] His deft arrangement of the chain enables both perceptions to be accommodated. Milton, on the other hand, characteristically minimizes the distance between man and the angels, making the difference between intuitive and discursive reason a difference

4. *Of Reformation,* in *Complete Prose,* 1:566.
5. *Of Education,* in *Complete Prose,* 2:368–69.
6. The Platonic strain in Browne is best brought out by Leonard Nathanson, *The Strategy of Truth: A Study of Sir Thomas Browne* (Chicago, 1967). For continuity and discontinuity in Milton, see my essay "Osiris and Urania," *Milton Studies* 13 (1979): 221–35.

of degree rather than of kind and foreseeing the likelihood of body evolving to spirit (V, 469–90).

The common ground, as elsewhere, covers instructive differences. For Milton, the lower book educates us in the reading of the higher; but it is the higher book that matters, since "the end then of learning is to repair the ruins of our first parents by regaining to know God aright."[7] Contemplation of the natural world and of our relationship to it may remind us of the divine image in ourselves; but the restoration of that image is only possible when we follow another book. For Browne, submission to the great wheel of the church surrenders the higher book to an institutional reading and leaves man free for "deliberate research" into the book of creation. That research is "the duty of a devout and learned admiration," "the debt of our reason wee owe unto God, and the homage wee pay for not being beasts" (*P*, 75). The book of the creatures is Browne's chosen text, and he reads the text persistently as literature, painting, and music. Nature is the art of God, the world is "Histrionical, and most Men live Ironically," the individual life is not history but poetry, the events of our lives are drawn "by a pencill that is invisible," and on the Day of Judgment "all the Actors must enter to compleate and make up the Catastrophe of this great peece" (*P*, 81, 114, 119, 153, 463; see also *P*, 375). Even the crudities of tavern music arouse Browne to "a profound contemplation of the first Composer" (*P*, 149). "The severe Schooles," he assures us, "shall never laugh me out of the Philosophy of *Hermes*, that this visible world is but a picture of the invisible" (*P*, 74). The language implies much—the constriction of the system-makers versus the exuberance of the real, and the abstraction of laughter versus the gaiety of truth. Browne's attention is to the language of the universal manuscript as much as to its propositions and above all to its status as metaphor and symbol. Nature provides to the student "in an ocular and visible object the types of his resurrection" (*P*, 121). Music furnishes us with "an Hieroglyphicall and shadowed lesson of the whole world, and Creatures of God" (*P*, 149–50). If the visible world is a picture of the invisible, it is a picture in which "things are not truely, but in equivocall shapes" (*P*, 74) that presumably require a skilled interpreter. Even in interpreting the higher book, literal readings result in the "grosse and duller sort of heresies." By not attaining "the deutoroscopy and second intention of the words," the reader leaves out of account "their superconsequencies, coherencies, figures, or tropologies" (*P*, 175). If Browne were alive today he would discern more than seven types of ambiguity.

With many good poems the end is in the beginning. In fact, the end precedes the beginning when the omniscient author writes out the poem according to his fore-conceit,[8] as the omniscient author of the arch-poem created it "Answering his great idea" (*P. L.*, VII, 557). When the poem is to

---

7. *Of Education*, in *Complete Prose*, 2:366–67.
8. The word is Sidney's. For elaboration see S. K. Heninger, *Touches of Sweet Harmony* (San Marino, Calif., 1976).

be composed of the ingredients of a historical rather than a fictive world, the omniscient author must also be omnipotent. Browne is attracted to the idea of the divine books as controlled works of literature in which pattern is everywhere manifest and in which all that happens is an unfolding from the origins. "In the seed of a Plant to the eyes of God, and to the understanding of man, there exists, though in an invisible way, the perfect leaves, flowers, and fruit thereof" (*P*, 124). As Browne proceeds to elevate the thought and to write it larger, it assumes a singular eloquence of paradox. "The world was before the Creation, and at an end before it had a beginning; and thus was I dead before I was alive, though my grave be *England*, my dying place was Paradise, and *Eve* miscarried of mee before she conceiv'd of *Cain*" (*P*, 132). Carried to its ultimate height the thought becomes one of the most powerful literary statements of the aesthetics of predestination:

> that terrible terme *Predestination*, which hath troubled so many weake heads to conceive, and the wisest to explaine, is in respect to God no prescious determination of our estates to come, but a definitive blast of his will already fulfilled, and at the instant that he first decreed it; for to his eternitie which is indivisible, and altogether, the last Trumpe is already sounded, the reprobates in the flame, and the blessed in Abraham's bosome. (*P, 72–73*)

The simultaneous present, the abolition of space and time in the quintessential unity of eternity, is also placed before us by Milton, as he contemplates that empyrean "High throned above all highth" from which God views "His own works and their works" (*P. L.,* III, 57–59). "In eternity there is no distinction of Tenses," Browne tells us (*P*, 72), and Milton's God enacts this recognition by recounting the Fall of Man in all three tenses. The motives behind this convergence of understanding are once again instructively different. For Browne, foreknowledge seems an insufficient force to form and maintain the simultaneous present. The unity of the divine poem, the actualization of latency, are perceptions so imperative that a "definitive blast" of will must drive them forward. Browne uses the word *blast* at one other crucial point in *Religio Medici*, when describing the Creation (*P*, 105). In both cases the Last Judgment is embedded in the anticipations of the language, joining the beginning and the end, with the imperative energy of "blast" seeming to compound the cementing force. Milton, on the other hand, uses the simultaneous present to stage a drama of heroic choice and to apply to that choice the maximum weight of consequence. The heresy that the older Milton shares with the younger Browne concerns the same literary purpose. To maximize the heroism of the exemplary choice, it is necessary to elevate its cost. The total death foreseen by mortalism raises that cost beyond that implied in other views of the atonement.

Browne's submission to the great wheel of his Church invited him to be a Calvinist, though he does point out, intriguingly, that he does not "approve all in the Synod of *Dort*" (*P*, 64). Milton may well have been a Calvinist at the time *Religio Medici* was published. His preference for the epicycle of his own brain eventually made him an Arminian, but Arminianism, which was ceasing to be a heresy by the time *Paradise Lost* was published, has important poetic consequences. Milton's universe of choice rests on the precarious gift of freedom at its center. Arminianism or something like it is necessary to maintain that freedom in a fallen world. The positing of a central indeterminacy does mean that, for Milton, the providential poem is fundamentally open-ended. It maintains itself as a poem by constantly combating its own subversiveness, the tragic propensity built into its core. Milton avoids underlining the divine omniscience too heavily, and in fact it is the reader rather than Adam and Eve who is advised of that omniscience. Milton's interest is rather in the poem as performance and in its freedom to become what the performers make of it. Providential regulation does not fully prescribe the internalities of the artwork, though it does insure that it remains a work of art. Browne, on the other hand, sees the providential poem as determinist, as definitively settled from its initiation. The divine nature might write a more open poem, but that poem would be aesthetically inferior and has therefore not been written.

Given Milton's commitment to right action in a world of cunning resemblances and his several dramatizations of education through experience, one might expect his approach to the natural world to be empirical. He does indeed counsel us not to wander from the "safe leading" of nature; but he describes that "leading" as "regenerate reason."[9] Browne, in a celebrated passage, points to the inability of reason to "display the visible and obvious effects of nature." It is educated by this failure "to stoope unto the lure of faith" (*P*, 71), thus displaying its characteristic arrogance even in its humiliation. Elsewhere, Browne refers to the element of divinity in those "workes of nature, which seem to puzle reason" (*P*, 110). Even Aristotle has frequently confessed "the reason of man too weake for the workes of nature" (*P*, 147). These disavowals of reason[10] indicate Browne's approach to the natural world, which is that of the poet-scientist scrutinizing the text of the universal and public manuscript for the revelatory nuances of its language. *The Garden of Cyrus* is hardly a rationalist document. Rather, it partakes of that "mysticall method . . . bred up in the Hieroglyphicall Schooles of the Egyptians" of which Moses, according to Browne, was also a practitioner (*P*, 104).

Browne's skepticism is similarly directed to restraining the excessive claims of reason. It is not the skepticism of methodical denial, in which a question mark is placed at the end of every affirmation so that the basis of the skepticism is laid in a failure to make the commitment to faith. Characteristically, for Browne the time for skepticism comes when systems of rational

9. *An Apology etc.*, in *Complete Prose*, 1:874.
10. Browne's language in these disavowals is close to Bacon's: "The subtlety of nature is greater many times over than the subtlety of the senses and understanding" (*Novum Organum*, I, 10). "The understanding, unless directed and assisted, is a thing unequal and quite unfit to contend with the obscurity of things" (ibid., I, 21). Bacon, of course, is not fascinated by the "lure of faith."

thought have had their day and when the mind recognizes that the effects of nature are too complex and too rich to be displayed in deductive arrangements. The natural world can be known, but not by the logical intellect. Browne seeks the poet's understanding, the right metaphor in an analogical universe, rather than the fideist's commitment. His opposition is to the Idols of the Theater,[11] to systems that inhibit our right to engage ourselves fully with the complexity of the actual. Janus, whose patronage Browne seeks, is, we must remember, the God of doors. The door of the actual gives entry into more than one room, while Philosophy holds all in the one room of its system.

In *The Garden of Cyrus,* Browne seeks to "erect generalities" and to "disclose unobserved proprieties, not only in the vegetable shop, but the whole volume of nature" (*P,* 386). The "delightful Truths, confirmable by sense and ocular Observation," yielded by this method seem to him "the surest path, to trace the Labyrinth of Truth." Discursive inquiry and rational conjecture "may leave handsome gashes and flesh-wounds" on the body of error, but "mortal blows" are only possible when the poet-empiricist enters the fray. In the preface to *Pseudodoxia Epidemica,* Browne notes that "we find no open tract, or constant manuduction" in the labyrinth and are therefore "fain to wander in the America and untravelled parts of Truth" (*P,* 167). He makes us aware less of the perils of the labyrinth than of the rewarding complexities that attend our journey through it. It is the proper image for the skeptic, stressing the sinuous movement of understanding, which recoils on and encircles itself, rather than the linear progress of "rational conjecture."

Milton speaks of the wandering mazes in which the angels lose themselves (*P. L.,* II, 557–61), the "surging maze" of the serpent tempting Eve (IX, 499), and the mazes through which Adam is led by the thread of grace to the admission of his responsibility for the Fall (IX, 829–33). The emphasis here is on the treacheries and deceptions of the maze. But there are also the "mazes intricate" of the "mystical dance" of the angels in heaven (V, 620–22) and the "mazy error" (IV, 239) of the brooks in paradise, where semantic innocence seems to anticipate the tragic mutations that language, like reality, can hold within itself. In a fallen world we find ourselves in the maze as the Lady in "Comus" finds herself in the dark wood. Our passage through the maze is a test to be undergone before mazyness can reassume its innocent or celestial meaning, but we need not expect to be guided in that passage by "delightful truths" and "unobserved proprieties."

Milton's conventional image of truth is the hill—the "guarded mount" of *Lycidas,* the hill on which Adam learns the consequences of his own destructiveness, and the hill on which the "greater man" makes himself. The hill is the correct image for the rational mind, with the field of understanding and relationship becoming more spacious as the ascent proceeds. But Milton also has an empiricist's image of truth— that of the torn body of Osiris put

11. *Novum Organum,* I, 64.

together by a community of believers. The finding of what we know not, by virtue of what we know, represents a step-by-step advance in which structure emerges from the gathering of fact. But the movement, though experiential, is not skeptical. It is dominated by the prospect of a "homogeneal and proportional" entity that will be approached steadily by enlightened reason. It is a movement, moreover, that engages itself with the religious and not the natural world.[12]

Milton and Browne may both be tolerationists, but Milton wishes to defend the seeking mind of the believer from the prescriptive force of the great wheel of the Church. He also enters debate with the unfaltering confidence that today's epicycle can be tomorrow's wheel. Browne's disposition is irenic: "I could never divide my selfe from any man upon the difference of an opinion" (*P,* 65). More disarmingly, Browne states that he is "of a constitution so generall, that it consorts and sympathizeth with all things" (*P,* 133). Nevertheless, the two writers are of one mind at more than one point. "They that endeavour to abolish vice," Browne says, "destroy also vertue, for contraries, though they destroy one another, are yet the life of one another" (*P,* 140). Milton's language is similar: "that which purifies us is triall, and triall is by what is contrary." "Look how much we thus expell of sin, so much we expell of virtue; for the matter of them both is the same; remove that and yet remove them both alike."[13] Browne, with an exuberance unusual in *Christian Morals,* which is not the most vivacious of his tracts, affirms that "Many positions seem quodlibetically constituted, and like a *Delphian* Blade will cut on both sides. Some Truths seem almost Falshoods, and some Falshoods almost Truths; wherein Falshood and Truth seem almost equilibriously stated and but a few grains of distinction to bear down the ballance" (*P,* 437–38). Milton, too, writes of the "cunning resemblance" between truth and error,[14] and where Browne talks of the "equivocall shapes" (*P,* 76) in which the visible counterfeits the invisible, Milton observes, as if in response, "Yet it is not impossible that she [Truth] may have more shapes than one, What else is all that rank of things indifferent, wherein Truth may be on this side, or the other, without being unlike herself?"[15] The ambiguities of truth are restricted to "things indifferent," but the enlargement of indifferency was a trend among dissenters, and the "rank" in any case covers nearly all of natural philosophy. Within that large field, Milton might be content not to divide himself from another man "upon the difference of an opinion" and to recognize that by tomorrow he might think so too (*P,* 65, 138). On more fundamental matters, Milton

---

12. In making use of the proverbial image of truth as lying at the bottom of a well (*P,* 184, 439), Browne refers twice to the "exantlation of truth" and suggests that in our time we cannot hope to behold "that obscured Virgin" even "half out of the pit." This awareness of truth as something lost and only gradually retrieved is shared with Milton's image of Osiris.

13. *Areopagitica,* in *Complete Prose,* 2:515, 527.

14. Ibid., 2:514.

15. Ibid., 2:563.

might have felt that charity was less to be admired than clarity, even if clarity could be attained only through the uncharitableness of debate. In saying this we must moderate our finding by the younger poet's statement that the house of God is meant to accommodate and indeed may be adorned by "brotherly dissimilitudes."[16] Much depends upon the extent of that adjective.

Browne refers often to the image of Janus not simply in connection with the problem of knowledge but also as a reminder that there is another side to every event.[17] In his main reference, which we have already twice traversed, he says that he has "runne through all sorts [of philosophers] yet find no rest in any." Our "first studies & *junior* endeavors" may "stile us Peripateticks, Stoicks, or Academicks," but "the wisest heads prove at last almost all scepticks" (*P*, 148). Much is cleverly implied here—the dissociation of skepticism from youthful inconoclasm, the addiction of young minds to masterful solutions, the false peace of mind promised by the securities of systematic thought, and the true peace conferred by open-mindedness before the complexities of the actual. The word *rest* points deftly to the claims of Epicureans and Stoics and to the "rest" paradoxically offered by skepticism's apparent restlessness.[18] Browne thinks of skepticism not as a philosophy but as an attitude, a resistance to systematic arrangements that should be attained by passing through and discarding those arrangements. Those who have not lived long enough and fully enough have not qualified themselves to be skeptics. Having "little behind them," they "are but *Januses* of one Face, and know not singularities enough to raise Axioms of this World" (*P*, 465). The turn of thought is deft here. Singularities resist axioms at least as much as they raise them; but generalizations, to be valid, must come to terms with the obstinacies of the singular, as Browne does in considering monstrosities in nature in *Religio Medici* (*P*, 80–81).

"Peace of thought" is the climax of Adam's education in *Paradise Lost* (XII, 558), and "calm of mind" is the climax of the chorus's education in *Samson Agonistes* (1758). The language may seem to echo Browne's "rest," but the "rest" is the result in one poem of a long course of instruction in the rhythms of history and in the other of the disclosure brought about by the lightning of a "great event." There is nothing Janus-faced about the Miltonic settlement. "Beyond is all abyss," Adam admits to Michael (XII, 555), but

16. Ibid., 2:555.
17. See, for example, *P*, 446, 450, 455, 465. At one point Browne says that "In Bivious Theorems and *Janus*-faced Doctrines," "Virtuous considerations" should "state the determination" (*P*, 450). It is the "Luciferous" side of opinions that should be embraced, and we should avoid choosing the "dark hemisphere" for contemplation.
18. In the *Outlines of Pyrrhonism*, I, iv, Sextus Empiricus defines skepticism as the "ability to place in antithesis, in any manner whatsoever, appearances and judgments and thus—because of the equality of force in the objects and arguments opposed— to come first of all to a suspension of judgment and then to mental tranquillity" (*Scepticism, Man, and God: Selections from the Major Writings of Sextus Empiricus*, ed. Philip P. Hallie [Middletown, Conn., 1964], pp. 32–33).

in the area of light, however restricted, the shapes of understanding and the answers are clear. Browne approves of those "who keep the temple of Janus shut by peacable and quiet tempers" (*P*, 466). Milton characteristically wishes the doors to be open: "The Temple of *Janus* with his two *controversal* faces might now not unsignificantly be set open. And though all the winds of doctrine were let loose to play upon the earth, so Truth be in the field, we do injuriously by licencing and prohibiting to misdoubt her strength."[19] Since the doors of the temple of Janus were open in times of war, Milton's commitment is clearly to the wars of truth, the unrestricted turbulence of the winds of doctrine. The purpose is not ambiguity, but the removal of ambiguity. Of the two faces, one is to be chosen.

To make this contrast is not to end the affair. After Browne has declared his approval of standing "like *Janus* in the field of knowledge," he proceeds as follows: "I have therefore one common and authentick Philosophy I learned in the Schooles, whereby I discourse and satisfie the reason of other men, another more reserved and drawne from experience, whereby I content mine owne" (*P*, 148). This is indeed a tantalizing admission. Is the skepticism part of Browne's public stance (it is, after all, a philosophy "learned in the Schooles" that the previous sentence has certified as "authentick"), or is it a characteristic of the "reserved" self? Which of the two selves is writing *Religio Medici*? Are we being advised, despite the tone of genial self-disclosure that dominates the work, that privacy has its province, that writers are unavoidably double-faced, that the book speaks to its author as it cannot to its audience? When Milton wrote *Paradise Lost* he was also writing *De doctrina christiana*. The public face of the poem stood by itself for over a century before the other side of the door was revealed. We now know what the poem meant to its author and to the enlightened consensus that Milton hoped history would bring about. Or perhaps we do not yet know. Browne may be suggesting that we do not.

19. *Complete Prose*, 2:561.

Sir Thomas Browne
and the Ethics of Knowledge

Leonard Nathanson

In the wars of truth that marked the seventeenth century, Sir Thomas Browne played the role of a double agent. His intellectual loyalties, though clearly announced, are difficult to categorize. Everywhere in his writings there is evidence of a dedication to scientific observation, to disclosing nature's secrets, and to unraveling apparent contradictions. But his conviction that nature is no mere series of phenomena but a vast network of meanings—Platonic and Christian in their final implications—appears even stronger. Browne's divergent commitments to Baconian experimentation and to religious mystery coexist in paradoxical balance, most readers agree, with the latter encompassing and even justifying the former. My own study of Browne, *The Strategy of Truth* (1967), took his epistemological pluralism as the groundwork for examining his major works. While these assumptions and the conclusions to which they led remain essentially intact, I find as I read Browne now an important shift of emphasis. The competing strategies of truth—the conflicts among faith, reason, empiricism, rationalism, authority—seem less engaging. Instead, I find increasingly that Browne focuses the reader's attention upon what I would call the ethics of knowledge.

It may be that the familiar issues of seventeenth-century epistemology, as offered by T. S. Eliot in the terms of literary criticism and as posed in our time by Basil Willey, are now resolved for us. Not that the relative strengths and weaknesses, uses and misuses, of the various ways of knowing can ever be really settled. Such basic questions in intellectual history and in the history of sensibility can never be answered with finality, though it is possible, probably inevitable, to reach after a time a settled view of their complexities and tensions. After a period of intense exploration and controversy, the pressing questions of truth or value that challenge an age begin to appear outworn and are put aside in favor of new questions that have become more urgent.

Accordingly, I propose to turn from Browne's explicit concern with the methodology of knowledge to his implicit involvement with the ethics of knowledge. By this I mean the validation of intellectual activity itself, as distinct from discriminations of the relative reliability of competing

12

methods. These two lines of interest do merge, since a thinker's views of the ends and the means of knowledge are bound to exert a mutual influence. We can say of Bacon, for example, that he argued for the prime legitimacy of empirical thought because he believed that the proper focus of human reason was to increase man's practical control of the natural and social world in which he lived. Browne, on the other hand, while fascinated by direct observation and experimentation, thought of intellectual endeavors as fulfilling a duty that man owed God for having been endowed with reason. Man's special gift of reason impelled him to glorify God through the pursuit of knowledge as well as through religious worship; this was a favorite idea of Browne's that inspired some of his most memorable passages.

Somewhere between the ultimate purpose of knowledge and the means propounded to reach it there lies a vast area of ethical issues about the value of knowledge. For the individual who undertakes to pursue the question of value, the actual enterprise, unlike its telos, is not likely to have a single definition. Instead, the individual thinker is likely to confront a series of definitions that may be opposed, or complementary, or hierarchical. The issue for the philosophical writer or the poet accordingly becomes more one of emphasis and priority than one of single-minded commitment.

As a physician, Browne was highly sensitive to the utilitarian value of knowledge, specifically to the biological and medical applications of the wide range of natural principles and curiosities that engaged his study. On the other hand, no man could respond more eloquently than Bacon to the elegance of knowledge, not only to the practical possibilities but also to the sheer aesthetic delight of understanding the world. Both of these imaginative minds were conscious of varying goals and values for knowledge as well as of competing methods. But it is in this former area that the questions that make for literary discourse are more likely to arise.

No less than epistemology in the usual sense, the ethics of knowledge represents a philosophical issue with a long historical continuity. An essay celebrating the three hundredth anniversary of the death of Sir Thomas Browne would hardly be the occasion for tracing that history, but one may note that the question is at least as old as Socratic humanism. The refocusing of philosophical inquiry upon the conduct of human life, away from the previous concern of the pre-Socratics with the nature of phenomena, marks the first chapter of that history. This refocusing established many of the basic questions about what human reason is for, what its primary object as well as its best means of operation should be. To ask what human reason is for is to ask several interrelated questions: What are the proper objects of reason? From what perspective should reason undertake the study of these objects? And most important of all, toward what end does reason pursue knowledge? Is that end or purpose inherent in the object? In the method of the pursuit? In the total existence of the pursuer? Or in the essence of the pursuer as distinct from any single faculty or activity? Further, may some quests for knowledge be validated in purely prudential terms? Or does every endeavor require, or at least invite, justification in the humanistic terms of self-knowledge or in the religious terms of knowledge of the creator?

The terms in which Browne grasped these issues were very much those that the seventeenth century inherited from previous centuries. It was assumed that the question of human knowledge, like any other human enterprise, could not be viewed apart from the issue of life's final concern: the drama of salvation. The traditional Christian answer found its fullest and most influential treatment in Augustine, who saw man as a being who sought knowledge with his natural and rational powers and whose soul aimed at salvation. The powers with which man uniquely among the creatures was endowed could not, Augustine believed, be inimical to the Christian's prime goal of salvation. Accordingly, Augustine defended the systematic understanding of the nature of things, which he called *scientia*, in the face of an antirational pietism on the part of some of the early fathers of the church who had rejected the learning of the classical world, which they felt to be irrelevant to the Christian. Augustinian orthodoxy embraced *scientia* as a legitimate activity of the Christian insofar as it could lead to *sapientia*, the knowledge of this world and of the next that is true wisdom.

In what became the orthodox view, knowledge of this world is a definite, though not an absolute, good. *Scientia*, whatever proportion of man's attention it may properly absorb, is not a self-validating activity. It is the epistemological basis of scientific knowledge and of technological progress, of things that are of great use to man, but not of what speaks to man's purpose in the final design. *Sapientia*, the wisdom that relates man to God, to his supernatural destiny in the next world, is also the form of wisdom necessary for self-knowledge, for the humanistic enterprise as it can be pursued within a Christian context. The distinction figures again and again in important ways in the literature of the period. It has often struck modern readers as pietistically anti-intellectual or as obscurantist, though expressed by men of the widest learning and with the greatest curiosity about new currents of thought. Donne offers as good an example as any in his *Second Anniversary* when he speaks contemptuously of man's epistemological status in this world:

> Poore soule, in this thy flesh what dost thou know?
> Thou know'st thy selfe so little, as thou know'st not,
> How thou didst die, nor how thou wast begot.
> Thou neither know'st, how thou at first cam'st in,
> Nor how thou took'st the poyson of mans sinne.
> Nor dost thou, (though thou know'st, that thou art so)
> By what way thou art made immortall, know.
> Thou art too narrow, wretch, to comprehend
> Even thy selfe: yea though thou wouldst but bend
> To know thy body. Have not all soules thought
> For many ages, that our body is wrought
> Of Ayre, and Fire, and other Elements?

And now they thinke of new ingredients,
And one Soule thinkes one, and another way
Another thinkes, and 'tis an even lay. (lines 254–68)

But the unavoidable lack of finality in man's knowledge—unavoidable precisely because knowledge progresses—is used by Donne as a reason to deride this knowledge for its pointlessness:

Wee see in Authors, too stiffe to recant,
A hundred controversies of an Ant;
And yet one watches, starves, freeses, and sweats,
To know but Catechismes and Alphabets
Of unconcerning things, matters of fact;
How others on our stage their parts did Act;
What *Caesar* did, yea, and what *Cicero* said.
Why grasse is greene, or why our blood is red,
Are mysteries which none have reach'd unto.
In this low forme, poore soule, what wilt thou doe? (lines 281–90)

By "unconcerning things, matters of fact," Donne calls into question the validity of the quest for *scientia,* not merely the dubiousness of the results. Donne's profoundest skepticism about *scientia* does not rise from the fact that knowledge is subject to constant revision and even reversal; this consideration excites and pleases the intellectual adventurer in him. The full measure of his skepticism arises from his conviction that *scientia* is not really relevant to man as man, that it is not a worthy human concern with value of its own:

When wilt thou shake off this Pedantery,
Of being taught by sense, and Fantasie?
Thou look'st through spectacles; small things seeme great
Below; But up unto the watch-towre get,
And see all things despoyl'd of fallacies:
Thou shalt not peepe through lattices of eyes,
Nor heare through Labyrinths of eares, nor learne
By circuit, or collections to discerne.
In heaven thou straight know'st all, concerning it,
And what concernes it not, shalt straight forget. (lines 291–300)

Donne criticizes promiscuous curiosity because it is a misplacement of intellectual energy. The crucial issue becomes the relevance of knowledge to man and consequently the distrust of an idolatrous obsession with knowledge as a self-validating, ever-expanding system of abstraction. The folly of sacrificing peculiarly human values for the sake of such a scientific edifice is clear whether one defines these values in the humanistic terms of the good life in this world or in the religious terms of salvation in the next. The most devastating assault upon abstract cerebral activity divorced from any human good was Swift's great satire of Laputa in *Gulliver's Travels,* a critique posed in humanistic rather than religious terms, yet carrying the larger implications of the Augustinian ethic of knowledge into an age in which the Augustinian theology and world view were quite forgotten.

In the age of Donne and Browne and Milton, the ethics of knowledge was inextricably bound up with the awareness that human curiosity can never be satisfied nor ever possess certainty. The assurance of the soul's total illumination in the next world should not be read, then, as mere Christian resignation, as a pious undercutting of intellectual effort as "vanity, vanity, all is vanity." What Donne underlines so insistently is that the distinction between the soul's pursuit of "concerning" and of "unconcerning" things corresponds to the difference between *scientia* and *sapientia,* between narrow knowledge grasped though specialized techniques and the wisdom that yields only to the total application of man's rational and spiritual powers. Donne in the *Second Anniversary,* Browne in the *Religio Medici,* and Milton in *Paradise Lost* are all painfully conscious that what man wants to know often bears little proportion to what he is capable of knowing and even less to what, in relation to life's main issues, he really needs to know. This ethic of knowledge and its accompanying critique of the limits of knowledge are mutually supportive and illuminating, though each reader must determine for himself where the emphasis lies for the particular writer.

Browne tends to consider these questions so as to emphasize their close conjunction. Characteristically, he expresses the issue as an insoluble paradox, but it is a paradox that, even more characteristically, he is quite comfortable with:

> Wisedome is his [God's] most beauteous attribute, no man can attaine unto it, yet *Solomon* pleased God when hee desired it. Hee is wise because hee knowes all things, and hee knoweth all things because he made them all, but his greatest knowledg is in comprehending that he made not, that is himselfe. And this is also the greatest knowledge in man. (*P, 74*)

These ideas recur again and again in Browne, though never in quite the same terms. The best-known presentation of the issue in the *Religio* takes on rather a different meaning from the one usually attached to it if we read it in the context I have suggested.

> I have runne through all sorts, yet finde no rest in any, though our first studies & *junior* endeavors may stile us Peripateticks, Stoicks, or Academicks, yet I perceive the wisest heads prove at last, almost all Scepticks, and stand like *Janus* in the field of knowledge. I have therefore one common and authentick Philosophy I learned in the Schooles, whereby I discourse and satisfie the reason of other men, another more reserved and drawne from experience, whereby I content mine owne. *Solomon* that complained of ignorance in the height of knowledge, hath not onely humbled my conceits, but discouraged my

endeavours. There is yet another conceit that hath sometimes made me shut my bookes; which tels mee it is a vanity to waste our dayes in the blind pursuit of knowledge, it is but attending a little longer, and wee shall enjoy that by instinct and infusion which we endeavour at here by labour and inquisition: it is better to sit downe in a modest ignorance, & rest contented with the naturall blessing of our owne reasons, then buy the uncertaine knowledge of this life, with sweat and vexation, which death gives every foole gratis, and is an accessary of our glorification. (*P,* 147–48)

Browne contrasts the schools of formal philosophy that he employs as an intellectual, speaking to his peers, with the more private and personal habits of thinking that he has drawn from his own experience and that answer his own concerns. It is clear that he suspects there may be something factitious about the "authentick," formal philosophies in which men argue with one another, that the results are not commensurate with the pride and dexterity of learning with which the philosophical arguments are handled. Coming to rest in the antischool of the Skeptics, he finds the truths he can confirm from his own experience to be both more certain and more relevant to him than the products of the public systems of thought that are the inventions of others. Skepticism about *scientia* becomes for Browne a springboard for greater reliance on direct experience, in both the existential and the intuitive sense. He expresses a position in this passage that links him, on one hand, with the Montaigne of the late *Essays,* often read as a precursor of existentialism, and, on the other, with the orthodoxy of Augustine that focuses upon the wisdom relevant to man's final destiny. Early in the *Religio,* Browne announces a ringing slogan for trusting the experience of his own reason: "I perceive every mans owne reason is his best *Oedipus*" (*P,* 66).

The assumed ease and the completeness of the knowledge available in the next world cast a shadow on the rational efforts—admirable and proper as they may be—that are expended in this world. Again, the superiority of the certain over the dubious, of the concerning over the unconcerning, parallels the basic superiority of *sapientia* over *scientia.* The questions about knowledge that lie at the center of the *Second Anniversary* take on, as one might expect, an even more specifically Christian emphasis in Donne's sermons. As Browne does in Part II of the *Religio,* Donne also links the ethical value and the wise use of knowledge to the relative difficulty and validity of different levels of knowledge:

> There our curiosity shall have this noble satisfaction, we shall know how the Angels know, by knowing as they know. We shall not pass from Author, to Author, as in a Grammar School, nor from Art to Art, as in a University; but, as that General which Knighted his whole Army, God shall Create us all Doctors in a minute.[1]

The Augustinian assumption of the transformation from rational knowl-

1. From "A Sermon Preached at the Spittle, Upon Easter-Munday, 1622," *The Sermons of John Donne,* ed. G. R. Potter and E. M. Simpson (Berkeley, 1953–1962), 4:128.

edge to intuitive wisdom permeates the quest for truth at every level. It provides, admittedly, a melancholy perspective, under the aspect of eternity, on the effort as well as on the results of rational inquiry. But for the more immediate sphere of man's intellectual duties in this world, a purposiveness emerges that is far from discouraging and that yields a sense of which paths of inquiry are most worth pursuing. A salient example of how this ethic of knowledge influences epistemology in a specific way can be found in Browne's use of the contrast between the totality of intuitive knowledge in the next world and the fragmentariness of discursive knowledge in this world. Though an eager investigator of all sorts of odd particulars, and always happy to reflect upon universal principles, Browne never loses sight of the greater value and reliability of the truths that come out of man's total apprehension of his own nature:

> I could never content my contemplation with those generall pieces of wonders, the flux and reflux of the sea, the encrease of Nile, the conversion of the Needle to the North, and have studied to match and parallel those in the more obvious and neglected pieces of Nature, which without further travell I can doe in the Cosmography of my selfe; wee carry with us the wonders, we seeke without us: There is all *Africa*, and her prodigies in us; we are that bold and adventurous piece of nature, which he that studies, wisely learnes in a *compendium*, what others labour at in a divided piece and endlesse volume. (*P*, 78)

Browne shares with Donne and Milton certain assumptions about what makes for seriousness of purpose in the pursuit of knowledge and what is merely frivolous. The Augustinian assumptions of men dedicated to the life of the mind cannot be dismissed as pious anti-intellectualism or obscurantism. The crucial consideration for Browne and his contemporaries is that the life of the mind is an inextricable part of the life of man and not simply an attempt to master a set of external problems. What is highly significant about this traditional Christian attitude is how well it meshes with the impulses of humanism. Both resist the subordination of man's well-being and chosen values to any enterprise of knowledge that has only its own procedures or its own contributions to itself to offer in support of the human sacrifice it demands. Our own century can probably respond more sympathetically to the seventeenth-century ethic of knowledge than could most of the intervening ages. Swift, for example, who seemed so reactionary and wrongheaded an enemy of progress to Macaulay, seems terribly prescient to us. His satiric vision of dehumanized technocrats, indifferent to the needless suffering they impose upon others, speaks all too clearly to our own time. Obviously, Sir Thomas Browne and his contemporaries assigned profoundly different aims to human life, and consequently different motives for the pursuit of truth, than we would assign today. But the twentieth-century reader is aware enough of the absurdities, not to mention the dangers, of the pursuit of knowledge when it serves only its self-defined purposes and addresses itself to no human value to be able to read Browne and his contemporaries with sympathetic understanding.

Sir Thomas Browne
and the Labyrinth of Truth

John R. Knott, Jr.

Near the end of *The Garden of Cyrus*, Sir Thomas Browne reluctantly gives up his search for quincunxes and speculates upon the large field left to those who will search out the order of God in the natural world, commending "sense and ocular Observation" as "the surest path, to trace the Labyrinth of Truth" (*P*, 386). One hears an echo of Browne's great predecessor Bacon here. In the preface to the *Novum Organum*, Bacon had argued, "The universe to the eye of the human understanding is framed like a labyrinth; presenting as it does on every side so many ambiguities of way, such deceitful resemblances of objects and signs, natures so irregular in their lines, and so knotted and entangled."[1] Bacon's goal was to make his way boldly through what he called "the woods of experience and particulars." For this to be possible, he argued, "the whole way from the very first perception of the senses must be laid out upon a sure plan," which he aimed to provide. Browne was not as interested in setting forth grand plans for arriving at the truth as he was in discovering the intricacies of God's designs, in the book of God's Word as well as in the book of God's works, the natural world. His fondness for the figure of the labyrinth reveals both an inclination to marvel at the complexity of the divine order and a tendency to dwell upon the human capacity for error, including his own.

Browne pursued what he called the "exantlation," or drawing out, of truth with a keen sense of the limits of human understanding. He characterized himself in the preface to *Pseudodoxia Epidemica* as wandering "in the America and untravelled parts of Truth." The "Labyrinth" of popular misconception—about Scripture as well as about natural phenomena—that he confronted offered no easy paths. Browne's emphasis, at the outset of his anatomy of popular errors at least, is upon the threat of error to engulf the searcher after truth: "Being now at greatest distance from the beginning of Error, [we] are almost lost in its dissemination, whose waies are boundless, and confess no circumscription" (*K*, 2:25). Like many Protestants of his

---

1. Hugh G. Dick, ed., *Selected Writings of Francis Bacon* (New York, 1955), pp. 433–34.

time, Browne made much of the consequences of the Fall. His own concern, particularly in *Pseudodoxia Epidemica,* was with the complications and difficulties of the search for truth. Having lost the "unthorny place of knowledge," as he called paradise, we must find our way back by learning to negotiate an intellectual landscape that can take on the character of a maze.

Margaret Wiley has suggested that "Browne's uniqueness lay in his decision to present himself, a man seeking the truth," rather than his conclusions.[2] Much of Browne's attraction for modern readers springs from his diffidence about his hold on the truth, however calculated for effect this diffidence may be at times. To get a sense of how extraordinary Browne's stance was for his times, one has only to turn to the prickly Alexander Ross, who felt compelled to attack Browne for his avoidance of controversy as well as for his tropes. Without a willingness to dispute matters of religion, the Presbyterian Ross protested, "I see not how against our learned adversaries wee should maintaine the truth. If there had been no dispute against *Arius* . . . and other Hereticks, how should the truth have been vindicated?"[3] The prayer with which Ross closed his tract ("The God of truth direct all our hearts into the way of truth") flaunts his confidence that God will make the truth plain. He betrays no doubts about his ability to find the one right way and proclaim it. For Ross, "to be still doubting, is a signe of a bad Christian."[4]

Browne declined to enter the wars of truth, preferring, with Paul, to think of his faith as a shield rather than as a sword. Although he proclaimed that he was "not a proper Champion for Truth" (*P,* 65) to explain his reluctance to "hazzard her on a battell" (*P,* 66), it is apparent that he had deep-seated philosophical and temperamental antipathies to controversy. To justify his stance, Browne most often invoked the principles of charity and harmony ("It is my temper . . . to affect all harmony" [*P,* 149]). In his *Christian Morals,* he enjoins his readers, "Live happily in the *Elizium* of a virtuously composed Mind" (*P,* 466) and, conversely, "Swell not into vehement actions which embroil and confound the Earth" (*P,* 424). Browne was, of course, notably tolerant of Roman Catholicism. He saved his least charitable comments for extremists of the left who pursued the Catholics, and each other, with what he called "Insolent zeales." Browne was less troubled by Rome than by the sects who "usurpe the gates of heaven, and turne the key against each other" (*P,* 130).

I cite these generalized attitudes toward the pursuit of truth by way of background to a more particular inquiry, into Browne's understanding of the truth of Scripture.[5] Browne saw in the book of God's Word some of the same mystery and complexity that he found in the book of nature: "What a

2. *The Subtle Knot* (London, 1952), p. 144.

3. *Medicus Medicatus; or, The Physician's Religion Cured by a Lenitive or Gentle Potion* (London, 1645), p. 8.

4. Ibid., p. 80.

5. See Basil Willey's relatively brief treatment of this subject in *The Seventeenth*

Labyrinth is there in the story of *Joseph*, able to convert a Stoick?" (*P*, 81). This story, of kidnapping and seemingly miraculous reunion, offered striking evidence of the hand of God. Along with the averting of Abraham's sacrifice of Isaac and the discovery of Moses by Pharaoh's daughter, Browne regarded it as an illustration of what he called the "cryptick and involved method" of God's providence, a way "full of Meanders and Labyrinths" (*P*, 81). While Browne could recognize and appreciate the simplicity of the basic message of the Gospel, he delighted in serpentine lines, mysteries, puzzles. Implicitly setting himself against the common Puritan characterization of the Bible as perspicuous and available to the most ordinary understanding, Browne kept returning to the complexities of the text. He was acutely aware of the obscurities of Genesis, as of the difficulties of knowing God: "For we behold him but asquint upon reflex or shadow. . . . therefore to pry into the maze of his Counsels, is not onely folly in Man, but presumption even in Angels" (*P*, 74–75).

With Protestants of varying persuasions, Browne celebrated the Bible as the "evidence of Truth" (*P*, 69) and insisted upon the supremacy and the durability of this truth over that of all other writings and works of man: "This onely is a Worke too hard for the teeth of time, and cannot perish but in the generall flames, when all things shall confesse their ashes" (*P*, 91). Beyond his youthful heresies, Browne was not troubled by doctrinal questions. In divinity he was content to "follow the great wheele of the Church" (*P*, 66), in matters of interpretation as well as in those questions not addressed by the Bible: "where the Scripture is silent, the Church is my Text" (*P*, 64). Yet Browne recognized, with other thoughtful readers, that the truth of Scripture was not always plain. He began his *Observations* upon the plants in Scripture by commenting upon the difficulty of the text, "Though many ordinary Heads run smoothly over the Scripture, yet I must acknowledge, it is one of the hardest Books I have met with: and therefore well deserveth those numerous Comments, Expositions and Annotations which make up a good part of our Libraries" (*K*, 3:3).

Browne was learned enough to recognize that no particular text of the Bible was without corruption, even the original Hebrew of the Old Testament, and that the various translations (Septuagint, Vulgate, and later English versions) differed in matters of fact such as chronology. He was sufficiently familiar with biblical commentaries to be aware of extensive speculations upon the nature of the events described in Genesis, among other biblical matters that aroused dispute. Old Testament narrative could appear fantastic to one of his sophisticated taste: "I confesse there are in Scripture stories that doe exceed the fable of Poets, and to a captious Reader sound like *Gargantua* or *Bevis*" (*P*, 87). Browne resolved his doubts about such improbabilities as the story of Samson—and about the "irregularities,

Century Background (New York, 1967; originally published 1933), pp. 57–61, 67–69.

contradictions, and antinomies" that he saw in the text—by a simple act of faith, opposing "the infallible voyce of God" to "the weaknesse of our apprehensions" (*P*, 87).

Browne had little patience with those who read Scripture with a persistent literal-mindedness, lacking his sense of its difficulties. The chief failing of such readers was blindness to the figurative sense of much biblical language.

> Their apprehensions are commonly confined unto the literal sense of the Text; from whence have ensued the gross and duller sort of Heresies. For not attaining the deuteroscopy, and second intention of the words, they are fain to omit their Superconsequencies, Coherencies, Figures, or Tropologies. (*P*, 27)

In other words, they are unaware of the need to look for the true meaning of the text, which may be hidden. In *Pseudodoxia Epidemica*, Browne argues the importance of recognizing the possibility of a "loose and popular delivery" in Scripture (*K*, 2:60). His scientific understanding recoiled from the description of the sun and moon as "the two great lights of Heaven" and likewise from the biblical account of the dimensions of Solomon's molten sea. The latter contradicts Archimedes, in Browne's view the better authority: "Now if herein I adhere unto Archimedes who speaketh exactly, rather than the sacred Text which speaketh largely; I hope I shall not offend Divinity: I am sure I shall have reason and experience of every circle to support me" (*K*, 2:61). The ability to see Scripture as speaking "largely" rescued Browne from any number of corners into which his scientific curiosity led him.

Browne also combats literalism by appealing to the familiar doctrine of accommodation, as in justifying his own unfettered interpretation of the Day of Judgment:

> I cannot dreame that there should be at the last day any such Judiciall proceeding, or calling to the Barre, as indeed the Scripture seemes to imply, and the literall commentators doe conceive; for unspeakable mysteries in the Scriptures are often delivered in a vulgar illustrative way, and being written unto man, are delivered, not as they truely are, but as they may bee understood. (*P*, 117)

Browne was comfortable with the prospect that the event would be interpreted differently "according to different capacities." Alexander Ross, on the other hand, rejected Browne's "mysticall" interpretation outright, insisting upon the reality of a "visible proceeding" as satisfying to saints and terrifying to the wicked.[6] Ross was even more troubled by Browne's "metaphoricall" versions of heaven and hell. Like some others of his time, including Milton, Browne believed that one could experience an inner hell or an inner heaven. He was more insistent than most, however, in his questioning of the physical representations of heaven and hell popularized

6. Ross, *Medicus Medicatus*, p. 51.

by the Bible. At bottom, Browne appears to have been reacting to the constraints imposed upon the imagination by the need to render these places concretely. The popular preoccupation with the physical torments of hell seemed to him too limiting, something for "grosser apprehensions" (*P*, 125). Likewise, the jewels of Revelation struck him as "too weake" a representation of heaven. Browne found the true reality of both places in states of the soul that he could "imagine," in the case of hell that of a devil, or anyone, who "needs not the misery of circumference to afflict him." Jewels have nothing to do with the kind of satisfaction that he regarded as the essence of heaven:

> Briefly therefore, where the soule hath the full measure, and complement of happinesse, where the boundlesse appetite of that spirit remaines compleatly satisfied, that it can neither desire addition nor alteration, that I thinke is truely Heaven. (*P*, 122)

In Browne's liberated vision the truest conceptions are those least restricted by physical appearances.

It is not hard to understand why Browne quarreled with the kind of literalism represented by Ross and by even more extreme Protestants, the Puritan "multitude" that Browne chided for zeal and crudeness in matters of religion. He was too charitable to be comfortable with representations of divine judgment or torment and too reticent in his approach to the "unspeakable mysteries" of God to want to accept simplifications of them. Browne's reaction to the tradition of learned commentary, which represented the other extreme in responses to the Bible, was more complex but sufficiently skeptical to make him regard this as a potential source of error as well as of enlightenment.

Browne was familiar with the kind of speculation on doctrine and matters of biblical fact that engaged Renaissance commentators, chiefly through the two large commentaries that he owned, those of Pererius and Mersenne.[7] He tends to counter excessive speculation of any kind by the exercise of reason and common sense, frequently observing that a particular line of inquiry is barren or unimportant. Browne's discussion of the rainbow of Genesis is typical. He challenges the view that God's use of the rainbow as a covenant with man after the Flood meant that rainbows were unknown before that time. His reasoning is scientific: "the Rain-bow hath its ground in Nature, as caused by the rayes of the Sun, falling upon a roride and opposite cloud" (*K*, 2:493). He is impatient as well with those who exaggerate its symbolic significance, "Cabalistical heads" and those Christians whose conceits "do seem to strain as high" (*K*, 2:495) in seeing the mysteries of baptism and of the Eucharist figured in the blue and red of the rainbow's spectrum of colors.

Browne's attempts in *Pseudodoxia Epidemica* to expose the errors of the

---

7. See Arnold Williams, *The Common Expositor: An Account of the Commentaries on Genesis, 1527–1633* (Chapel Hill, N.C., 1948), p. 32.

commentators can try the patience of a reader not concerned with such questions as which son of Noah was the oldest or whether we can be sure that *three* kings traveled to honor the birth of Christ. The amount of attention that he gives to some matters, such as the belief that the earth was sparsely populated before the Flood, suggests that he could be caught up in the kind of speculation that he frequently dismisses as pointless. In this particular case, Browne painstakingly demonstrates that, given the longevity of the early inhabitants and the number of generations reported, we must conclude that well over a billion people lived on earth before the Flood. The striking thing about this instance, given Browne's general tendency to see the Bible as speaking "largely," is his willingness to build an argument from biblical "facts." He does end this chapter with a characteristic qualification: "Thus have I declared some private and probable conceptions in the enquiry of this truth; but the certainty hereof let the Arithmetick of the last day determine; and therefore expect no further belief than probability and reason induce" (*K*, 2:438).

Browne's emphasis in *Pseudodoxia Epidemica* upon the limitations of human understanding, often wittily expressed, saves him from becoming just another in a long line of somber commentators on Genesis. The real aim of his arguments is to illustrate the intellectual folly of trying to resolve questions that will admit no certain answers. Thus he debunks the notions that the world was created in a particular season and that the forbidden fruit was an apple, the latter by showing that the text offers no basis for such an assumption. In this case he concludes:

> Since therefore after this fruit, curiosity fruitlesly enquireth, and confidence blindly determineth, we shall surcease our Inquisition; rather troubled that it was tasted, then troubling our selves in its decision; this only we observe, when things are left uncertain, men will assure them by determination. (*K*, 2:488–89)

Pseudodoxia Epidemica abundantly illustrates Browne's own curiosity about scriptural matters, as he attempts to unravel some of the tangled strands of biblical chronology and to make sense of problems that had taxed the ingenuity of the commentators, but it reveals as well his sharp eye for the pretensions and the limits of rational inquiry.

In the first chapter of *Pseudodoxia Epidemica*, Browne examines the Fall in order to display the fundamental human infirmity that he saw as the source of so much error; yet he cuts short his discourse by excluding many standard topics:

> Whether the transgression of Eve seducing, did not exceed that of Adam seduced . . . we shall refer it to the Schoolman; Whether there was not in Eve as great injustice in deceiving her husband, as imprudence in being deceived her self . . . we leave it unto the Moralist. Whether the whole relation be not Allegoricall . . . we leave it unto the Thalmudist. (*K*, 2:20)

Other questions Browne leaves to the lawyer, still others, to God,

For he alone can truly determine these, and all things else; Who as he hath proposed the World unto our disputation, so hath he reserved many things unto his own resolution; whose determination we cannot hope from flesh, but must with reverence suspend unto that great Day, whose justice shall either condemn our curiosities, or resolve our disquisitions. (*K*, 2:20–21)

Browne's mild irony has the effect of casting doubt upon the ability of the various experts to answer the questions proper to them and even upon the significance of the questions themselves; they may turn out to be "curiosities."

In *Religio Medici*, Browne had condemned the tendency to pursue "niceties" in divinity as unbecoming to those who "peruse so serious a Mystery" as the Bible. Yet he did this from the perspective of one who had looked deeply enough into the text to be aware of "irregularities, contradictions, and antinomies" that invited speculation. Browne's affirmations of the truth of Scripture carry more weight because the reader knows that he has overcome his own "catalogue of doubts"; one feels the tug of Browne's curiosity in the examples that he gives, despite his dismissal of them:

> I can read the history of the Pigeon that was sent out of the Ark, and returned no more, yet not question how shee found out her mate that was left behind: That *Lazarus* was raised from the dead, yet not demand where in the interim his soule awaited. (*P*, 88)

Browne's discussion of Satan in *Religio Medici* offers glimpses of his struggles with doubt. Where the devil of Bunyan's *Grace Abounding to the Chief of Sinners* whispers blasphemies, Browne's more subtle devil whispers scientific explanations of biblical miracles:

> Having seene some experiments of *Bitumen*, and having read farre more of *Naptha*, he whispered to my curiositie the fire of the Altar might be naturall, and bid me mistrust a miracle in *Elias* when he trench'd the Altar round with water. (*P*, 85)

The workings of Browne's curiosity become instances of the devil playing at chess with him, as he puts it. His frequent references to Satan can be seen as the obverse of his insistence upon the mysteriousness of God's ways. The "invisible world" of spiritual presences in which Browne believed so strongly could be threatening as well as reassuring.

Browne pursued his quest for religious truth partly by exposing what he saw as the frauds of the "enemy of God, and the hater of all Truth" (*K*, 2:23). He explained the persistence of errors that undermined belief in the one true God by pointing to the mission of this "invisible Agent":

> Maligning the tranquility of truth, he delighteth to trouble its streams; and being a professed enemy unto God (who is truth it self) he promoteth any Error as derogatory to his nature; and revengeth himself in every deformity from truth. (*P*, 75)

Satan's most subtle tactic, in Browne's view, was to make us believe that he did not exist; thus he would "lead us farther into darkness, and quite . . . lose us in this maze of Error" (*K*, 2:69). Browne saw Satan's maze of error as the perversion of the divinely ordered labyrinth. To come under his spell was to lose the thread and be doomed to confused wandering.

Browne charges Satan not only with such traditional activities as fostering belief in a multiplicity of gods and deceiving people with oracles but also with laboring "to destroy the evidence of Truth, that is the revealed verity and written Word of God" (*K*, 2:69) by leading some to repudiate books of the Bible. This was to attack the very foundation of truth. Browne's defense against this error, made by a growing number of rationalistic critics of the Bible in the seventeenth century, was to assert confidently that the survival of the Bible and "the providence of that Spirit, which ever waketh over it," would overcome it at last: "This is a stone too big for Satan's mouth, and a bit indeed Oblivion cannot swallow" (*K*, 2:70). Browne rejected the popular superstition that the words of Scripture could serve as a charm to drive off Satan, but he found an efficacy in "the life and animated interior" of the Word lacking in "the letter and dead verbality" (*K*, 2:68). While Browne did not identify the source of this power, it can only be the Holy Spirit, pictured by him as a watchful presence. Browne had to believe that demonic fraud would be defeated by the Word of God; otherwise one could never hope to escape from Satan's maze of error.

Browne's diagnoses of the errors of interpretation and their causes reveal several related assumptions that underlie his approach to Scripture. The first and most basic of these is that the Bible embodies mysteries that one must not question. This attitude is all the more significant for coming at a time when the Bible was being subjected to increasingly rationalistic inquiry.[8] Browne was quick to credit the extraordinary effect of the hand of God in miracles and in improbable stories and to insist that God should not be restrained by the limits of our intellectual capacities. He did not hesitate to apply his reason to scriptural puzzles, but when reason failed to provide an explanation, he fell back upon his faith that the Bible provided unchallengeable evidence of the workings of divinity. He could have said of Scripture what he said of Christian doctrine: "me thinkes there be not impossibilities enough in Religion for an active faith" (*P*, 69).

A corollary of Browne's belief in the essential mysteriousness of much of Scripture is his readiness to accept uncertainty about the meaning of the text. In fact, he relished it as a test of faith and scorned those who would restrict the sense of the words by the limits of their own understanding. Thus he could pronounce the time of the Second Coming of Christ "a professed and authentick obscurity, unknown to all but to the omniscience of the Almighty": "Certainly the ends of things are wrapt up in the hands of God, he that undertakes the knowledge thereof, forgets his own beginning, and disclaims his principles of earth" (*K*, 2:410).

8. For a discussion of this trend, with regard to the text and to such questions as the universality of the Flood, see Don Cameron Allen's *The Legend of Noah* (Urbana, 1963; originally published 1949), especially chaps. 3–5.

Another assumption that helps to explain Browne's faith in the fundamental truth of Scripture is that biblical language frequently demands a figurative reading. He was alert to what he called the "deuteroscopy," or "second intention," of such language. To explain difficulties in the early chapters of Genesis, Browne suggested "allegorical interpretations" appropriate to "the mysticall method of *Moses* bred up in the Hieroglyphicall Schooles of the Egyptians" (*P,* 104). Ross's accusation that Browne offered "mysticall" interpretations was one that Browne might well have welcomed. Although he avoided the obsessive concern with typology that characterizes some seventeenth-century commentaries, he could slip easily into typological readings: "Christ was mystically slain in Abel" (*K,* 2:23). In fact, he envied those who lived before the birth of Christ and achieved a "bold and noble faith" by believing in "obscure prophesies and mysticall Types" (*P,* 70). The Jews erred, Browne believed, in deriving "literal and temporal expectations" from prophecies of the Messiah, in much the same way that followers of Pythagoras erred in converting "Metaphors into proprieties, and receiving as literal expressions, obscure and involved truths" (*P,* 32).[9] Browne's respect for the complexity of truth is inseparable from his sensitivity to the figurative properties of biblical language. He attacks not only misconstructions of prophecy but also "all deductions from Metaphors, Parables, Allegories, unto real and rigid interpretations" (*K,* 2:34). The rigidity comes from squeezing the mystery out of the language by reducing it to a single, literal sense. Browne's frequently remarked aversion to definition arises from a reluctance to limit the significations of words by insisting upon a too simple and too readily discernible version of the truth. He preferred to keep alive a sense of the mystery of biblical language, through it reaching for connections with the invisible world of divine truth: "I am now content to understand a mystery without a rigid definition in an easie and Platonick description" (*P,* 70).

Despite his endorsement of "allegorical interpretations" of Genesis, Browne read Scripture in ways that bear little resemblance to the systematic allegorizing of the Alexandrian fathers or the hunting after multiple senses of the text that characterizes much medieval commentary. His "mysticall" method was that of a Protestant with strong Platonizing tendencies who delighted in finding evidences of the unseen world of divinity in the historical fabric of the Bible: chiefly in miracles, typological or symbolic revelations of divine truth, and manifestations of divine order in this world. Browne looked for hieroglyphs in Scripture as in the natural world, yet in *Pseudodoxia Epidemica* he complained that "the Hieroglyphical Symboles of Scripture," which he found in such events as sacrificial offerings and Pharaoh's dreams, "are oft-times wrackt beyond their symbolizations, and inlarg'd into constructions disparaging their true intentions" (*K,* 2:381).

9. John Mulder has written suggestively on the opposition of Aristotle and Moses in *Religio Medici,* showing the latter to be allied with Hermes Trismegistus, Pythagoras, and Plato in understanding the visible world to be a hieroglyph of the invisible. See *The Temple of the Mind* (New York, 1969), pp. 54–62.

Browne was cautious enough to be wary of symbolic interpretations that run away with the text. A similar caution surfaces in the fifth book of *The Garden of Cyrus,* in which Browne's search for quincunxes leads him into observations about the occurrences of the number five in Scripture: "Many Expressions by this Number occurre in Holy Scripture, perhaps unjustly laden with mysticall Expositions, and little concerning our order" (*P,* 382). He nonetheless goes on to pose some tantalizing questions (Why does Christ feed five thousand people in the wilderness with five barley loaves? Why does David take "just five pibbles out of the brook" to use against Goliath?), which he coyly avoids answering: "We leave it unto Arithmeticall Divinity, and Theologicall explanation" (*P,* 384).

Browne sometimes advances a "mysticall" reading to invest a seemingly straightforward passage with greater meaning. In the course of his largely technical *Observations* upon the botanical characteristics of biblical plants, he suggests that the fig tree that Christ finds in leaf but barren (Mark 11:13) should be understood as the synagogue and rulers of the Jews, who could have been expected to bear the fruit of good works early. "In this account of the Figg Tree," Browne observes, "the mystery and symbolical sense is chiefly to be looked upon" (*K,* 3:41). In *The Garden of Cyrus,* he finds in the description in the Song of Solomon of the beloved looking through the lattice both another evidence of divine order (in the network of the lattice) and a symbolic statement about the nature of Christ: "partly seen and unseen, according to the visible and invisible side of his nature" (*K,* 3:336). Browne found the ancient habit of reading the Canticles as an allegory of Christ congenial and was obviously attracted by an image suggesting the interpenetration of the two worlds in which he moved in his imagination.

When a picture or a text cried out for a symbolic reading, Browne was quick to respond. He observed in *Hydriotaphia* that the cells of the early Christian martyrs contained pictures of biblical stories, including the "mysticall Figures of Peacocks, Doves, and Cocks" and portraits of Enoch, Lazarus, and Jonas. He saw these as "hinting imagery of the Resurrection; which is the life of the grave, and sweetens our habitations in the Land of Moles and Pismires" (*P,* 290). Browne clearly was fascinated by such symbolism, his wry conclusion notwithstanding. This attraction comes through even more clearly in a reference in *The Garden of Cyrus* to the symbolism of the Tabernacle, described in Hebrews:

> The greatest mystery of Religion is expressed by adumbration, and in the noblest part of Jewish Types, we finde the Cherubims shadowing the Mercy-seat: Life it self is but the shadow of death, and souls departed but the shadows of the living: All things fall under this name. The Sunne it self is but the dark *simulachrum,* and light but the shadow of God. (*P,* 376)

Browne was drawn to the description of the cherubim "shadowing the Mercy-seat" because he saw in it an anticipation of the coming of Christ.[10]

10. See the note by C. A. Patrides on this passage (*P,* 376).

Divine mysteries expressed through biblical types interested him more than plain statements of gospel truth because they invited "mysticall" readings in which he could exercise his imagination in trying to apprehend the divine plan behind the apparent sense of a passage. The concluding words of the commentary quoted here translate the phrase *Lux est umbra Dei,* derived ultimately from Marsilio Ficino, which Browne had quoted in *Religio Medici* to illustrate the value of using "a description, periphrasis, or adumbration" in cases "where there is an obscurity too deepe for our reason" (*P,* 71). Browne's leap from biblical symbolism to the idea of light as the shadow of God takes us to the heart of the mystery of man's relationship to the divine as Browne understood it. The startling paradox has the effect of forcing the reader to recognize the inadequacy of his normal way of understanding the world in which he lives and the primacy of divine truth.

A further assumption that underlies Browne's approach to the Bible is that the evidence of truth contained there reflects the unity and the order of Creation. In *The Garden of Cyrus,* he explores evidences of divine order in the Bible as well as in the book of nature. The greatest of these appears near the end of the fifth chapter, in Browne's evocation of the heavenly Jerusalem: "All things began in order, so shall they end, and so shall they begin again; according to the ordainer of order and mystical Mathematicks of the City of Heaven" (*P,* 387). Browne refers to the square design of this ultimate city in his second chapter, comparing it with that of Babylon; he may have been thinking also of its twelve gates, representing the twelve tribes of Israel. The pattern of "Quincunciall Ordination" that Browne looked for in biblical gardens as well as in the garden of Cyrus involves the crossing of rows of trees within a four-sided figure. He finds this in Eden on the rather slender evidence that since the tree of knowledge was planted in the center of the garden, "there wanted not a centre and rule of decussation" (*P,* 333), and assumed that the same pattern was likely to have appeared in the grove of Abraham and the garden of Solomon. The pattern appeared clearly in the lattice- and stonework of the temple of Solomon. Browne also found imitations of divine order in various rectangular shapes that appear in Scripture: the Ark of the Covenant, the stone in which the names of the twelve tribes were engraved, the tablets bearing the Ten Commandments.

Such tracing of patterns reveals as much about Browne's need to find order as it does about any figures he discovered in the carpet of biblical narrative. His need to believe in the possibility of unity as well can be seen in his striking renderings of the Apocalypse. Browne's dismissal of the idea of a judicial proceeding at the last day, seized upon by the literalistic Ross as an indication of the punishment awaiting the wicked, reflects not only his charity but also his attraction to a more compelling vision of the "corrupted reliques" of men, "scattered in the wilderness of formes," miraculously restored to their original condition:

> I beleeve that our estranged and divided ashes shall unite againe, that our separated dust after so many pilgrimages and transformations into

the parts of mineralls, Plants, Animals, Elements, shall at the voyce of God returne into their primitive shapes; and joyne againe to make up their primary and predestinate formes. (*P,* 120)

In *Pseudodoxia Epidemica,* he offers another version of this restoration of primal order, using biological imagery to forge a startling linkage between the creation of Eve, seen as "in a manner seminal," and the rebirth of mankind at the last day, "For then indeed men shall rise out of the earth: the graves shall shoot up their concealed seeds, and in that great Autumn, men shall spring up, and awake from their Chaos again" (*K,* 2:399). Browne imaginatively re-creates Scripture in passages such as these, going beyond "mysticall" readings of particular texts to shape his own vision of the restored union of God and man.

Browne's Platonism comes to the fore in such passages. The chaos from which he sees men recalled by the "powerfull voyce" of God reflects both the corruption and the fragmentation of the original unity of Creation that he saw as resulting from the Fall. A yearning for the recovery of this unity colors his thought: "For things as they recede from unity, the more they approach to imperfection and Deformity; for they hold their perfection in their Simplicities, and as they nearest approach unto God" (*K,* 2:397). Browne found adumbrations of this unity in the scriptural types that appealed to him so strongly. Through his "mysticall" readings he established a connection with the invisible world that he saw as containing the patterns that made sense of the visible one, looking for hieroglyphs and adumbrations that promised glimpses of the divine order. His awareness of the imperfections of human understanding entailed by the loss of paradise was counterbalanced by a serene confidence that this divine order could be apprehended, in the Bible as in nature, by those who knew how to look. Its supreme symbol, the city of heaven, can be set against the figure of the labyrinth, which Browne used to express both the intricacy of the natural world and the complexity of scriptural truth. The clarity of his vision of God's "mystical Mathematicks" explains Browne's confidence that the "Labyrinth of truth" need hold no confusion for one who respects its mysteries.

"The Best Part of Nothing": Sir Thomas Browne and the Strategy of Indirection

C. A. Patrides

> his delights
> Were dolphin-like, they show'd his back above
> The elements he lived in
> (Shakespeare)

I

The creative mind can be perverse. It introduces exceptions when we aspire to study an artist's work in toto, and embarrassments when we fabricate schemes to accommodate the given vision. In the case of T. S. Eliot, for example, while we endeavor to align *The Waste Land* with the *Four Quartets*, he confronts us with his performance in that improbable cluster of poems, *Old Possum's Book of Practical Cats*. In the case of Browne, while we labor mightily to unravel the oddities of *Religio Medici* or *The Garden of Cyrus*, he provides us with the ultimate oddity, the short piece entitled *Musæum Clausum, or Bibliotheca Abscondita: containing some remarkable Books, Antiquities, Pictures and Rarities of several kinds, scarce or never seen by any man now living (K, 3:109–19)*.

Not many have read the piece; and those who have, behave as if they have not. *Musæum Clausum* is but the inventory of a collection, its three parts devoted to rare books, rare paintings, and rare items "of several sorts." At the outset of the inventory we are informed that the collection is not readily accessible ("I may justly say you have not seen [it] before"); and at the end, that its location is unknown ("He who knows where all this Treasure now is, is a great Apollo. I'm sure I am not He"). In point of fact, the collection is inaccessible, and its location unknown, for one very good reason: it has never existed.

The farcical situation is ill-concealed. True, a number of the items

31

enumerated might have belonged to an actual collection, however odd the description of each ("A *Sub Marine* Herbal, describing the several Vegetables found on the Rocks, Hills, Valleys, Meadows at the bottom of the Sea"). Most of the items, however, are so utterly and absurdly improbable that it is positively impossible to mistake their burden. It is more likely, indeed, that Browne endeavored not to obscure but actually to underline the inherent absurdity. In this respect, the context he provides for the collection ("There are many Collections of this kind in Europe") argues an effort to call attention to yet another "vulgar error" of his time, the indiscriminate accumulation of "rarities" by scientists who should have displayed less virtuosity and more judgment. One of several such collections in England was gathered by the Tradescants, father and son, and exhibited at the Ashmolean Museum in Oxford; another was detailed by Nehemiah Grew, F.R.S., in *Musæum Regalis Societatis. Or a Catalogue of Description of the Natural and Artificial Rarities belonging to the Royal Society and preserved at Gresham Colledge* (1681), and contained, side by side with eminently respectable items, objects that ranged from the tears of a stag to an unspecified stone "anomalously shaped" and the like.[1] Browne's inventory parallels such standard collections by citing inter alia "A Ring found in a Fishes Belly taken about Gorro," its potential utility promptly undercut by the added supposition that it is "conceived to be the same wherewith the Duke of Venice had wedded the Sea." The evident restraint here is in other instances so delivered as to intimate a sense of veritably black humor, especially when the given item is visualized. Thus of several paintings mentioned by Browne, one is "of Tamerlane ascending his Horse from the Neck of Bajazet"; another, "of Œdipus when he first came to know that he had killed his Father, and married his own Mother"; and a third—the most deliciously gruesome of all—"of Thyestes when he was told at the Table that he had eaten a piece of his own Son."

The humorous dimension of *Musæum Clausum* is inescapable; but so is the serious one. As much can certainly be said of a parallel compilation, Donne's *Catalogus Librorum Aulicorum incomparabilium et non vendibilium* (circa 1603–1611), which ascribes thirty-four imaginary books to real authors.[2] Elaborate jests of this order, in fact, were rather widely dissemi-

1. In Grew's *Catalogue*, pp. 21, 189, and so forth. For the inventory of the Tradescant collection, see R. T. Gunther, *Early Science in Oxford* (Oxford, 1925), 3:200 ff. and 391 ff. I am grateful to Robin Robbins for directing me to these materials.

2. Donne, *The Courtier's Library, or Catalogus Librorum Aulicorum*, ed. and trans. Evelyn M. Simpson (London, 1930); first published in the *Poems* of 1650. One of the thirty-four imaginary books, for example, is ascribed to Pico della Mirandola ("The Judaeo-Christian Pythagoras, proving the Numbers 99 and 66 to be identical if you hold the leaf upside down"); another, to the celebrated Elizabethan *magus* John Dee ("On the Navigableness of the Waters above Heaven; and whether a ship in the firmament will in the Day of Judgment land there or in our harbours"). The satiric intention is clearly apparent: it partakes, as Evelyn Simpson rightly observes, of the impulse informing the *Satires* written some ten years earlier.

nated, their format—the inventory as inventory—determined by the example of Rabelais. Accordingly, just as Donne's ambition was to satirize the extravagant labors of some of his predecessors and contemporaries, and Browne's was to parody the indiscriminate collecting of "rarities" by scientists in the seventeenth century, the ambition of Rabelais had been to lampoon the equally indiscriminate books written by authorities in his time. In detailing the contents of the Library of St. Victor, where Pantagruel was to expand his educational horizons (book 3, chap. 7), Rabelais augmented the credible volumes by adding others, whether on jurisprudence ("The Flimflams of the Law"), pharmacy ("The Bumsquibcracker of Apothecaries"), or social activities ("The Trictrac of the Knocking Friars").[3] Still another title is mentioned by Browne himself, in the course of his castigation in *Religio Medici* of that

> bundle of curiosities, not onely in Philosophy but in Divinity, proposed and discussed by men of most supposed abilities, which indeed are not worthy our vacant houres, much lesse our serious study; Pieces onely fit to be placed in *Pantagruels* Library, or bound up with *Tartaretus de modo Cacandi*. (*P*, 88)

Tartaretus was real enough, an authority of the Sorbonne much given to esoteric elaborations of medieval arcana; but I need hardly insist that the book ascribed to him by Rabelais could scarcely have existed! Its admission by Browne into *Religio Medici* is the closest he ever came to a scatological reference.

Browne's seriousness of purpose, it is clear, is bisected by "a most uncanonical levity" (to borrow the phrase that Emerson applied to Montaigne).[4] The strategy was described best in Coleridge's commendation of "that grave Humour that renders Sir T. B. so delightful to a learned Reader."[5] Placed within a broader context, this "grave Humour" attests to Browne's affiliation with that Greek tradition for which the ideally balanced man is σπουδαιογέλοιος or "grave-merry," his life fully responsive to the Platonic precept that "fun and gravity"—or indeed comedy and tragedy— "are sisters." Peculiarly relevant to Christianity's paradoxical affirmation of the joy that emanates from the tragedy of the Crucifixion, the tradition evolved in time into a *theologia ludens* that posited not only a Church that "plays" *(ludet in pace / omnis Ecclesia)* but also a *Deus ludens*: "the Logos on high plays (παίζει), stirring the whole cosmos back and forth, as he wills,

3. *The Complete Works of . . . Rabelais,* trans. Sir Thomas Urquhart and Peter Motteux (London and New York, 1927), 1:257–83.
4. *Representative Men,* rev. ed. (Boston, 1888), p. 158. It should be pointed out that A. C. Howell has written persuasively on "Sir Thomas Browne as Wit and Humorist" (*Studies in Philology* 42 [1945]: 564–77), but his exclusive concern with Browne's "peculiar sense of humor" is clearly only one aspect of the total vision examined here.
5. *Coleridge on the Seventeenth Century,* ed. Roberta F. Brinkley (Durham, N.C., 1955), p. 462.

into shapes of every kind," to quote a hymn by St. Gregory of Nazianzus.[6] Such, in very broad terms, is the background to Browne's "grave Humour"; in mentioning it here at all I mean not to prescribe but to suggest that the three works we are to consider next form part of the seventeenth century's inurement to "art as play,"[7] but part, too, of a more comprehensive *philologia ludens* that derives its orientation from the Logos that plays on high. And so to that improbable discourse, *Hydriotaphia*.

II

The immediate occasion of *Hydriotaphia* was the discovery in Norfolk of some forty or fifty urns, thought by Browne to have been Roman even as he recognized that some individuals "might somewhat doubt" whether they were not of a later provenance (*P,* 281). Connected with funerary rites as these "sad and sepulchral Pitchers" were, they incited Browne to examine in detail a prodigious number of obsequial traditions drawn from his considerable experience and polymorphic reading. A treatise devoted largely to funerary habits is likely, I should have thought, to arouse at best expectations of a rebarbative dissertation, and at worst suspicions of a rather necrological obsession. Oddly enough, however, the tone of *Hydriotaphia* is not even remotely lugubrious, nor even—if one dares to use the word in this context—grave. The convergence of the lusory and the solemn is indeed an elemental aspect of Browne's rhetorical tactics, sustaining his argument in providential ways.

The argument unfolds in proportions directly inverse to the occasion of the discovery of the urns. In spite of the work's specific title—"A Discourse of the Sepulchrall Urnes lately found in Norfolk"—Browne focuses on the discovered objects but once, at the outset of Chapter II. The treatise otherwise advances in a variety of directions, immediately to consider funerary customs across time and space, but mediately to place them within a distinctly moral framework. The pattern is first sounded within range of the opening paragraph, in a sentence that forms part of a larger structural unit, to the effect that "men have been most phantasticall in the singular contrivances of their corporall dissolution" (*P,* 268). Thus discreetly

6. The tradition is outlined in a most eloquent survey by Hugo Rahner, S.J., *Man at Play,* trans. Brian Battershaw and Edward Quinn (London, 1965); I have quoted especially from pp. 9, 23, and 51, where full documentation will be found. It should be emphasized that Rahner's thesis—and by extension my own—is distinctly different from modern theories of "play" inclusive of Johan Huizinga's emphases in *Homo ludens* (English trans., London, 1949). These latter are deployed in connection with Browne by Anna K. Nardo in "Sir Thomas Browne: *Sub specie ludi,"* *The Centennial Review* 21 (1977): 311–20.

7. See Frank J. Warnke, "Art as Play," in his *Versions of Baroque: European Literature in the Seventeenth Century* (New Haven, 1972), chap. 5. Consult also Judith Dundas, "Levity and Grace: The Poetry of Sacred Wit," *The Yearbook of English Studies* 2 (1972): 93–102.

announced, the pattern is orchestrated thereafter fully. It reaches a resonant pitch at the ingress to the centrally placed Chapter III:

> Playstered and whited Sepulchres, were anciently affected in cadaverous, and corruptive Burials; And the rigid Jews were wont to garnish the Sepulchres of the righteous; *Ulysses* in *Hecuba* cared not how meanly he lived, so he might finde a noble Tombe after his death. Great Princes affected great Monuments, And the fair and larger Urnes contained no vulgar ashes, which makes that disparity in those which time discovereth among us. (*P,* 284)

The pattern peals last in the final pages of *Hydriotaphia,* during that sonorous peroration that is generally regarded as Browne's ultimate achievement in the modulation of auditory cadences: "man is a Noble Animal, splendid in ashes and pompous in the grave, solemnizing Nativities and Deaths with equall lustre, nor omitting Ceremonies of bravery, in the infamy of his nature" (*P,* 313).

Within the unfolding argument, the quotation from Chapter III cited above encompasses inter alia two dimensions that invite further comment. The first involves the apparent reappearance of the urns as urns; the other, the casual reference to "time." The urns are indeed the actual "Sepulchrall Urnes lately found in Norfolk"; concurrently, however, they have been transmuted by Browne into symbolic entities that elicit a diversity of fully premeditated responses. The transmutation is evident as early as the opening paragraph of *Hydriotaphia,* where the urns—again in conjunction with "time"—are said to symbolize man's ignorance of the very world he inhabits:

> The treasures of time lie high, in Urnes, Coynes, and Monuments, scarce below the roots of some vegetables. Time hath endlesse rarities, and shows of all varieties; which reveals old things in heaven, makes new discoveries in earth, and even earth it selfe a discovery. That great Antiquity *America* lay buried for a thousand years; and a large part of the earth is still in the Urne unto us. (*P,* 267)

Other urns attest other attitudes, like the interment of ashes in silver urns (*P,* 269)—indicative yet again, of course, of man's propensity ever to be "splendid in ashes, and pompous in the grave." Jointly, it is clear, the absurd customs enumerated by Browne argue the absurdity of man. They argue more particularly folly, recurrently if diversely emphasized as "vanity, feeding the winde, and folly" (*P,* 312), "a vanity almost out of date, and superanuated peece of folly" (*P,* 308).

As with the urns, so with time: the spiriform pattern woven by Browne depends on such a multiplicity of references to time that they may fairly be claimed to encompass his argument. These references, inaugurated in the opening paragraph of *Hydriotaphia* as we have observed, proliferate most persistently in its fifth and final chapter. Their admonitory role is clear: time resists us, misleads us, defeats us. It resists us where we endeavor to establish the time of the urns, only to discover "nothing of more uncertainty" (*P,*

279); it misleads us where we hope "to subsist in bones, and be but Pyramidally extant," only to be confronted by "a fallacy in duration" (*P*, 308); and it defeats us where we entertain great expectations, only to realize that time itself is far from timeless: "The great mutations of the world are acted, or time may be too short for our designes" (*P*, 309). The ultimate irony is that time becomes most meaningful when it ceases to exist, its mission accomplished precisely when it ushers in that "day" which according to "the decretory term of the world" is to be the last (*P*, 313). Not in time but beyond time is time finally comprehensible, in the "infallible perpetuity" espoused by the Christian faith (*P*, 314). Hence that polyphonic peroration which, quoted earlier but in part, in full display conjoins Browne's variegated sounds inclusive of "folly" and "duration":

> There is nothing strictly immortall, but immortality; whatever hath no beginning may be confident of no end. All others have a dependent being, and within the reach of destruction, which is the peculiar of that necessary essence that cannot destroy it self; And the highest strain of omnipotency to be so powerfully constituted, as not to suffer even from the power of it self. But the sufficiency of Christian Immortality frustrates all earthly glory, and the quality of either state after death, makes a folly of posthumous memory. God who can only destroy our souls, and hath assured our resurrection, either of our bodies or names hath directly promised no duration. Wherein there is so much of chance that the boldest Expectants have found unhappy frustration; and to hold long subsistence, seems but a scape in oblivion. But man is a Noble Animal, splendid in ashes, and pompous in the grave, solemnizing Nativities and Deaths with equall lustre, nor omitting Ceremonies of bravery, in the infamy of his nature. (*P*, 312–13)

The solemnity of the argument is beyond dispute. Yet it is a measure of Browne's complexity that the solemnity is pervaded by a playfulness of considerable latitude, its purpose as much to deride the funerary customs he records as to subvert his own prodigal ostentatiousness. We have already noted the oddity of a treatise which, nominally devoted to "Sepulchrall Urnes lately found in Norfolk," attends to those urns but once, and even then all too laconically; and we have noted, too, the unexpectedness of a work of scholarship that marshals countless details concerning funerary rites primarily in order to render them equally absurd. The mode of thought witnessed by these tactics is amply confirmed by the use of a telling phrase or even a word, and often by an abrupt change in the tone, to remind us of Browne's unflagging amusement over man's boundless capacity for folly. To be informed of the cremation of a hero, for instance, disposes us one way, but to be told of his "solemn combustion," quite another (*P*, 268). Our response is similarly qualified when faced by "the *Ichthyophagi* or fish-eating Nations about Ægypt" (*P*, 271), especially if we recall—as recall we might—Othello's equally pompous "Anthropophagi, and men whose heads / Do grow beneath their shoulders" (I, iii, 144–45). The impact of several other references is measurably more substantial if each is visualized:

the corpse of Pyrrhus cremated successfully enough save for his toe, which could not be burnt (*P*, 291); the Balearians bruising the flesh and bones of their dead in order to crowd them into urns (*P*, 271); the Hebrew patriarchs insisting that they be buried in Canaan so as to be among the very first to be resurrected (*P,297*); or the numerous pagans, Jews, Christians, and Muhammadans who dispatch their remains into the grave sometimes feet first, sometimes headfirst, and who position each cadaver supine or prone or pendulous or indeed erect (*P*, 300). As Browne noted drily, "Men have lost their reason in nothing so much as their religion" (*P*, 299).

The conflation of the serious and the lusory in *Hydriotaphia* is most evident in the relentless roll call of individuals, tribes, nations, and sects that cumulatively testify to the awesome extent of human desipience. Cosmic as it is in its compass, the strategy is reminiscent of the procession of the demonic agents in *Paradise Lost*. However, Browne's most noteworthy effects are achieved after the fashion not so much of Milton as of Erasmus, Rabelais, and Shakespeare. *Hydriotaphia* is like *The Praise of Folly* in that both deploy a serrated irony that with sustained gaiety discloses the reality beneath the appearance and the folly beneath the wisdom. *Hydriotaphia* is also like the Rabelaisian magnum opus in that both attend through playfulness to the regression of erudition into absurdity and of credulity into fanaticism. And it is like *King Lear* in that both resort to a purgatorial "comedy" that inverts wisdom to behave as if it were folly in order to expose the turpitude pretending to be rectitude. In short, *Hydriotaphia* enacts the principle sanctioned by the playful Logos on high: "God hath chosen the foolish things of the world to confound the wise" (1 Corinthians 1:27).

III

Hydriotaphia is an entity unto itself that attains its maximal significance beyond itself, in the treatise with which it was jointly published in 1658, *The Garden of Cyrus*. The two works are intimately related in accordance with the principle of "nexus through contrast" so brilliantly explicated by Frank L. Huntley.[8] The principle as a principle is the most meridian of oddities yet, for it aspires to link the mutually exclusive and to connect the strictly incompatible: death and life, mutability and immutability, darkness and light. But it is in the nature of *Hydriotaphia* and *The Garden of Cyrus* to be in terms of their unity dependently independent of one another, and in terms of their strategy exclusively inclusive, incompatibly compatible, and indeed negatively positive. In the face of such tonitruous ingenuity, Browne's

8. Frank L. Huntley, "Sir Thomas Browne: The Relationship of the *Urn Burial* and *The Garden of Cyrus,*" *Studies in Philology* 53 (1956): 204–19; revised in his *Sir Thomas Browne: A Biographical and Critical Study* (Ann Arbor, 1962), chap. 13; reprinted in *Seventeenth-Century Prose,* ed. Stanley Fish (New York, 1971), pp. 424–39.

reader is likely to be rather concerned, perhaps apprehensive, and possibly even vexed. But in due course concern yields to delight, apprehension to exhilaration, and vexation to a palpable joy.

Delight, exhilaration, and joy are the unmistakable effects of *The Garden of Cyrus*. One must be constantly alert, however, since the tone is likely to change ever so imperceptibly in order to intimate attitudes substantially more ambiguous than the stated ones. The epistle dedicatory to Nicholas Bacon is in this respect characteristic of the entire work:

> You have been so long out of trite learning, that 'tis hard to finde a subject proper for you; and if you have met with a Sheet upon this, we have missed our intention. In this multiplicity of writing, bye and barren Themes are best fitted for invention; Subjects so often discoursed confine the Imagination, and fix our conceptions unto the notions of fore-writers. Beside, such Discourses allow excursions, and venially admit of collaterall truths, though at some distance from their principals. Wherein if we sometimes take wide liberty, we are not single, but erre by great example. (*P*, 319–20)

We mark that the passage on the one hand refers pejoratively to the "trite learning" about to be displayed by Browne and on the other refers favorably to his "invention"—a term which in the vocabulary of Renaissance rhetoric was pregnant with laudative implications. We mark also the description of his approach by way of "excursions . . . at some distance from their principals," which we later find are not excursions so much as errant perambulations, nor "at some distance" so much as at distances thrice as far as is the center from the utmost pole. We mark finally—that is, if we remember to consult Browne's marginal clarification—that the "great example" he invokes as precedent for his own "wide liberty" is Hippocrates, who digressed in one work on tonsillitis, and in another on sexual intercourse. Improving even on such an authority, however, Browne did not provide digressions from his nominal subject: he provided a nominal subject for his digressions.

The stage of *Hydriotaphia* is the world; that of *The Garden of Cyrus* is the universe. Browne's range, appropriately cosmic, draws freely on any number of his manifold interests such as biblical scholarship, astronomy, zoology, archaeology, history, and literature. But his primary concern is with botany, in keeping both with his nominal subject of gardens and with his ambition to ascend by means of those gardens to the Creator, "that eminent Botanologer" (*P*, 333). There is certainly no lack of gardens in *The Garden of Cyrus*, ranging as they do from the grove of Abraham through the hanging gardens of Babylon to the gardens variously of Solomon and of Homer's Alcinous. But as gardens have a certain shape, not infrequently rhomboidal, Browne's fecund imagination explodes in search of rhombi throughout the created order. Within his gardens, moreover, he discerns further evidence of "the higher Geometry of nature" (*P*, 353–54) in the proliferation of figures such as the circle, the ellipse, the cone, the rectangle, the isosceles triangle— and, the most remarkable figure of all, the quincunx.

It would be a gross understatement to propose that the quincunx fascinated Browne. It propelled him, rather, into ecstasy—yet an oddly *controlled* ecstasy that allowed him to delineate nature's geometric disposition after an orderly fashion, advancing eventually to suggestions of its "mystical" import in the last two of his inevitably five chapters. "The greatest mystery of Religion," we are informed, "is expressed by adumbration" (*P,* 376), and it is by adumbration—the "wide liberty" sanctioned in the epistle dedicatory, the "soft and flexible sense" endorsed in the preface to *Religio Medici* (*P,* 60)—that the quincunx can be understood best. The fugatious figure is, as it were, the capital ideogram within "the great Volume of nature" (*P,* 374), tolerant even of that saltatorial excursion into "the Emphaticall decussation, or fundamental figure," that is to say, the first letter of Christ's name in Greek—the letter *chi* (χ)—formed whenever the five points said to constitute the basic design of all gardens are intersected (χ), also whenever the Roman numeral five is "doubled at the angle" to produce a like effect ($>$ and $<=X$), and especially whenever the circle is observed to be but the figure X turned about on its axis (*P,* 328, 378). A cardinal lesson in "Christian signality," the decussation is also the cardinal symbol within "the orderly book of nature" (*P,* 330, 360).

But the delight, exhilaration, and joy generated by *The Garden of Cyrus* are not the consequences merely of ingenuity. They depend in particular on the "signality" of Browne's creativity in maintaining a fimbriated discourse with boundless zest. It is nevertheless true that while we are transported by the wittily extravagant first and fourth chapters, and by the extravagantly witty second and fifth, we may be less than patient with the third chapter, which is both the longest and the most expressly botanical one. If so, we have not fully discerned that Browne's intent in that chapter, like Milton's in the equally underestimated account of creation in Book VII of *Paradise Lost,* was not only to celebrate God's creative prowess but also to enact it through a disclosure of Browne's own talents at "invention." The details so dazzlingly flaunted by Browne do not of themselves attest much more than his prodigal knowledge; but animated imaginatively, they proclaim the fecundity of Providence, and urged creatively, they assert the harmony of the cosmic order. To cite two examples where any would have served as well, first:

> The exiguity and smallnesse of some seeds extending to large productions is one of the magnalities of nature, somewhat illustrating the work of the Creation, and vast production from nothing. The true seeds of Cypresse and Rampions are indistinguishable by old eyes. Of the seeds of Tobacco a thousand make not one grain. From such undiscernable seminalities arise spontaneous productions. He that would discern the rudimentall streak of a plant, may behold it in the Originall of Duckweed, at the bignesse of a pins point, from convenient water in glasses, wherein a watchfull eye may also discover the puncticular Originals of Periwincles and Gnats. (*P,* 351–52)

And next:

> The *Arbustetum* or Thicket on the head of the Teazell, may be observed in

this order: And he that considereth that fabrick so regularly palisadoed, and stemm'd with flowers of the royall colour; in the house of the solitary maggot, may finde the Seraglio of *Solomon,* And contemplating the calicular shafts, and uncous disposure of their extremities, so accommodable unto the office of abstersion, not condemne as wholly improbable the conceit of those who accept it, for the herbe *Borith.* (*P,* 344–45)

The two passages define Browne's creative language at the service of his art: the unfamiliar words about to emerge into our understanding, the improbable connections galloping in search of compaction, the underlying nervous rhythm suggestive of the effort, the onward movement expressive of the eventual resolution. More critically still, the solemnity is ingested by the creator's sheer delight in words and their potential concent. So throughout *The Garden of Cyrus* the sounds support the argument in a sustained playfulness that terminates in joy.

Dr. Johnson—not a man easily impressed—was quite enchanted. He aligned *The Garden of Cyrus* with the *Muiopotmos* of Spenser as well as with the *Batrachomyomachia* and the *Culex* formerly attributed to Homer and Virgil respectively in that all four demonstrate to what extent "it is a perpetual triumph of fancy to expand a scanty theme, to raise glittering ideas from obscure properties, and to produce to the world an object of wonder to which nature had contributed little" (*P,* 494). No less appropriately, however, one could apply to Browne's strategies in *The Garden of Cyrus* the claim advanced by Erasmus on behalf of *The Praise of Folly,* that "just as nothing is more trivial than to treat serious matters in a trivial way, so too nothing is more delightful than to treat trifles in such a way that you do not seem to be trifling at all."[9] The finality of the claim is itself qualified, of course, by the elastic nature of the "trifles" at the heart of *The Praise of Folly.*

As with Erasmus in one respect and with Dr. Johnson in a second, so with the invariably perceptive Coleridge in a third: in Browne "the Humorist [is] constantly mingling with and flashing across the Philosopher" (*P,* 21, 40).[10] Such flashing is most often immediate, sometimes prolonged, and not infrequently "at some distance from [its] principals." Immediate where the effect depends primarily on Browne's creative language, it is prolonged where the given pattern is articulated incrementally after the fashion of "the Emphaticall decussation" or, even more spectacularly, after the fashion of that spirited discourse in Chapter II that encompasses rectangular patterns ranging from bricks and beds and windows to the Macedonian phalanx, the shape of Nineveh, and the Ark of the Convenant—but mercifully *not* the Tables of the Law since Browne was, he tells us, "unwilling to load the shoulders of *Moses* with such massive stones" (*P,* 342). The flashing is "at some distance" where Browne derives much of his gardenist lore from

9. *The Praise of Folly,* trans. Clarence H. Miller (New Haven and London, 1979), p. 4.
10. *Coleridge on the Seventeenth Century,* p. 448.

treatises like Benoît Court's *Horti* (1560) or Giambattista della Porta's *Villa* (1592),[11] which are indeed quite relevant, but also excruciatingly dull. More to the point, Browne's reiterated unwillingness to record any more material than absolutely necessary—an unwillingness invariably beginning with "We shall not call in . . . ," or "we shall not insist . . . ," or "to omit . . ." (*P*, 330, 335, 336, and elsewhere)—is always followed by a detailed list of the items he has vowed to bypass. The most delightful example of this tactic is the entire last chapter, which begins with a ringing declaration of his refusal to indulge in Pythagorean speculations on the number five, yet promptly overtakes every numerologist ambling along:

> To enlarge this contemplation unto all the mysteries and secrets, accommodable unto this number, were inexcusable Pythagorisme, yet cannot omit the ancient conceit of five surnamed the number of justice; as justly dividing between the digits, and hanging in the centre of Nine, described by square numeration, which angularly divided will make the decussated number; and so agreeable unto the Quincunciall Ordination, and rowes divided by Equality, and just *decorum*, in the whole com-plantation; And might be the Originall of that common game among us, wherein . . .

and so on to the end of *The Garden of Cyrus* (*P*, 379 ff.). Coleridge, for one, was overjoyed: "Quincunxes in Heaven above," he exclaimed, "Quincunxes in Earth below, & Quincunxes in the water beneath the Earth; Quincunxes in Deity, Quincunxes in the mind of man, Quincunxes in optic nerves, in Roots of Trees, in leaves, in petals, in every thing!" (*P*, 383).[12] Yet numerologists dare not enlist Browne as an ally since his enthusiasm for "inexcusable Pythagorisme" is, like so much else in *The Garden of Cyrus*, turned upside down. After all, where they favored numbers like three and seven—each diversely regarded as "a most holy and potent number," "a most powerfull number," "an universall & absolute number," "the nombre of fulnes," "the most sacred of Numbers," and the like[13]—Browne focused with an optimum of eccentricity on five; and, in "proving" its truth, he disproved both his case and theirs. The approach appears to be nihilistic, and in a sense it is. But in a much more fundamental sense it is mimetic of the Creator's "vast production from nothing" (as above, p. 39), while in the last analysis it reflects too the fondness of the *Deus ludens* for inversion which proscribes the folly that passes for wisdom and commends the folly that is wisdom.

11. See Jeremiah S. Finch, "Sir Thomas Browne and the Quincunx," *Studies in Philology* 37 (1940): 274–82.
12. *Coleridge on the Seventeenth Century*, p. 439.
13. *Seriatim* as claimed on behalf of the numbers three and seven by Thomas Tymme, *A Dialogue Philosophicall* (London, 1612), p. 38; Heinrich Cornelius Agrippa, *Three Books of Occult Philosophy*, trans. J. F. (London, 1651), p. 179; Pierre de la Primaudaye, *The French Academie*, trans. T. B. (London, 1586), p. 563; Heinrich Bullinger, *A Hvndred Sermons vpō the Apocalips*, trans. John Daws (London, 1561), p. 165; and David Person, *Varieties* (London, 1635), 5:10.

The penultimate paragraph of *The Garden of Cyrus* translates the "wide liberty" Browne has taken up to that point into a refulgent statement of his major motif: "All things began in order, so shall they end, and so shall they begin again; according to the ordainer of order and the mystical Mathematicks of the City of Heaven." But the ultimate paragraph is much more characteristic in its relaxation of the erstwhile somber tone into a conspicuously whimsical one:

> Though *Somnus* in *Homer* be sent to rowse up *Agamemnon*, I finde no such effects in these drowsy approaches of sleep. To keep our eyes open longer were but to act our *Antipodes*. The Huntsmen are up in *America*, and they are already past their first sleep in *Persia*. But who can be drowsie at that hour which freed us from everlasting sleep? or have slumbring thoughts at that time, when sleep it self must end, and as some conjecture all shall awake again? (*P*, 387–88)

Philologia ludens has not often scaled higher.

IV

To consider *Religio Medici* third and last when it was the very first of Browne's works to be published (1643) might be construed as a tactic pregnant with numerological import or, worse still, as a distant reflection of Browne's own predilection for inversion. But such ambitions, I should insist, would have been far less tolerable had they been far more modest. *Religio Medici* is here placed after *Hydriotaphia* and *The Garden of Cyrus* strictly because it anticipates those symbiotic works in some respects and, just as strictly, because it does not.

It does not anticipate the other two in its carefully designed title page, for example. Frontispieces to Renaissance books were, we know, rarely if ever merely decorative. As they were also invariably wrought under the supervision of the given author—the elaborate title page for Sir Walter Raleigh's *The History of the World* (1614) is an extravagantly eloquent case in point[14]— we could accept that Browne was not altogether averse to the design prefixed to *Religio Medici;* indeed, as that design was the same for both the authorized edition and for the earlier, pirated version, it could even appear that the unauthorized edition was not entirely unauthorized. At any rate, in displaying the hand of God arresting a man's fall into the sea (*P*, 55), the design invites attention to a pattern iterated within *Religio Medici* with such frequency as to coincide with the axis of Browne's argument. The first reference, fully congruent with God's "cryptick and involved method," is obliquely to a Spanish salute—"bezo las manos": "I kiss the hands"—which

14. Reproduced, and remarked upon, in my edition of *The History of the World* (London and Philadelphia, 1971), pp. xv–xvi. But see especially the more comprehensive study by Margery Corbett and Ronald Lightbrown, *The Comely Frontispiece: The Emblematic Title-Page in England, 1550–1660* (London, 1979).

is promptly transposed from its naturalistic context to suggest with ironic understatement "the meere hand of God" (*P*, 81–82). Expansively applied thereafter, the pattern encompasses references to secondary causes as the "visible hands of God" (*P*, 84) and to the Primary Cause as "that invisible hand" (*P*, 102) or "that hand which doth uphold [our] natures" (*P*, 152). Moreover, the intervention of the divine through miracles is described as "the extraordinary effect of the hand of God" (*P*, 95), while a normal disclosure of the divine is said to be simply "the hand of God" (*P*, 114), more expressly his "hand or providence" (*P*, 161), and lastly "the finger of God" (*P*, 126)—or, more adventurously, "the little finger of the Almighty" (*P*, 87). In brief, *Religio Medici* is concerned with Providence in general while *Hydriotaphia* and *The Garden of Cyrus* attend to its manifestation through order in particular.

Religio Medici anticipates the other two in several illuminating ways, each apocalyptic of Browne's evolving thought and artistry. Order, certainly, is already a major preoccupation. But not yet articulated with the ardent commitment to the fecundity of Providence so clearly impressed upon *The Garden of Cyrus*, it is still confined to mere affirmations of hierarchy in the universe as in society (*P*, 101, 134), and especially to reiterated invocations of the commonplace parallelism between the macrocosm of the universe and the microcosm of man, for example, "every man is a *Microcosme*, and carries the whole world about him" (*P*, 152). The exception is that sustained paean to cosmic hierarchy in Part II:

> there is a musicke where-ever there is a harmony, order or proportion; and thus farre we may maintain the musick of the spheares; for those well ordered motions, and regular paces, though they give no sound unto the eare, yet to the understanding they strike a note most full of harmony. Whatsoever is harmonically composed, delights in harmony; which makes me much distrust the symmetry of those heads which declaime against all Church musicke. For my selfe, not only from my obedience but my particular genius, I doe imbrace it; for even that vulgar and Taverne Musicke, which makes one man merry, another mad, strikes in mee a deepe fit of devotion, and a profound contemplation of the first Composer, there is something in it of Divinity more than the eare discovers. It is an Hieroglyphicall and shadowed lesson of the whole world, and Creatures of God, such a melody to the eare, as the whole world well understood, would afford the understanding. In briefe, it is a sensible fit of that Harmony, which intellectually sounds in the eares of God. (*P*, 149–50)

Even more evidently anticipatory of *Hydriotaphia* and *The Garden of Cyrus* is Browne's fully evolved attitude toward time. The "day" that the later treatises proclaim in accordance with "the decretory term of the world" to be the last, already figures prominently in that magniloquent meditation on "the great Jubilee" of the Day of Judgment and the end of the time-bound world:

> This is the day that must make good that great attribute of God, his

justice, that must reconcile those unanswerable doubts that torment the wisest understandings, and reduce those seeming inequalities, and respective distributions in this world, to an equally and recompensive Justice in the next. This is that one day, that shall include and comprehend all that went before it, wherein as in the last scene, all the Actors must enter to compleate and make up the Catastrophe of this great peece. This is the day whose memory hath onely power to make us honest in the darke, and to bee vertuous without a witnesse. (*P,* 119)

Even as time advances relentlessly toward timelessness, however, never does it exist in God save in a strictly metaphorical sense, in the manner of that "easie and Platonic description" or "easie Metaphor" commended in *Religio Medici* (*P,* 70; compare 160). God may indeed be styled the Ancient of Days (Daniel 7:9), yet he "cannot receive the adjunct of antiquity, who was before the world, and shall be after it, yet is not older then it: for in his yeares there is no Climacter, his duration is eternity, and farre more venerable then antiquitie" (*P,* 96–97). By the same token, the biblical claim that in his sight a thousand years are only a day (2 Peter 3:8) is hazarded rather too "modestly":

> for to speake like a Philosopher, those continued instances of time which flow into a thousand yeares, make not to him one moment; what to us is to come, to his Eternitie is present, his whole duration being but one permanent point without succession, parts, flux, or division. (*P,* 73)

But time may be annihilated even by the believer whose "memory" of the future permits him to recognize that he died before he was born and that the last trumpet heralding the end of history has already sounded (*P,* 73, 132). So, too, can he nightly close his eyes in security, "content to take [his] leave of the Sunne, and sleepe unto the resurrection" (*P,* 157).

Religio Medici foreshadows the later treatises in still other respects that, not yet fully regulated by Browne, are conspicuous precisely because of their distance from their later manifestations. Thus the hyperborean prospect of *The Garden of Cyrus* may in *Religio Medici* be scanned solely through the analogy of God to "a skilfull Geometrician" on the one hand, and the commendation of "the mysticall way of *Pythagoras* and the secret Magicke of numbers" on the other (*P,* 73, 80), insofar as Browne had not yet mounted an effort to elevate the former into a cosmic principle or to depress the latter into an inversion of its essential truth. Thus, too, the placement in *Hydriotaphia* of men's aspirations after temporal perpetuity merits in *Religio Medici* but a passing reference devoid of the later sonority:

> This conceit and counterfeit subsisting in our progenies seems to mee a meere fallacy, unworthy the desires of a man, that can but conceive a thought of the next world; who, in a nobler ambition, should desire to live in his substance in Heaven rather than his name and shadow in the earth. (*P,* 11)

Nor is folly mentioned in *Religio Medici* except within the conventional framework of objurgations whether directed passionately against our prejudices ("folly and madnesse" [*P*, 140]), uncharitably against the multitude ("fooles" [*P*, 134]), or amusingly against sexual intercourse ("an odde and unworthy piece of folly" [*P*, 149]). One other manifestation of folly is said to be man's frequent indulgence in activities of scant consequence:

> What a Βατραχομνομαχία [*Batrachomyomachia*], and hot skirmish is betwixt *S.* and *I.* in *Lucian?* How doth Grammarians hack and flash for the Genitive case in *Jupiter?* How doe they breake their owne pates to salve that of *Priscian?* (*P*, 138)

In time, of course, Browne would indulge in a scanty excursion of his own. But in *Religio Medici* the mental disposition that was to create the quincunx is evident but tangentially.

As it is in the nature of a tangent to meet a curved surface, however, so *Religio Medici* touches the later treatises at a specific point, the point of indirection implicit in Browne's espousal of a "soft and flexible sense" (*P*, 60). Particularly apposite in this respect are the principles of organization upon which *Religio Medici* rests—the "order or œconomy" Browne invokes in another context (*P*, 69)—and the tonal range of seriousness not exclusive of playfulness, and of gravity not exclusive of "a most uncanonical levity." The principles of organization are accessible though oblique and apprehensible though abaxial. The division of *Religio Medici* into two parts, for example, revolves about the three cardinal virtues, with Faith and Hope apportioned to Part I and Charity to Part II. At the same time, the two parts unfold with an unremitting commitment to the vertical dimension that links man to God, even as the first part advances more specifically along a horizontal line that in coincidence with the Christian view of history extends from the initial act of Creation to the last scene of the Day of Judgment. Correspondences, moreover, are well-nigh numberless, informed throughout by the seminal parallelism between the macrocosm and the microcosm already noted and reinforced persistently by several "easie" metaphors: manuscripts, books, registers, letters, characters, figures, abbreviations, hieroglyphs, and the like. The elaborate structure is intended to uphold unity against plurality and congruence against dissonance. Nominal dichotomies, whether of reason versus faith or of philosophy versus divinity, are only nominal; the actual opposition is rather of truth against its perversion: "the right rule and law of reason" in agreement with divine precepts against "insolent" or "arrogant" reason (*P*, 127), and "mysterious Philosophy" in alliance with divinity against "the rules of our Philosophy," "common Philosophy," "meere Philosophy" (*P*, 107, 123, 101, 120). Browne's emphatic partiality to "mysterious Philosophy"—"such," he adds, "as reduced the very Heathens to Divinity"—accounts also for his seduction by all manner of "*Ænigmaes,* mysteries and riddles" finally dependent on "the mysticall method of *Moses* bred up in the Hieroglyphicall Schooles of the Egyptians," *id est,* those supposed Egyptians who like the legendary Hermes Trismegistus were regarded as "addicted" to "abstruse and mysticall sciences" (*P*, 143, 104, 136). The approach was eminently suitable to

Browne, temperamentally inclined as he was to favor indirection or—to use the term deployed in both *Religio Medici* (*P,* 71) and *The Garden of Cyrus* (above, p. 39)—"adumbration." It will be observed that Browne's repeated description of himself as "irregular" (*P,* 66, 132) describes also his method, which is at once entirely singular to him and yet conformable to God's prototypically "cryptick and involved method" (above, p. 42).

Indirection is also fundamental to Browne's proclivity to inosculate the serious and the playful. The diverse manifestations of his "grave Humour"—to quote Coleridge's apt phrase yet again—are wont in some instances to take the form of an expeditious passage from analogy to analogy, so that the implicit parallel between the creator of *Religio Medici* and the Creator of the world—himself "an excellent Artist" (*P,* 79)— involves also relationships between the book that is *Religio Medici* and the books of nature and of God, or (as noted above) the "irregular" methods alike of Browne and of God. In other instances Browne toys so extravagantly that we behold him as his friends did, "but in a cloud" (*P,* 140). Thus a celebrated metaphor in Isaiah (40:6) occasions a discourse that confirms Browne's pursuit of unity in a characteristically paradoxical way:

> *All flesh is grasse,* is not onely metaphorically, but literally true, for all those creatures we behold, are but the hearbs of the field, digested into flesh in them, or more remotely carnified in our selves. Nay further, we are what we all abhorre, *Antropophagi* and Cannibals, devourers not onely of men, but of our selves; and that not in an allegory, but a positive truth; for all this masse of flesh which wee behold, came in at our mouths: this frame we looke upon, hath beene upon our trenchers; In briefe, we have devoured our selves. (*P,* 107)

Even more arresting is the serious yet playful pirouette danced about the doctrine of creation ex nihilo, or that "vast production from nothing" (as above, p. 39). First, the angels are wittily described as "the best part of nothing" (*P,* 103); and two pages later Browne returns to elaborate on a related oddity: "God being all things is contrary unto nothing out of which were made all things, and so nothing became something, and *Omneity* informed *Nullity* into an essence." Coleridge's response was, for once, rather scalene: "An excellent *Burlesque* on some parts of the Schoolmen, tho' I fear an unintentional one" (*P,* 105).[15] It is more likely, however, that Browne aspired not so much after any outward-looking burlesque as after an inwardly directed gaiety over the surprising ways of God. Only four lines later, after all, God is said to have "played the sensible operator" in creating man (*P,* 105), which in turn echoes the assertion a few pages earlier that his Spirit "playes within us" (*P,* 99). The implications of "playing" are of course suggestive of doing or acting no less than of toying and sporting, and certainly of performing on the stage as well as on a musical instrument.

When all is said, however, indirection as a strategy is most impressively

15. *Coleridge on the Seventeenth Century,* p. 442.

operative in the ever seasonable dimension of man's fallen state. True, *Religio Medici* appears on the face of it to be concerned with the Fall only spasmodically if not indeed almost accidentally. But such absentmindedness is peculiar rather to Browne's narrator than to Browne. Here more than anywhere else in *Religio Medici* the distance between the two is measurably spacious; for if Browne's narrator eschews the Fall with an almost religious zeal, Browne himself presses hard to bring its reality within range of our consciousness. The transition from the first part of *Religio Medici* to the second should in this respect be noted because it is a transition from an agreeably irenic voice to a frequently prejudiced one. In Part I, Browne's narrator is of the commendable opinion that "It is the method of charity to suffer without reaction" (*P,* 65); but in Part II—the part expressly devoted to Charity—we are confronted by a violent reaction against the multitude ("fooles"), supported by an unwarranted appeal to "canonicall Scripture" (*P,* 134). A fundamental truth uttered subsequently—"all is but what we all condemne, self-love," that is to say, pride (*P,* 141)—leads to an equally firm declaration that "Pride [is] a vice whose name is comprehended in a Monosyllable, but in its nature not circumscribed with a world" (*P,* 146). Browne's narrator, obviously unaware that his tintinnabulary generalizations apply as much to himself as they do to others, hastens proudly to detail his understanding of "no less then six Languages" besides the chorography of several countries, the topography of their cities, the structure of their laws, and so on (*P,* 147). The ensuing tirade against sexual intercourse ("an odde and unworthy piece of folly") is a manifestation of another form of pride—the pride of prejudice—which is all the more eloquent because of its disclaimer ("I speak not in prejudice"). In like manner the narrator of *The Praise of Folly* inverts the attitude of Erasmus himself by asserting that "the human race is propagated by the part which is so foolish and funny that it cannot even be mentioned without a snicker."[16]

Browne's irony, like that of Erasmus, is unmistakable; yet it is deployed with gentle humor and an infinite good will, precisely because Browne was so unlike his narrator in his recognition that the dimensions of pride are indeed "not circumscribed with a world." The strategy of indirection has plainly illuminated a vital issue yet again, especially in that its gravity is at once intensified and tempered by a playfulness assertive of a sympathetic response to the oddities of human behavior. To speak parabolically after Browne's own "soft and flexible sense," the discernment by Yeats that at the heart of *Hamlet* and *King Lear* lies a "Gaiety transfiguring all that dread"[17] is no more eccentric in itself than it is irrelevant to the vision of Sir Thomas Browne.

"The whole creation," Browne maintained in *Religio Medici*, "is a mystery" (*P,* 105). The unexceptionable subject is a variation on a theme

16. *The Praise of Folly,* p. 18.
17. "Lapis Lazuli," line 17.

sounded by St. Paul as by many others, that we now see God "through a glass darkly." But Browne's idiomorphic formulation of the same premise is no less solemn than it is witty: "we behold him," he wrote, "but asquint upon reflex or shadow" (*P*, 74–75).

Dare one visualize "asquint"?

A Hook for Amphibium:
Some Reflections on Fish

Frank J. Warnke

It was in some ways refreshing when, in his *Self-Consuming Artifacts* of 1972, Stanley Fish attacked Sir Thomas Browne as being "the bad physician."[1] Not since Sir Kenelm Digby's contemporaneous *Observations* had the worthy doctor been really strenuously condemned, and, after some three centuries of laudatory appreciations and respectful analyses, the bristling rejection was stimulating. It gave one the warm feeling one gets on hearing motherhood maligned, or patriotism, or apple pie. Yet, unless one is relentlessly frivolous (as I may yet prove to be), Fish's attack must, I think, be refuted—not by rejecting his aesthetic and methods (which I think have much to recommend them) but by applying that aesthetic and those methods more rigorously, more radically, than Professor Fish himself has done, though assuming, be it admitted, a rather different set of beliefs concerning the nature and function of art.

Although Fish grants a grudging admiration to Browne's skill, to the superb mastery with which he pulls rugs from under the reader, he is finally compelled to condemn him on the grounds that the author is not honest, is misleading, is either unwilling or incapable of conveying a sound moral experience. That last phrase is important: Fish is by no means naive, and he surely does not expect simple didactic messages from the great masters of baroque prose (on the contrary, his entire method would deny the separability of texture and "message"). He does, however, expect the *experience* of the work to be a moral experience, the kind he receives from other seventeenth-century authors. But let us have his own words on the subject:

> What sets Browne apart from those with whom he shares so much is the absence in his work of their intentions, which are rhetorical in a very special sense. They seek to *change* the minds of their readers; they have designs on us; they are out to do us good; and they require our

---

1. *Self-Consuming Artifacts: The Experience of Seventeenth-Century Literature* (Berkeley, 1972), chap. 7.

participation in what is, more often than not, the painful and exhausting process of self-examination and self-criticism. Bacon's style of
presentation provokes the reader to question the adequacy of his
received opinions and the completeness of his received systems of
knowledge; the "present satisfaction" of a coherent literary experience
is deliberately sacrificed for an uneasiness that is a stimulus to "further
inquiry"; in Herbert's poetry the reader is required to give up, one by
one, his claims to an independent existence, even to the extent (in some
poems) of surrendering his powers of interpretation; when Bunyan
promises "This book will make a traveller of thee," he keeps his promise
by forcing the reader to claim a share in the errors and sins of Christian
and his companions; at least half of Milton's readers are alienated and
discomforted when he insists that each of us measure himself against
an unyielding standard of righteousness and illumination; in *Death's
Duell,* the reader is teased into asking questions that only point up his
inability to answer them, and in the end he is brought literally to his
knees; and if the reader is the *subject* of the *Anatomy of Melancholy,* he is
in his preeminence the *object* of taunts, laughter, rebukes, and scorn. In
all of these works, an uncomfortable and unsettling experience is
offered as the way to self-knowledge, in the hope that self-knowledge
will be preliminary to the emergence of a better self, with a better (or at
least more self-aware) mind. And by offering that experience rather
than another, these works shift the focus of attention from themselves
and from what is happening in their formal confines to the reader and
what is happening in the confines of his mind and heart.[2]

I have quoted at some length, and absolutely without omissions, because I
want to make certain that I allow Professor Fish to speak for himself, with
full clarity. And I haven't finished yet; I shall be quoting the continuation of
this passage below. But I do want to pause briefly to consider some of the
implications of what I have already quoted. When Fish affirms that the
reader of *Death's Duell* is brought *literally* to his knees, I pay him the respect
of assuming that he means what he says: *literally.* Surely this can only mean
that a proper experience of Donne's great sermon can only be an experience
at least in part religious, an experience that enforces the full personal
acceptance of Donne's religious position, complete with the repellent and
vicious theology that that position has in common with those of other
seventeenth-century religious writers. In this case I am personally obliged to
say that, though I yield to no reader in my love for Donne, I experience him
differently. *Death's Duell* brings tears to my eyes, but it has never brought
me to my knees, even metaphorically.

    This digression anticipates a little of what I shall have to say in attempted
refutation of Fish's position. But, for the moment, let me return to the text
of *Self-Consuming Artifacts* and to the paragraph following the one just
quoted. Here we find the core of Fish's rejection of Browne:

> These, then, are the characteristics of what I have called the aesthetic
> of the good physician (actually an anti-aesthetic), and on every point
> Browne stands on the opposite side. He draws attention not *away*

2. Ibid., p. 371. Subsequent references to this study are in the text.

from, but *to,* himself; his words are not seeds, spending their lives in salutary and self-consuming effects, but objects, frozen into rhetorical patterns which reflect on the virtuosity of their author; the experience of his prose has its climaxes not in moments of insight and self-knowledge, but in moments of wonder and admiration for the art that has produced it; rather than provoking us to a distrust of its procedures and conclusions, the *Religio Medici* solicits and wins our confidence. It is therefore not self-consuming, but self-indulgent, and in two directions: for the confidence it wins is reflected in the confidence it leaves us, a *self*-confidence, which is the result of never having been really pained or challenged; Browne does not say to us, "awake, remember, change," but "take it easy, don't let it bother you, let it be." (p. 372)

This characterization strikes me as partly right, partly wrong. I shall attempt to demonstrate the wrongness of some parts, and I shall attempt to maintain that the accurate parts of the characterization refer to things more deserving of praise than censure, but first I should like to draw attention to one aspect of Fish's own phrasing. In the earlier paragraph certain artists are singled out for praise: those who "have designs on us . . . are out to do us good . . . and . . . require our participation in . . . [a] painful and exhausting process," those who leave us "alienated and discomforted," those who offer us "an uncomfortable and unsettling experience." In the latter paragraph Browne is condemned for not leaving us "pained or challenged." One wonders if it is not so much the good physician whom Fish seeks as the good dentist—and one who is conservative in the use of Novocain.

The last remark is facetious, of course, and probably tasteless, but it suggests, I think, what is wrong with Fish's approach to Browne. Fish is a puritan—not an uppercase Puritan, like Milton and Bunyan (as contrasted with Burton, Donne, and Herbert), but a lowercase puritan, like a distressingly large number of other American literary intellectuals. Some of the assumptions of the lowercase puritan literary intellectual are: if the literary work doesn't give you a sound moral experience, there's something wrong with it; if it doesn't hurt, it's not good for you; if it's frankly and cheerfully "aesthetic," it's corrupt. Browne, in contrast, is the least puritan of authors, with the possible exception of Shakespeare.

Browne, we are told, fails to participate in the "anti-aesthetic" of some other baroque authors. I agree. In what does Browne's *aesthetic* exist? It exists, I believe, in freeing us—an accomplishment that is not, I submit, without value. Professor Fish himself knows this: he draws attention frequently to the manner in which Browne's stylistic effects and syntactic constructions produce in us a feeling of release, as distinctions and definitions are established only to be annihilated, leaving us with only a vertiginous "O altitudo!" Let us consider one passage from the *Religio Medici* that Fish chooses for comment:

The earth is a point not onely in respect of the heavens above us, but of that heavenly and celestiall part within us: that masse of flesh that circumscribes me, limits not my mind: that surface that tells the

> heavens it hath an end, cannot perswade me I have any; I take my circle
> to be above three hundred and sixty; though the number of the Árke do
> measure my body, it comprehendeth not my minde: whilst I study to
> finde how I am a Microcosme or little world, I finde my selfe
> something more than the great. (*P*, 153)

As the critic notes, the first part of the quoted sentence "seems to confirm
our everyday sense of a world where objects occupy discrete places at
measurable distances from one another" (p. 362), but, with the appearance
of the word *within,* "the objects that had been fixed in their respective
positions become interpenetrable, and the largest of them is discovered to
reside 'within' the smallest" (p. 362). Fish continues: "The language of
spatial configuration has been retained, but in a context—of inner space—
that makes nonsense of it, and of the proportional statement we have half
formulated: as we are to the earth, so is the earth to the heavens. Once again
the demonstration (the syntax is itself a form of demonstrative argument)
falls to the ground along with the superstructure of assumptions it implies"
(pp. 362–63).

Fish's concern, as we know, is with "literature in the reader," with what
texts *do* to us. But what does the quoted passage do to the reader? More, I
think, than simply sending him skidding on an intellectual pratfall, as Fish
implies. It subjects the reader to an experience that liberates him/her from
the rational world of spatial configurations and consistent relations; only
through such an experience (frequent in Browne) can the reader be liberated
into that larger, sublimely paradoxical world in which his/her immortal and
eternal being is confirmed—confirmed, let me stress, not by assertion or
demonstration but by the *experience* of the sentence. One might object that
we are in fact not possessed of an immortal and eternal being, that Sir
Thomas is thus misleading us, however innocently, and that the passage is
therefore without moral value for us. To approach the text thus would
surely be to grab it by the wrong end, as I'm sure Fish would agree. If we
start judging texts by their verifiability, we're going to have to throw out an
awful lot, starting with the Bible. As it happens, I don't share Browne's
optimistic belief in the immortality of the soul, though I rather wish I did. I
don't even *want* to believe certain other propositions—innate depravity,
predestination, eternal punishment, the sole efficacy of faith as an agency of
justification—that are conveyed with feverish enthusiasm by a number of
the seventeenth-century worthies whom Fish finds to be purveyors of
wholesome moral experience. Clearly, a noble and humanly worthy belief,
even if mistaken, is, when clothed in fine invention and appropriate rhetoric, something deserving of our admiration.

Admiration: the word may be a key. Some readers may be pardoned for
finding in Fish's strictures on Sir Thomas Browne not merely critical
disapproval but also downright dislike. If such readers (and I am one) are
correct in their suspicion, the grounds may be present in such a passage as
the following, from Fish:

> What is required of the reader of *Religio Medici* is . . . admiration. In the

prose of Donne and Milton, and the poetry of Herbert, the stylistic effects—the dislocations, ambiguities, confusions of tenses—are in the service of the commonplaces of Christian belief. In the *Religio Medici,* the commonplaces of Christian belief are in the service of a succession of stylistic effects, and our attention is continually being diverted from the implications (personal and cosmic) of Browne's statements to the skill he displays in making them. (p. 365)

Leaving aside the surprisingly crude dichotomy between form and content here implied, we might note that what Fish is really saying here is that Sir Thomas is a smart-ass and a show-off, unlike solid, serious Donne, Milton, and Herbert. Maybe. But it's hard to understand how anyone who can't tolerate show-offs can have much fondness for baroque literature. For "admiration" is at the very core of its aesthetic—even for Donne and Herbert, even for Milton. Not "admiration" in the common sense of the English word, but *admiration* in the sense of the French word. That is to say, not "admiration" meaning "approval," with a strong connotation of "moral assent," but rather *admiration* meaning "astonished wonder," with a strong admixture of helpless pleasure. For example, here is Pierre Corneille, in his *Discours de l'utilité et des parties du poème dramatique* of 1660, speaking of his bloody tragedy *Rodogune* and then of his great comedy *Le Menteur:*

Cléopâtre, in *Rodogune* [she is not, by the way, to be confused with Cleopatra the Queen of Egypt] is very evil . . . but all her crimes are accompanied by a grandeur of soul which has something so elevated that, at the same time that one detests her actions, one wonders at [in Corneille's phrase, *on admire*] the source from which they spring. I would dare to say the same of *Le Menteur.* No doubt lying is a vicious habit; but the hero presents his lies with so much presence of mind and so much vivacity that this flaw assumes a kind of grace in his personality and forces the audience to recognize that the talent of lying is, after all, a vice of which fools are not capable.[3]

As Georges May observes, "In his comments and critical writing as well as in the plays themselves Corneille so clearly expressed his intentions that we know what fundamental emotion he wished to arouse: he called it *admiration,* that is, in his terms, the emotion we feel when confronted with extremes in human behavior. Admiration, for Corneille, does not necessarily imply moral approval or disapproval. It is closer to a kind of wonder, of amazement."[4]

This baroque view is not a doctrine for puritans—uppercase *or* lowercase. It is the same doctrine that the baroque poet Giambattista Marino expressed in equally memorable terms:

E del poeta il fin la meraviglia,
(Parlo del eccelente, e non del goffo):
Chi non sa far stupir, vada alla striglia!

3. My translation, from Corneille's *Polyeucte and Le Menteur,* Introduction and Notes by Georges May (New York, 1963), pp. 21–22.
4. Ibid., p. 20.

The purpose of the poet is marvel,

(I speak of the excellent one, not of the hack):

He who does not know how to stupefy, let him curry horses![5]

And it is Sir Thomas Browne's aesthetic.

What is the aesthetic of stupefaction, and can we justify it morally? Probably not, but let us try. Corneille typically achieves his effects through the representation of "extremes in human behavior." Marino, like Donne, achieves his through the *presentation* of extreme phenomena of rhetoric and imagery, those phenomena that we normally label *wit* and *conceit*. Mastery of these arts could be depended on, in the baroque age, to earn one a reputation as a wit—not "wit" meaning "smart aleck," but "wit" meaning "man of perception, insight, wisdom, combined with grace of expression." The astounding combinations and recombinations proferred us by the baroque artist are not merely, pace Dr. Johnson, the fabrications of perverse human cleverness; they are rather creations of God, the master fabricator, the artist who created the world as a metaphysical poem. This view is supported by the writings of such seventeenth-century theorists as Baltasar Gracián in Spain and Emmanuele Tesauro in Italy, as we are reminded by a number of modern scholars.[6] The witty poet does not fabricate his astounding effects; he discovers them—*ad majorem Dei gloriam*.

Nevertheless, if all creation is a metaphysical poem, the work of a witty God, then there is something about it that is, despite its seriousness, downright amusing. Perhaps that is why our response to so much baroque literature—even when it is most relentlessly doing us good, even when the author is "holy Mr. Herbert" himself—includes as one component a snort of delighted and astonished laughter. We laugh because the literary text is, however serious, also amusing, and it is amusing because reality—or what we can know of it—is amusing. Cosmic play is what baroque literature is all about, and this cosmic play is what Professor Fish fails to appreciate in the writings of Sir Thomas Browne.

Is this laughter good for us, or is this sense of the universe as cosmic play, reflected in playful artifacts, good for us? I'm not really sure that I care, having not yet been persuaded that it is beneficial to confuse the function of the literary artist (let alone that of the critic) with the function of the preacher. If compelled, I suppose I should say that I *feel* that it is good for us. The sense of play encourages humility, perhaps; it makes a little less practicable the terrible sense of self-importance that is the besetting vice of our species. Donne, Marino, Herbert, Sir Thomas Browne—all had the sense of

---

5. My translation, from Marino's *Poesie Varie*, ed. B. Croce (Bari, 1913), p. 345.

6. See H. M. Priest, *Adonis: Selections from "L'Adone" of Giambattista Marino* (Ithaca, N.Y., 1967); Joseph A. Mazzeo, *Renaissance and Seventeenth-Century Studies* (New York, 1965); S. L. Bethel, "Gracián, Tesauro, and the Nature of Metaphysical Wit," *Northern Miscellany of Literary Criticism* 1 (Autumn 1953): 19–40. The matter is also dealt with by Ann Hurley in an unpublished study entitled "Wit's Re-Creation: A Study of the Poetry of John Donne."

play. John Calvin did not have it: if he had, he might not have ordered Servetus burned; he might not even have written the *Institutes,* and, by not doing so, have given us all cause for gratitude. Milton had some of it, as witness "L'Allegro" and "Il Penseroso," but one could wish he had had a bit more. Oliver Cromwell did not have it, nor did Tomás de Torquemada. The sense of cosmic play might even tend to discourage human beings from the systematic destruction of the enviroment of human and other life.

But, before I get carried away by my claims any further than I already have, perhaps we should return to Sir Thomas Browne and to some specific examples of his art. Here is a typical passage from early in the *Religio Medici:*

> I could never divide my selfe from any man upon the difference of an opinion, or be angry with his judgement for not agreeing with mee in that, from which perhaps within a few dayes I should dissent my selfe: I have no Genius to disputes in Religion, and have often thought it wisedome to decline them, especially upon a disadvantage, or when the cause of truth might suffer in the weaknesse of my patronage: where wee desire to be informed, 'tis good to contest with men above our selves; to confirme and establish our opinions, 'tis best to argue with judgements below our own, that the frequent spoyles and victories over their reasons may settle in our selves an esteeme, and confirmed opinion of our owne. Every man is not a proper Champion for Truth, nor fit to take up the Gantlet in the cause of Veritie: Many from the ignorance of these Maximes, and an inconsiderate zeale unto Truth, have too rashly charged the troopes of error, and remaine as Trophees unto the enemies of Truth: a man may be in as just possession of Truth as of a City, and yet bee forced to surrender; 'tis therefore farre better to enjoy her with peace, then to hazzard her on a battell. (*P,* 65–66)

This passage begins with a statement that leads us to expect simply another bit of naive self-commendation of the sort so familiar in the *Religio:* "I could never divide my selfe from any man upon the difference of an opinion." More precisely, we think we hear Sir Thomas claiming to possess the virtue of charity. More of that later. But the sentence continues, "or be angry with his judgement for not agreeing with mee in that, from which perhaps within a few dayes I should dissent my selfe." The continuation complicates matters: the speaker claims that he is not moved to anger by a conflicting opinion not merely because he is of a charitable, or perhaps phlegmatic, temperament, but rather (or perhaps also) because he holds all his views in a tentative manner, undogmatically, and with a constant awareness of the possibility of error. But the sentence is not yet over, and in the phrases that follow a new idea is introduced to modify the meanings that we, the readers, have thus far absorbed. This idea is that a person in possession of truth may nevertheless not be equipped with the skills of disputation that would enable him effectively to defend that truth. Such a person Sir Thomas claims himself to be—whether sincerely or not, I would not presume to say.

In developing this point about the incompetent champion of truth, Browne comes up with a recommendation that is bound to amuse us—that we seek the conversation of clever people on only those matters on which we have not yet formed opinions and that we discuss our *opinions* only with dummies, so that we may bolster our egos in holding those opinions. I used to teach this passage as a charming example of the quaint and faintly dotty way Browne's mind often works, as an example, in short, of his naiveté. It is only more recently that it has occurred to me that the passage may have been intended to be funny, part of the creation of the persona in a work that follows many of the principles of fiction. The comic self-characterization, if that is what it is, leads directly into a significant passage in which Browne humbly affirms his submission to the doctrines of the Church:

> If therefore there rise any doubts in my way, I doe forget them, or at least defer them, till my better setled judgement, and more manly reason be able to resolve them . . . In Philosophy where truth seemes double-faced, there is no man more paradoxicall then my self; But in Divinity I love to keepe the road, and though not in an implicite, yet an humble faith, follow the great wheele of the Church, by which I move, not reserving any proper poles or motion from the epicycle of my own braine. (*P*, 66)

Fish speaks much about the *experience* of the text, about "literature in the reader." I would submit that what we find in this passage of the *Religio* is the *experience* of humility, in which we are forced, by the author's admiration-awakening skill, to participate. The creation and projection of a slightly dotty narrator—with whom we identify—is a part of that skill. We are prepared thus for a passage that occurs only two sections later, one of the most justly famous passages of the entire work:

> As for those wingy mysteries in Divinity, and ayery subtilties in Religion, which have unhing'd the braines of better heads, they never stretched the *Pia Mater* of mine; me thinkes there be not impossibilities enough in Religion for an active faith; the deepest mysteries ours containes, have not only been illustrated, but maintained by syllogisme, and the rule of reason: I love to lose my selfe in a mystery to pursue my reason to an *oh altitudo*. (*P*, 69)

Humility, charity, awe—such emotional attitudes are perhaps good for us, whoever runs the cosmos, and whether or not there is a theology capable of giving us some contact with that force. They are emotional attitudes with immensely serious implications, and Sir Thomas Browne renders them a part of our experience through an artistry that includes among its principal devices comedy and playfulness. Through comedy and playfulness, among other devices, the author liberates us into the aesthetic. And there is nothing trivial about such liberation.

I have stressed frequently the "experience" of reading Sir Thomas Browne, indicating thereby a conception of "literature in the reader" that to some extent agrees with that of Professor Fish. I think, however, that Fish errs in seeming to imply that we read a text only once, or, more accurately, that the first reading possesses somehow a definitive authority. I should think it obvious that, in our experience of literature as in our experience of music, subsequent exposures add new dimensions to our experience. Knowing what is coming, we find new meanings in what was always there. Even the element of surprise, so important in Browne, continues to operate, aesthetically, as surprise, and thus to arouse our admiration, but the flavor of surprise is a bit different when we know we are going to be surprised. An appropriate analogy might be the "magic modulation" near the end of Mozart's *Nozze di Figaro,* which is as entrancing, aesthetically as "surprising," the five hundredth time as it was the first, but even richer after continued exposures.

The reader experiences not merely sentences, paragraphs, and pages; he experiences whole texts. And after repeated experiences of the same text he is bound to respond differently and, I would think, more richly to any single passage. On our first reading of the *Religio Medici* we do not, I suspect, recognize that beneath its apparently aimless and casual surface there is a deeper structure based on an examination of the virtues of Faith, Hope, and Charity.[7] The work is divided, with seeming arbitrariness, into "The First Part" and "The Second Part." Upon examination we note that Part I ambles from casual reflections having to do mostly with the author's faith to casual reflections having to do with the author's hope and that Part II, beginning "Now for that other Vertue of Charity, without which Faith is a meer notion" (*P,* 133), is devoted entirely to reflections on that virtue. Only Charity receives an entire section of the work to itself—properly so, since, as we know, "the greatest of these is Charity." Having noted this, we note, on our second or third time through the experience of the text, that even the sections dealing primarily with the virtues of Faith and Hope are saturated with thematic references to Charity. Such a saturation is present, for example, in the passage previously discussed in which Sir Thomas observes that he "could never divide his selfe from any man upon the difference of an opinion." Indeed, many traits of the persona we come to know so well in reading the *Religio*—including several traits that are cunningly devised to operate as comic or as self-depreciatory—work cumulatively to illustrate the theme of Charity that is central to the work. But we are not likely to be aware of this on our very first experience of the text.

Comparably, in reading the *Hydriotaphia* for the first time, we are likely to feel that there is a ragged discrepancy between some of the more practical, precise, and (if I may venture the phrase) down-to-earth passages in the earlier chapters and the glorious and transcendent perorations of Chapter V. Let me illustrate, citing first a couple of passages from Chapters II and III:

> In a Field of old *Walsingham,* not many moneths past, were digged up between fourty and fifty Urnes, deposited in a dry and sandy soile, not a yard deep, nor farre from one another: Not all strictly of one

7. This is also noted by Joan Webber in her *The Eloquent "I": Style and Self in Seventeenth-Century Prose* (Madison, 1968), p. 161.

figure, but most answering these described: Some containing two
pounds of bones, distinguishable in skulls, ribs, jawes, thigh-bones,
and teeth, with fresh impressions of their combustion. Besides the
extraneous substances like peeces of small boxes, or combes
handsomely wrought, handles of small brasse instruments, brazen
nippers, and in one some kinde of *Opale*. (*P,* 274)

A little later on:

How the bulk of a man should sink into so few pounds of bones and
ashes, may seem strange unto any who considers not its constitution,
and how slender a masse will remain upon an open and urging fire of
the carnall composition. Even bones themselves reduced into ashes do
abate a notable proportion. And consisting much of a volatile salt,
when that is fired out, make a light kind of cinders. (*P,* 292)

Let us compare these two passages with a passage from Chapter V:

There is nothing strictly immortall, but immortality; whatever hath
no beginning may be confident of no end. All others have a dependent
being, and within the reach of destruction, which is the peculiar of that
necessary essence that cannot destroy it self; And the highest strain of
omnipotency to be so powerfully constituted, as not to suffer even
from the power of it self. But the sufficiency of Christian Immortality
frustrates all earthly glory, and the quality of either state after death,
makes a folly of posthumous memory. (*P,* 312)

And, finally, the concluding passage of the work:

To subsist in lasting Monuments, to live in their productions, to
exist in their names, and praedicament of *Chymera's,* was large
satisfaction unto old expectations, and made one part of their *Elyziums.*
But all this is nothing in the Metaphysicks of true belief. To live indeed
is to be again our selves, which being not only an hope but an evidence
in noble beleevers; 'Tis all one to lye in St *Innocents* Church-yard, as in
the Sands of *Ægypt:* Ready to be any thing, in the extasie of being ever,
and as content with six foot as the Moles of *Adrianus.* (*P,* 315)

On our first experience of the text, we are likely to take the two earlier
passages as straightforward, workmanlike examples of descriptive prose, in
short, as examples of scientific writing. At the same time, however, whether
we know it or not, they are doing work of a different sort, driving upon us
with terrible force the sense of our pathetic and doomed materiality: "a light
kind of cinders." In the first passage, the initial description of the contents of
the urns, the bones juxtaposed to boxes, combs, handles of brass instruments, nippers, and "some kinde of *Opale*" have the effect not merely of
catalog but also of rhetorical zeugma. As I have remarked elsewhere,[8] such
passages ask King Lear's question: "Is man no more than this?" Chapter V
gives us Browne's answer, the Christian answer. If we have missed the full

8. *Versions of Baroque: European Literature in the Seventeenth Century* (New
Haven, 1972), p. 211.

force of the question on our first reading of the work, we are not likely to miss it the second time round, with the solemn cadences of Chapter V ringing in our memories.

In summary, Fish's condemnation of Browne seems to me misdirected in a number of important ways. First, he fails to take sufficient account of the fact that readers *reread* texts, and that subsequent experiences of a text are modified by the memory of previous experiences. In the case of Browne, particularly, the larger and more serious responses to his work are likely to come after repeated experiences of a given text. Second, Fish underrates the seriousness of the playful, both in the sense in which playful techniques may be agencies of serious insights (George Herbert) and in the sense in which the playful itself *is* serious (Andrew Marvell) in that it enables us to transcend—not "to escape," but "to transcend"—the mundane and quotidian and, even more importantly, to transcend ourselves, to become more than those small and brief entities. Or it gives us the illusion of such transcendence. But perhaps the selves themselves are illusion. In any case, art itself, the aesthetic itself, exists in the realm of illusion. The art of Sir Thomas Browne, as I have maintained earlier, "liberates us into the aesthetic," and the third and final weakness of Fish's position is his underrating of the aesthetic itself.

With his emphasis on the moral and the didactic, on the ways in which the experience of literature may "do us good," Fish inevitably risks both a misleading separation of content and form and a sadly restrictive distrust of what some morally oriented critics have called the "merely aesthetic." There is, I think, nothing "mere" about the truly aesthetic. It is what remains after the ideas have died. In order to respond fully to the poetic art of George Herbert, must I share his religion? I hope not, and I think not. George Herbert is good for me—not because of his religion or his ideas but because of his art. So is Sir Thomas Browne. This is not to say that ideas and attitudes are irrelevant to aesthetic experience. Great literature cannot be made of ideas and attitudes that are base or ignoble or unworthy of our humanity. But it can surely be made of ideas that are erroneous or inadequate and attitudes that are partial or limited. In Sir Thomas Browne there is much that is quirky or irrelevant or eccentric, but nothing that is ignoble or unworthy of humanity. And, as an artist, he makes few mistakes and achieves an extraordinary number of triumphs. His art survives, and continues to enrich us every time we experience it. As Carducci said of an even greater author, Dante, "Giove muore, ma l'inno del poeta resta"—"Jove dies, but the hymn of the poet remains."

The Play of Mind:
Self and Audience in *Religio Medici*

J. R. Mulryne

I

Criticism of *Religio Medici* is extensive and on the whole approving. Almost since the book's appearance, readers have found it pleasing in its literary and instructive in its religious dimension. Yet the chorus has not been quite of one voice. Browne had "a special good opinion of himself" thought Sir Kenelm Digby,[1] and an intermittent but persistent strain of disapproval runs up to at least James Winny's edition of *Religio Medici* in 1963. Even Browne's admirers feel there is perhaps something to explain or forgive. Coleridge, with philosophy in mind, urged that Digby "ought to have considered Religio Medici in a *dramatic* & not in a metaphysical View—as a sweet Exhibition of character & passion, & not as an Expression or Investigation of positive Truth."[2] But, as I hope to show, character and philosophy do not so easily part company in *Religio Medici*. Others, like Digby, have found the "character and passion" no more palatable than Coleridge found the philosophy. Browne has been thought self-recommending, complacent, and vain. C. A. Patrides warns that "it is an error readily to identify the narrative voice of *Religio Medici* with its author" (*P*, 22), thus joining Coleridge in proposing a dramatic or literary reading of the work. We must separate, that is to say, the person from the persona, the Truth from the truth. *Religio Medici* offers itself, ambiguously I shall suggest, as a personal essay, intimate and confessional; its real existence, its admirers claim, bears a distant or ironic relationship to this naive stance. The interest of the work, considered as literature, lies in the tensions between the two and in the ways in which such tensions predicate and comply with the demands of an alert audience, the reader. Failures of complicity explain, I believe, the discomforts of the disapproving critic.

1. Quoted in Joan Webber, *The Eloquent "I": Style and Self in Seventeenth-Century Prose* (Madison, 1968), p. 150.
2. Quoted in *P*, 47–48.

II

One way of expressing the tensions of *Religio Medici* is to see them as a conflict between personality and style. For Walter Pater, Browne's work is that of a stylist, "a writer in whom mere style counts for so much."[3] The style, it is true, is not uniform; it "has its garrulity, its various levels of painstaking, its mannerism, pleasant of its kind or tolerable, together with much, to us intolerable, but of which he was capable on a lazy summer afternoon down at Norwich." (Browne's informal manner seems to affect even the normally fastidious Pater.) But besides being stylish, Browne's writing is also egocentric: "it is certain that Browne's works are of a kind to directly stimulate curiosity about himself—about himself as being manifestly so large a part of those works." And here the difficulty arises, for style ought to discipline, not express, personality. "If the style be the man," wrote Pater in his essay "On Style," "in all the colour and the intensity of a veritable apprehension, it will be in a real sense 'impersonal.'" In Pater's view, Browne's work cannot reach the level of art: "his religion is only the correlative of himself, his peculiar character and education, a religion of manifold association." *Religio Medici* is dismissed as "a contribution, not to faith, but to piety." Pater's criticism, perhaps unjustly, now tends to be regarded as interesting only as a reflection of his age and as an influence, broadly malign, on the life and art of the future.[4] But the concept of "impersonality" has remained and been strengthened. By its light, even if such light falls differently now, Browne's work will often be judged embarrassingly personal.

For Pater, art is consolation or inspiration, "a refuge, a sort of cloistral refuge, from a certain vulgarity in the actual world." From a different but not wholly unrelated point of view, Browne's fault is not defect of style but too much stylishness. Browne, according to Stanley Fish, diverts attention from moral truth to "a succession of stylistic effects."[5] The characteristic of "self-consuming artifacts" is to become themselves invisible while freeing the mind for contemplation. "Browne's prose," says Fish, "betrays no such modesty." It is self-indulgent, not self-consuming. For a critic like Joan Webber, apparent style is acceptable: "Anglican Browne liberates himself from Baxter's pain by emphasising style more than meaning. . . . He makes a game of doubt and allows himself much play of fancy in his style."[6] But for Fish, who admires literature that *does us good*, this is irresponsible. Browne, for prescribing too much style, becomes the "bad physician."

Both Pater and Fish think of art as purposive, the one to shelter from and the other to confront the actual world. Browne's admirers free themselves

3. *Appreciations, with an Essay on Style*, 4th ed. (London, 1901), p. 158. The following quotations from Pater are on pp. 126, 129, 31, 18, 37, 137, 138.
4. For a discussion of Pater's influence, see Harold Bloom, *Yeats* (New York, 1970), chap. 2.
5. *Self-Consuming Artifacts: The Experience of Seventeenth-Century Literature* (Berkeley, 1972), p. 365. The following quotation is on p. 367.
6. Quoted in Fish, ibid., p. 372.

from the embarrassments of self-consciousness, in the style or in the man, by fully embracing it. Joan Webber stresses the seventeenth-century prose writer's "crucial and unremitting awareness that he is the subject of his own prose"; such an awareness, however, the Anglican writer in particular transmutes into "the play of art."[7] In Browne, "every picture he draws of himself is a fully posed one";[8] the conceit of the world as the Art of God, and of man's art as recreation (in a double sense), sanctions and even sanctifies this self-conscious activity. Browne is therefore linked with Johan Huizinga's concept of "man at play."[9] Before Webber, at the beginning of the century, Edward Dowden thought of Browne's writing as a species of playing: "As a transcript from its author's spirit at the age of thirty, *Religio Medici* must not be taken in a literal sense; Browne plays around his own mind, and discovering a germ of feeling here, a suggestion of thought there, he develops these and refashions the whole substance of his being in an ideal mould."[10] Frank J. Warnke asks us to make an even more distinct separation between artist and created image. Warnke connects the popularity of the theater metaphor with "the concern with the illusory quality of experience which runs obsessively through the literature of the first two thirds of the seventeenth century."[11] Art takes on an ironic quality, with the author watching himself at work; even such "profoundly serious" books as *The Anatomy of Melancholy* and *Religio Medici* "operate through the projection of a persona, an image of the author's self which some other aspect of the author regards with a curious combination of delight, astonishment, trepidation, and bemused fascination." This stance, Warnke thinks, frees the artist from false theory, and the reader from an awkwardly unliterary relation to the given work: "not misled by either a naive faith in art as the mimesis of observed reality or a naive faith in art as expression of the self, the Baroque artist was free to create his art as art."

Religio Medici seems to me a work for which none of these approaches consistently accounts. I do not find it continuously a triumph of art, with a detached, even ironic, author consciously crafting a mask for himself; nor do I find it consistently naive and confessional. All self-description entails selection and so tends toward art; but the spectrum that runs from admission to art is a broad one. The interest of *Religio Medici* lies in how much of that spectrum it is able to occupy. We all live in divided worlds of adopted role and simple feeling; Browne's essay, it could be urged, reflects that division; so that even naiveté becomes the product of art. To some extent, this must be true, insofar as *Religio Medici* is interpreted as literature. But regarding the book as literature to some degree at least undermines its

7. Webber, *The Eloquent "I,"* pp. 4, 8.
8. Ibid., p. 156.
9. Webber, ibid., makes this reference on p. 179.
10. *Puritan and Anglican: Studies in Literature* (London, 1900), p. 44.
11. *Versions of Baroque: European Literature in the Seventeenth Century* (New Haven, 1972), p. 67. The following quotations from Warnke are on pp. 97–98, 220.

success. Around this paradox play some of the book's more interesting tactics and tensions.

III

For those who wish to emphasize the ironic author in *Religio Medici*, the preface "To the Reader" provides valuable evidence. This preface, in the authorized edition, alludes to a version of the book "corrupted" "by transcription" and already in print. Browne expresses his sense of doing what he is obliged to do in now offering "a full and intended copy of that Peece which was most unperfectly and surreptitiously published before" (*P,* 59). While it is difficult in these days of misuse of the press, he asserts, to counteract "things evidently false," one can and should do something about "things of truth falsly set forth" (*P,* 59). The alert reader may already feel some small adjustment in the relationship between himself and the author, who submits his essay to him not directly but as a service to "truth." More remarkable, the second paragraph is strikingly evasive about the status of the book now in the reader's hands. Browne explains that the unauthorized text, as a result of the copyists' endeavors, "arrived in a most depraved copy at the presse." He goes on:

> He that shall peruse that worke, and shall take notice of sundry particularities and personall expressions therein, will easily discerne the intention was not publik; and being a private exercise directed to my selfe, what is delivered therein was rather a memoriall unto me then an example or rule unto any other. (*P,* 59–60)

The reader prepares for a contrast between "that work" and the present work. Such a contrast never develops. Succeeding sentences begin: "It was penned . . . ," "It was set down . . . ," "There are many things delivered Rhetorically, many expressions therein . . . ," "Lastly all that is contained therein. . . ." The inexplicit prepositions and pronouns leave the reader entirely unclear about the distinction, if any, between the "private exercise" and the version now prepared for public attention. The disqualifications of the unauthorized edition blur into disclaimers about the kind of reading appropriate to the work now before us. This may be maladroitness on Browne's part. I prefer to think it a matter of tactics or guile. The seventeenth-century preface is a literary kind a contemporary audience would recognize as traditionally beset with irony. Browne makes use of it to detach himself from the text that follows. He concludes:

> Lastly, all that is contained therein is in submission unto maturer discernments, and as I have declared shall no further father them then the best and learned judgements shall authorize them; under favour of which considerations I have made its secrecie publike and committed the truth thereof to every ingenuous Reader. (*P,* 60)

We are unsure, as I have said, of the exact referent of "therein"; Browne will not "father" what is contained "therein" further than "learned judgements" will allow (the suppression of "I" before "shall" is characteristic and reduces a little Browne's presence: there is a witty play between "father" and "authorize"); yet, within these constraints, every "ingenuous" reader will receive the "truth." Commitment balances detachment in about as complicated a relation as it is possible to conceive. Entry to the essay under such auspices guarantees an open relationship between reader and author and construes the text as something other than personal utterance (it is not what Browne would say *now;* it is not what he would say at all were his discernment "maturer"; the writing is located somewhere between private musing and public utterance).

Of course, such tactics are traditional, save that Browne gives a further turn of the screw to the usual self-protective disclaimers, thus moving the text nearer to theater and the included "I" closer to persona. Within the text, the difficulty for the reader lies in maintaining critical distance from that persona. A vital cause of enjoyment in the theater is a knowledge of the distinction between actor and role, even in the most neo-naturalist forms. In social intercourse, too, we deal with mask-wearing by assuming (unconsciously, through habit) a similar distinction. In *Religio Medici* it is hard to separate Browne from "Browne," author from persona. Despite the elaborate preface, the convention within the text is that there is no such separation to make; the manner is confessional, the tone intimate, the implied contract with the reader one of admitting everything. Considered as literature, or even as social transcript, there is not background enough or perspective enough; the social or literary engagement loses its depth, and we are cheated of our interpretive role. Browne looms up and fills the screen. Joan Webber has noticed something of the kind but offers a debatable response. Remarking Browne's habit of referring to others by synecdoche (calling them "heads" or "judgments," but without further naming them), she writes: "His readers are able to keep liking him, and even thinking of him as really tolerant and modest, largely because it is easier for them to belong to his cosmic personality, for which he claims these attributes, than to the vulgar crowd."[12] Not every reader will think the preferred alternative desirable; to be swallowed up in another's "cosmic personality" will be seen by some as inherently objectionable, and certainly as violating the reservation of self that literary (and theatrical) manners normally require. Yet some such sacrifice of independence is entailed by the rhetoric of Browne's essay and is one of the responses that *Religio Medici* calls on us to make.

If some of the time we feel overwhelmed by the author's looming personality, perhaps more often we find ourselves negotiating a complex of uncertainties as to that personality's whereabouts; and this restores to us, though in an unsettling way, some role as interpreters. For example, Browne, when he flirts with heresies, flirts with them in a deliberately

12. Webber, *The Eloquent "I,"* p. 166.

blurred fashion. Mortalism, or psychopannychism, alleging the soul's mortality till Judgment Day, he deals with by distancing it first in time: like other errors it was a product of "my greener studies"; furthermore, as a heresy, it was "old and obsolete, such as could never have been revived" (*P*, 66).[13] The intellectual status of this heresy's appeal is thus confused, and Browne goes on to compromise the degree to which he is or was committed to it: "not that I did absolutely conceive a mortality of the soule" (*P*, 67). Nonetheless, the heresy becomes at the last if not a matter for pride, then an instance of humility; and by a sleight of hand with tenses it is brought uncertainly past error or present inclination:

> A serious reflex upon my owne unworthinesse did make me backward from challenging this prerogative of my soule; so I might enjoy my Saviour at the last, I could with patience be nothing almost unto eternity. (*P*, 67)

This is not to accuse Browne of deceit or self-deceit; it is to see that the relationship his awareness holds to this heresy is a shifting, adjusting, or, better, a dramatic one. Such a perception allows literary distance to flow back once more into our experience of the text. Something of the same kind could be said of Browne's well-known employment of negative constructions, a technique used with some complexity in the passage discussing the cessation of miracles:

> That Miracles are ceased, I can neither prove, nor absolutely deny, much lesse define the time and period of their cessation; that they survived Christ, is manifest upon record of Scripture; that they out-lived the Apostles also . . . we cannot deny, if wee shall not question those Writers whose testimonies wee doe not controvert, in points that make for our owne opinions; therefore that may have some truth in it that is reported by the Jesuites of the Miracles in the Indies, I could wish it were true, or had any other testimony then their owne Pennes. (*P*, 95)

Other passages employ negatives more forcefully to jolt or mislead the reader and thus set up a dramatic relationship; here the contract is more subtle. The apparently decisive "therefore" is in fact much less than decisive because of the tentative inquiries of the preceding clause; what positive charge it has is dissolved in the compounded hesitations of the clauses to follow. Again we are aware of Browne's hovering consciousness. But more interesting is the ungrammatical intervention of "I could wish it were true," prefaced only by a comma. For a moment we glimpse Browne (or his persona) perplexed and wistful among the bric-a-brac of his own thinking. Such glimpses permit us to see "round" the offered persona and thus as readers feel neither oppressed nor impotent.

There is a side to Browne's self-image in *Religio Medici* that is almost opposite to the dominating consciousness of which Joan Webber writes. A

13. Patrides (*P*, 67, n. 31) notes, however, that Calvin was obliged to write a treatise against the error in 1542.

remarkable instance occurs when Browne considers that topic of permanent fascination to the Renaissance mind, metempsychosis:

> for as though there were a *Metempsuchosis,* and the soule of one man passed into another, opinions doe finde after certaine revolutions, men and mindes like those that first begat them. (*P,* 66)

Characteristically, the analogy with metempsychosis is weakened, like a modified virus almost ("as though there were"), yet the implications are accepted. Opinions "find" men's minds and enter them. So the opinion-holding mind receives, or is occupied by, the opinions it holds. It is true that opinions find "mindes like those that first begat them"; and so a certain autonomy is restored to the mind as agent. But this irresolved liaison between the mind and its ideas seems descriptive of much that occurs in *Religio Medici.* A sort of psychomachia is played out, with Browne's persona as participant—and protagonist—but not as creator. Again, this clears a little space for the reader's sympathy and judgment. As the passage ends, it returns to the analogy of metempsychosis:

> men are lived over again, the world is now as it was in ages past, there was none then, but there hath been some one since that parallels him, and is as it were his revived selfe. (*P,* 66)

This is, as ever, rhetorically guarded ("as it were," "parallels"). Yet Browne appears to regard without uneasiness the prospect of unoriginality in ideas, and even the loss of a separate identity ("men are lived over again"). An outlook like this not only opposes the dominant self but seems to construe the reader's as the major consciousness. In theater, loss of identity terrifies, for the only existence the actor has lies in his role (many instances from *Richard II* through *King Lear* to Beckett could be cited). Browne, in these moments, appears to forsake, with equanimity, his existence as persona; the balance between reader and authorial "performance" alters again.

The imagery of *Religio Medici* is usually allusive and associational, and this accords with a first-person work where the exploring mind (not the narrative or the doctrine) determines content. But from time to time another kind of imagery is used. A well-known passage offers illustration:

> Yet have I not so shaken hands with those desperate Resolutions, who had rather venture at large their decaied bottome, then bring her in to be new trim'd in the dock; who had rather promiscuously retaine all, then abridge any, and obstinately be what they are, then what they have beene, as to stand in diameter and swords point with them. (*P,* 62)

The implicit drama of shaking hands and assuming a fencing stance is both spatially exact and yet spatially confusing, partly because of the negative construction, partly because of the way the evoked actions ambiguously recall and oppose each other. (There is also an associational ambiguity: shaking hands means farewell, but also betokens friendship.) Moreover, the incongruous image of a ship in need of repair interposes itself and renders absurd any spatially consistent reading. The metaphysical conceit is normally strict, if daring, in its treatment of spatial relationships. So too is Milton, though Marvell draws effects from conflation and confusion. Browne, I have suggested, provides access for the reader in certain ways, but when he writes in this vein his work recalls in its enclosed quality not the theatricality of the metaphysicals or Milton but rather Marvell. Theatrical "space" is denied.

For the most part, Browne conducts the emotional life of *Religio Medici* with control, sometimes to the point of its seeming false. But on occasion, emotion overrides control and allows us to read the text as we should a soliloquy. A poignant section near the book's end (II. 10) declares, no more than half-consciously it seems, the man within the image. The section opens with what we have come to recognize with no resentment as the customary mask: "For my conversation, it is like the Sunne's with all men, and with a friendly aspect to good and bad" (*P*, 151). This genial persona we accept, as we should accept someone who performed with success a similar role in everyday life. The movement of the prose is secure, and Browne's mind goes on to play some characteristically agile variations on the theme of human goodness and evil. At this point the rhythms change, and a new urgency of reference and expression enters:

> 'Tis that unruly regiment within me that will destroy me, 'tis I that doe infect my selfe, the man without a Navell yet lives in me; I feele that originall canker corrode and devoure me, and therefore *Defenda me Dios de me,* Lord deliver me from my selfe, is a part of my Letany, and the first voice of my retired imaginations. There is no man alone, because every man is a Microcosme, and carries the whole world about him. (*P*, 152)

Evidently a nerve is touched; the prose carries the note of a man under emotional strain. The repetitions have the effect not of rhetorical balance but of cries of distress: " 'Tis that unruly regiment . . . 'tis I that doe infect." The movement of mind from an agency that destroys, albeit an internal agency, to the self that destroys confirms the intensifying emotion. The following clause ("I feele that originall canker") is confessional, not in the familiar way Browne uses the *device* of confession throughout *Religio Medici,* but with the effect of emotion that demands expression. The preoccupation with solitude that emerges as the passage unfolds takes its place aptly within the inconsequential thinking that characterizes Browne's prose. But the insistence on being alone and not alone, in the quoted passage and after it, betrays a consciousness behind the given text, intuited through it (as we intuit a consciousness in social encounters or in the theater). The section gradually recovers equanimity, with Browne reflecting how God sustains the personality by his presence. He resolves the matter in the idiom of Neoplatonic philosophy: "In briefe, there can be nothing truely alone, and by its self, which is not truely one, and such is onely God: All others doe transcend an unity, and so by consequence are many" (*P*, 153). In a fashion characteristic of the whole book, the subject matter of the section is held as it

were in a field of force, coherent if hardly continuous. But here at least the
"real" emotion breaks free of the fictional; it is hard to read this passage as
intentional mask-wearing, and impossible to read it as irony.

There is a sense in which *Religio Medici* cannot be other than dramatic,
for, as critics have noted, Browne's conception of experience correlates
directly with the familiar topic of the world as stage. Life is perpetually in
process of transformation; reality as well as solitariness inheres only in God.
Death is the *mutatio ultima*, "a preparative way unto that last and glorious
Elixar which lies imprison'd in the chaines of flesh" (*P,* 110, n. 245). This
unstable world of appearances evokes inevitably the image of theater:

> mee thinkes I have outlived my selfe, and begin to be weary of the
> Sunne, I have shaked hands with delight in my warme blood and
> Canicular dayes, I perceive I doe Anticipate the vices of age, the world
> to mee is but a dreame, or mockshow, and we all therein but Pantalones
> and Antickes to my severer contemplations. (*P,* 112)

It is one thing to summon the conventional image, quite another to convey
its emotional potency. Here, the crowded syntax, the emotional rather than
witty logic, and the simple vocabulary (with scarcely an exception) show
Browne as a player on his own stage. Just such a perspective must in the end
certify the whole work, for Browne as artist shares the privilege of God's
creativity; but he is creature as well as creator. The mask may not be held
constant, but must imply or reveal the individual wearing it. Sufficiently
often, I think, in *Religio Medici* it does.

There is a last sense and a comprehensive one in which it might be argued
that *Religio Medici* approaches the condition of theater and in so doing
admits its reader as audience. That is the literary style itself, at its most
characteristic and successful. If fact and experience are the imprint of God's
mind, then describing them from our partial perspective becomes a hazard-
ous venturing among impressions, where the penalty for error is blasphemy.
Browne's sentence structures thus become philosophic, not stylish. Crossing a minefield requires wary walking, and the zigzag phrases and starts in
new directions that characterize Browne's prose may be thought appropriate tactics. If we can see only dimly the hidden glory, then questing and
wonder are the apt response, so that Browne's suspended sentences and
trailing clauses, so well described by Croll and others, dramatize the mind's
due activity. The tension of Browne's prose arises from such considerations
as these. Browne did not write, like Milton, "as ever in my great Taskmas-
ter's eye," at least not in the sense in which Milton felt that obligation.
Browne's world is no less sacramental than Milton's, but it is more hazard-
ous for the exploring mind. From such a double sense evolves at its best the
theater of Browne's prose.

The "Doubting" Thomas

Murray Roston

A perennial delight in reading the *Religio Medici* is the warmth of Browne's personality that shines throughout—a quality that Joan Webber has termed "the eloquent I."[1] The man himself is there before us, admitting with an engaging candor to his own idiosyncrasies and individual tastes in a manner that evokes the reader's indulgence and thereby establishes rapport before the author embarks on his more universal musings upon death or the cessation of oracles. "I love to lose my selfe in a mystery" (*P*, 69), he confides; and of his own religious doubts he concedes, "More of these no man hath knowne than my selfe, which I confesse I conquered, not in a martiall posture, but on my knees" (*P*, 85). The work, as he informs us in the preface, was composed as "a private exercise directed to my selfe," and although he remains conscious of his reader's presence as he writes, that self-contemplative mood is the starting point for any wider circlings of thought, and it is to that central self that the meditation will keep returning. A discourse on the decay of human flesh begins not, as one might expect, with a physician's account of postmortems he has performed nor with theological animadversions on mortality but with a confession, a personal disclosure of a trait rare in others; and if the "I" shifts soon to a more general "us," the note of intimacy has been struck and echoes on in the mind as he proceeds to the larger axioms:

> I have one part of modesty, which I have seldome discovered in another, that is (to speake truly) I am not so much afraid of death, as ashamed thereof; tis the very disgrace and ignominy of our natures, that in a moment can so disfigure us that our nearest friends, Wife, and Children stand afraid and start at us. (*P*, 111)

Sir Kenelm Digby, responding to *Religio Medici* within a few days of its publication, could see no possible justification for such self-centeredness. He was merely irritated by it: "What should I say of his making so particular a Narration of personal things, and private thoughts of his owne; the

1. *The Eloquent "I": Style and Self in Seventeenth-Century Prose* (Madison, 1968).

69

knowledge whereof can not much conduce to any man's betterment?"[2] Modern criticism has tended toward the opposite direction. That personal element in Browne's writings, the "self-exploring curiosity" of a mind pursuing the truth, actively engaged at the moment of setting pen to paper in an individual quest for verity, has come to be regarded not only as characteristic of Browne's own style but also in broader terms as the distinguishing mark of the new prose that was emerging in the late sixteenth and early seventeenth centuries. Since Morris Croll's seminal essay on the "baroque" style, which selected the *Religio Medici* as the main exemplar of the English mode, such writing has been seen, in contrast to the more formal rhetoric of the previous age, as offering to the reader "not the result of a meditation, but an actual meditation in process."[3] In a classic formulation, Croll pointed to the new preference for forms that express "the energy and labor of minds seeking the truth, not without dust and heat," over those expressing a contented sense of the enjoyment and possession of it. More specifically, he perceived within Browne's own work a struggle between the outward Pyrrhonist *ataraxia* and an inner dissatisfaction, between the fixed pattern of the more measured prose rhythms and an agitated forward movement, an energetic effort at imaginative realization creating, as in an El Greco painting, tortuous lines that "leap upward beyond the limit of the canvas." Austin Warren has written similarly of this personal search in progress, of the elements in the *Religio Medici* that, he affirms, display "the movement of ordering the mind in the process of thinking."[4] That inner movement D. C. Allen attributed to the spiritual distress of a Jacobean era unable to accept the Renaissance certitudes,[5] and Margaret Wiley in the same tradition has discerned behind Browne's protective quaintness and the cadences of his Latinity "an exciting search for truth" in a world torn by the conflicting claims of the new philosophy and the old faith.[6]

It is curious that such valuable insights into one of the emerging styles of the period should have been applied to a writer for whom they are so inappropriate; for a close reading of the *Religio Medici* suggests that Browne will not conform to the formula and that he belongs to a very different stylistic mode emerging within that period. Where those insights into seventeenth-century prose do apply, their relevance is impressive. Donne's writings, for example, even in so public a genre as the sermon, do indeed display the drama of a personal meditation in process, a probing inquiry into the isolated self. In place of the more authoritative Ciceronian phrases, there is an urgent, often labyrinthine movement toward some luminescent

2. *Observations upon Religio Medici*, 3d ed. (London, 1659), p. 33.

3. "The Baroque Style in Prose," in *Studies in English Philology in Honor of Frederick Klaeber,* ed. K. Malone and M. B. Ruud (Minneapolis, 1929), pp. 427–56.

4. "The Styles of Sir Thomas Browne," *Kenyon Review* 13 (1951): 674–87.

5. "Style and Certitude," *Journal of English Literary History* 15 (1948): 168.

6. *The Subtle Knot: Creative Scepticism in Seventeenth-Century England* (New York, 1968), p. 137.

truth whose import is only fully grasped at the climactic moment of final perception. The religious message, universal though it may be, is presented from the viewpoint of the lone meditator, visualizing with anguish the series of discoveries by which his spiritual journey proceeds, and we are permitted to witness that process of discovery in action:

> when I shall need peace, because there is none but thou, O Lord, that should stand for me, and then shall finde, that all the wounds that I have, come from thy hand, all the arrowes that stick in me, from thy quiver; when I shall see, that because I have given my selfe to my corrupt nature, thou hast changed thine; and because I am all evill towards thee, therefore thou hast given over being good towards me; When it comes to this height, that the fever is not in the humors, but in the spirits, that mine enemy is not an imaginary enemy, fortune, nor a transitory enemy, malice in great persons, but a reall, and an irresistible, and an inexorable, and an everlasting enemy, the Lord of Hosts himselfe.[7]

This is indeed a prose that catches in its rhythms and sequences the motion of a soul rather than its state of rest.

In Browne's writing there are certain affinities. Providence, he argues at one point, is not an outside force exerted upon nature but is intrinsic to the lifespan of all creatures. He too narrows down the focus from the universal to the sole self contemplating the possibility of its early death, and then moves upward toward the hand of God that determines all:

> Let them not therefore complaine of immaturitie that die about thirty, they fall but like the whole world, whose solid and well composed substance must not expect the duration and period of its constitution, when all things are compleated in it, its age is accomplished, and the last and generall fever may as naturally destroy it before six thousand, as me before forty, there is therefore some other hand that twines the thread of life than that of nature; wee are not onely ignorant in Antipathies and occult qualities, our ends are obscure as our beginnings, the line of our dayes is drawne by night, and the various effects therein by a pencill that is invisible; wherein though we confesse our ignorance, I am sure we doe not erre, if wee say, it is the hand of God. (*P*, 114)

It is a remarkable passage, powerful in its rhetorical force and, though Browne has been reproved for the poverty of his metaphors, concluding with a haunting image; but there is no energetic forward movement of spontaneous thought here such as would distinguish a mind progressing "without meditation, stating its idea in the first form that occurs." Donne, we may assume, had also established his theological tenets before composing the sermon, yet, in the tradition of the religious meditation intended to revitalize faith by stimulating the imagination, the act of writing itself, as

---

7. "Second Prebend Sermon" delivered 29 January 1625; in *The Sermons of John Donne*, ed. E. M. Simpson and G. R. Potter (Berkeley, 1962), 7: 57.

well as the oral delivery of the sermon, is aimed at conjuring up afresh the immediacy of the visionary experience and of the deepening emotional response it evokes. The progression of "when I shall need . . . and then shall finde . . . when I shall see . . ." creates the momentum that Croll so rightly discerned; but it is a momentum absent from Browne's treatise. His is an assertion of a belief already formed and personally confirmed. The "therefores" do not mark stages in a developing argument but serve as buttresses to the main structure, strengthening a concept already propounded. With that broad tolerance that constitutes one of Browne's greatest charms, he presents his conclusion with a modicum of caution ("I am sure we doe not erre, if we say . . ."), but he is in fact restating the view offered more confidently a few lines before the quoted passage, his conviction that God's wisdom both determines and accomplishes the "secret glome or bottome of our dayes."[8] This is not a difference merely of intensity but of the thought patterns themselves. The Donne passage is dramatically alive, producing the effect of ideas conveyed instantaneously as they are struck out in the mind, while Browne's is a more formal discourse, presenting in reasoned periods the author's beliefs offered for the reader's interest and delectation.

The assumption that Browne's outward calm is offset by an agitated inner exploration finds little support even in those endearing admissions of personal idiosyncrasy with their aura of introspective discontent. Frequently couched in confessional terms, they arouse in the reader's mind, particularly within this context of a meditation on faith, associations with the dissatisfied self-searchings of the religious penitent. "I am, I confesse, naturally inclined to . . . ," "I could never hear the *Ave Marie* Bell without . . . ," "I confesse I have had an unhappy curiosity. . . ." Such phrases recall the yearning for self-improvement that the meditation in both the Loyolan and Protestant versions of the *Spiritual Exercises* sought to encourage, the reviewing of the worshiper's own sins before he posed to himself the urgent questions, "What have I done for Christ? What am I now doing for Christ? What ought I do for Christ?"[9] There is, however, a strange consistency in Browne's confessions: despite their penitential and self-critical phrasing, they lead to the acknowledgment not of personal failings but of virtues, or, at the very least, of traits that ultimately redound to the confessor's credit. The first of the above quotations continues, "I am, I confesse, naturally inclined to that, which misguided zeale termes superstition" (*P*, 63), which is subsequently justified as a civility that serves to increase his devotion. Although as a Protestant he admitted he could never hear the Ave Maria bell without elevation, we are soon to learn that, while the Catholic worshipers "directed their devotions to her, I offered mine to God, and rectified the

---

8. Croll does acknowledge, as a variation, the statement of a truth followed by different aspects of it, but even there he sees the sequel as consisting of "new apprehensions" of that truth like the successive flashes of a revolving jewel.

9. *The Spiritual Exercises of St. Ignatius*, trans. A. Mottola (New York, 1964), p. 56.

errours of their prayers by rightly ordering mine owne"; and of his "unhappy curiosity" that led him to question the veracity of the Scriptures, we are told that he laughed himself out of it with a piece of Justin (*P*, 97). To deduce from such personal revelations that there exists below the surface a dissatisfied self-probing is to relate only to the opening phrases and to ignore their conclusions.

The list of such "confessions" is long. Browne admits to being uncontentious, immune to fears of death or hell, he could lose an arm without a tear, would never think of himself before God, country, or friends, gives charity only to fulfill the word of God, has escaped the vice of Pride (a comment that aroused the ire of his contemporary, Alexander Ross), loves music because he himself is harmoniously composed, and, though he grants in the accepted language of devotional works that he is the heir to Adam's vices and acknowledges his own unworthiness compared to the true Elect, he seems serenely confident that, if he will not be in the first ranks of the saints, he will at least bring up the rear. Significantly, when he does admit to a failing, it is always placed firmly in the past, as something manfully overcome and long settled. The manifold religious doubts he confesses to in the passage quoted at the beginning of this essay were, he concedes, conquered not in a martial posture but on his knees (itself a creditable admission); yet conquered they were. Where the disturbed religious meditator would despair of forgiveness for the enormity of his past sins, and often seems to reach back to them as a means of intensifying his present anguish and hence his awareness of a final dependence on the blood of the Crucifixion, Browne cheerfully dismisses his own sins with an easy finality as having been fully expiated and therefore as being worthy to be forgotten:

> For my originall sinne, I hold it to be washed away in my Baptisme; for my actuall transgressions, I compute and reckon with God, but from my last repentance, Sacrament or generall absolution: And therefore am not terrified with the sinnes or madnesse of my youth. (*P*, 145)

Cumulatively, these personal passages create the picture of a man not perhaps complacent, for he knows well his ultimate need for divine mercy, but certainly confident that he has won through to a sane outlook on life and a healthy balance between the realities of this world and the mysteries of the next. It is ironic, in fact, that the very writer selected by Croll to represent a rejection of any contented "enjoyment and possession" of truth should in fact have used the same words to defend the opposite view in his dislike of controversy: "A man may be in as just possession of Truth as of a City, and yet bee forced to surrender; tis therefore farre better to enjoy her with peace then to hazzard her on a battell" (*P*, 66). It would seem that at the time of writing the *Religio Medici* Browne felt himself to be already in possession of the truth or, at the very least, of those truths meaningful for him.

Browne contradicts himself, of course, as he shifts from mood to mood. He will declare at one moment with the pride of a patient displaying his wounds that he is deeply melancholic, "the miserablest person extant" (*P*,

109), and at the next that he is of a happy disposition (*P*, 154). He reveals his unique traits and preferences but then insists blithely that he has no idiosyncrasies (*P*, 133). He assures us that his many attainments such as his knowledge of "no lesse than six languages" have left him free of any sense of superiority toward his fellowmen, yet a few lines later he allows us a truer insight into his real self by displaying his resentment when those attainments are not acknowledged.

> I know the names, and somewhat more, of all the constellations in my Horizon, yet I have seene a prating Mariner that could onely name the Poynters and the North Starre, out-talke mee, and conceit himselfe a whole Spheare above mee. (*P*, 147)

If such glimpses allow the reader to form a more rounded impression of his character, including his weaknesses as well as his strengths, the author remains genially impervious to such contradictions in himself. Paradoxes he certainly affirms with that love of mystery in which he delights, but they are not the riddling paradoxes of a character torn within itself, nor even the theological paradoxes that leave the believer in despair of ever finding his salvation. His are *resolved* paradoxes, where the soul recognizes the limits of reason and bows respectfully to the religious truths that lie beyond: "and this I think is no vulgar part of faith to believe a thing not only above, but contrary to reason, and against the arguments of our proper senses" (*P*, 72).

Yet something is missing in the picture. Browne does not turn his back on the darker aspects of human life, nor ignore the problems and doubts that arise in the minds of men. We trust him because his range is so wide, his vision so inclusive. He is the physician who is familiar with our human ills, who acknowledges our suffering, and, if he encourages us to bear the pain with fortitude, who is sufficiently aware that the disease is fatal. It is, indeed, that calm self-assurance as he attends upon us, the sympathy of one who has himself experienced the grievous malady, that wins our confidence even as he presses upon the tenderest points of pain.

The *Religio Medici,* then, is not a tortuous search for certitude as we have been led to believe, but rather the celebration of an achieved equilibrium of spirit. Its brilliance as a literary work and, indeed, its enduring attraction derive to no small extent from its ability to avoid any impression of complacency despite that self-confidence, and it does so by carefully introducing the doubts and fears of mankind while avoiding any disturbance of the overall equilibrium. Browne obtains this effect partly, as we have seen, by subtly relegating such torments to the past as stages in his own movement toward maturity, and partly by his technique of deceptive first-person "confessions" that really lead toward affirmations of that calm of mind. So far from there being a visible struggle between inner agitation and outward calm, there is, I would suggest, only an *illusion* of personal disturbance to that overall serenity of spirit, its purpose being to acknowledge the existence of the darker shadows in the human condition and to strengthen our own confidence in the author's wider experience. To put it differently, Browne deliberately creates a momentary impression of emotional tribulation in order to heighten the subsequent triumph of the sane, reasoning self that has assigned the paradoxes and mysteries to the realm of faith. Thereby it has fortified its own dominion elsewhere, creating a division of kingship between Reason and Faith, with each "exercising his Soveraignty and Prerogative in a due time and place, according to the restraint and limit of circumstance" (*P*, 85).

The following must surely rank among the most affecting passages in the work, seeming to reveal as we read it a deep spiritual ordeal; yet it is really trompe l'oeil:

> But it is the corruption that I feare within me, not the contagion of commerce without me. 'Tis that unruly regiment within me that will destroy me, 'tis I that doe infect my selfe, the man without a Navell yet lives in me; I feele that originall canker corrode and devoure me, and therefore *Defenda me Dios de me*, Lord deliver me from my selfe, is a part of my Letany, and the first voyce of my retired imaginations. There is no man alone, because every man is a *Microcosme*. (*P*, 152)

If one were to ask precisely what fear disturbs him, the answer would be hard to come by. The fear is diffused into generalized terms. The "unruly regiment within" or "that originall canker" inherited from Adam is resorted to in place of specifics, and the purpose, it transpires, is really to lead up to "the Apophthegme of a wise man," the Ciceronian axiom that no man is less alone than when he is alone. For some critics, such last-minute withdrawals from a direct confrontation with his own doubts and fears have seemed to mark a failure in Browne's art. Stanley Fish particularly has faulted Browne within the context of the searching dialectical tradition of the seventeenth century for revealing a basic indifference to pain, for being more concerned with the making of a better artifact "than with the sounding of souls and the making of better persons."[10] But if Browne does not belong within that context at all, then the criteria themselves are inapplicable. It may be that Browne's artistic purpose has been misunderstood, that he should be placed not within the category of meditative self-probing but elsewhere in the developing patterns of seventeenth-century thought.

Since the "baroque" identification of his prose began in the context of the visual arts, perhaps we should return there. Aesthetically, the *Religio Medici* has little affinity to the paintings of El Greco with which it has long been compared. In those canvases, anguished figures stretch upward in religious ecstasy, striving away from this world in their yearning for the eternal. Theirs is a faith snatched from despair, echoing the tormented cry of Fulke Greville at the wearisome condition of man, divided between reason and passion:

10. *Self-Consuming Artifacts: The Experience of Seventeenth-Century Literature* (Berkeley, 1972), p. 373.

> Born under one law, to another bound,
> Vainly begot, and yet forbidden vanity,
> Created sick, commanded to be sound.

> *(Mustapha,* V, iv)

Such religious mannerists (as they would now be called, rather than "baroque" artists[11]) escaped from the dictates of reason and the new empiricism by placing their hope in an agonized transcendence of reality, a closing of the shutters on this world, whose forms lose their accustomed shape to the spiritual vision of a soul reaching beyond. Browne, with his sharp interest in natural phenomena, his careful tabulation "of places, beasts, fowles, & fishes," the depth of mines and the subsistence of cities, has no part in this rejection or derogation of actuality. Although he declares that he will not "so forget God as to adore the name of Nature" (*P,* 79), seeing in it the wisdom of the divine plan, he does believe that to study and engage in deliberate research into His creatures is "the debt of our reason wee owe unto God" (*P,* 75). While never underestimating the significance of eternal life, he can, because of his firm awareness of the division of realms, indulge his empirical bent to the full. Hence the absence of any tension between his tasks as a physician and his religious beliefs as a Christian; hence his achievement of a resolution between the natural and the spiritual.

If we must beware of any easy classifications of the various aesthetic forms in which the conflict between reason and faith expressed itself in that era, at least the broader groupings are comparatively clear within the visual arts. The baroque may be defined as a paean to divine splendor, to an infinite power that incorporates reason, energy, and the wealth of this material world as aspects of its plenitude, while mannerism, as has been noted, is the disturbed search for an inner spiritual truth outreaching the merely physical or logical. Both rely on the emotional response to actuality, one glorifying it, the other rejecting it. But there was a third style emerging in the early seventeenth century, exactly contemporaneous with Browne's treatise, and this style may be more relevant to his writings.

After a number of unsuccessful attempts in Rome to imitate the opulence of the Italian baroque artists, upon his return to France Nicolas Poussin inaugurated a style that involved the portrayal of apparently passionate scenes, in which the calm dictates of rational restraint prevailed nonetheless. The technique he employed to achieve that effect is instructive. *The Adoration of the Golden Calf,* for example, which he painted about 1636, depicts the fervor of religious celebrants as they dance in honor of their new god. In the tradition of Titian's scenes of bacchanalian orgy, the figures are presented at the moment of revelry; but where Titian swings the spectator into

11. Since the appearance of Walter Friedlander's *Mannerism and Anti-Mannerism in Italian Painting* in 1925, there has been a growing tendency to distinguish from the larger grouping of the baroque those painters to whom Vasari would have applied the term *mannerist.* See, for example, John Shearman, *Mannerism* (Harmondsworth, 1967); for the literary application, see Arnold Hauser, *Mannerism,* trans. E. Mosbacher (New York, 1965).

Nicolas Poussin, *The Adoration of the Golden Calf* (circa 1636). Reproduced by courtesy of the Trustees, The National Gallery, London.

the sweeping movement of Bacchus's own leap from the chariot, Poussin remains quietly aloof. He creates only an illusion of revelry rather than genuine abandonment. Only on closer scrutiny does one perceive that each figure, seemingly whirling in a circle of dancers, is, in fact, carefully poised upon one leg in perfect equilibrium, so that even were the dancers to release hands, each would remain upright and stable.[12] We are led to imagine that we are witnessing a scene of human surrender to passion, but, since the passion is posed, we are artistically prevented from surrendering to it ourselves and hence our confidence in rational control is strengthened.

The "modes" or rules for painting that Poussin introduced into France, and that, through his pupil Charles Le Brun, were to dominate the French Royal Academy throughout the reign of Louis XIV, established the so-called classical style with its respect for rationalism. "We must not judge by our senses alone," Poussin declared, "but by reason"; and he demanded "a certain restraint and moderation" in the portraying of all scenes however violent or passionate they might be in theme.[13] To achieve such restraint, a

12. His *Bacchanalian Revel,* painted about 1637, employs the same technique. It is also in The National Gallery, London.

13. Quoted in Anthony Blunt, *Nicolas Poussin* (New York, 1967), p. 220. Blunt discusses at length the stoical elements that entered Poussin's work at about that period. The second quotation is from a letter to Paul de Fréart, Sieur de Chantelou, dated 24 November 1647 and appearing in E. G. Holt, ed., *A Documentary History of Art* (New York, 1958), 2:155.

El Greco, *The Resurrection of Christ* (circa 1598). Courtesy the Prado, Madrid.

method he adopted in his own paintings was to avoid the depiction of spontaneous emotion by employing instead dramatic gestures that would serve to indicate it. Where the figures in an El Greco canvas, such as his *Resurrection,* are caught at the very moment of the revelation, writhing in torment or flung violently backward by the immediate shock of the vision, the worshipers to the right in Poussin's painting are calm and motionless. Their inner feelings are not displayed but rather suggested by their stance— an outstretched hand, a turn of the head, a pointing finger. The only real passion seen in action, Moses' fury as he dashes the holy tablets to the ground, is significantly relegated to a dark patch in the background where it could easily be missed were it not for the heads of the two revelers below turned away from the celebration to gaze at the source of the disturbance. The religious fervor of Moses, therefore, although intrinsic to the biblical event, is by that means separated from the main action, alluded to, but not permitted to affect the dominant calm of the picture.

So it is with Browne's *Religio Medici,* which reflects in literature that movement toward rational control that found its culmination in Dryden's writings. In the latter's heroic dramas, such as *The Conquest of Granada,* however impassioned his characters may be, they seem to be standing outside themselves, calmly measuring the degree of anger or frustration to which their emotions have succumbed, and commenting upon those emotions rather than offering any demonstration of the passion itself:

> *Abdelmelech:* She's gone; and now
> Methinks there is less glory in a crown;
> My boiling passions settle and go down.
>
> (II, i, 178–80)

In Browne's writings the religious ardor he experiences is never condemned. On the contrary, it is validated as an integral part of Christian worship; but it is moved into the background as belonging to the past or, indeed, to any period other than the moment of writing. He will allude to an *O altitudo!,* to his "untamed affections," to his abundant weeping at religious ceremonies, but we are never permitted to watch the author actually engaged in mystic or devotional meditation, or to see his soul struggling toward the realization of a truth.

At his most personal moments, therefore, with assurances that he speaks from his soul, he encourages us to believe that an act of intimate self-revelation is about to occur; but the potential confession is carefully dissipated into abstract terms such as "a mass of mercies," or "favours of his affection," and the passage proceeds not toward a personal discovery that we may share, but toward the promulgation of a universal religious truth, an assertion of the established tenet that "God is mercifull unto all":

> And to be true, and speake my soule, when I survey the occurrences of my life, and call into account the finger of God, I can perceive nothing but an abysse and masse of mercies, either in generall to mankind, or in

particular to my selfe; and whether out of the prejudice of my affection, or an inverting and partiall conceit of his mercies, I know not, but those which others terme crosses, afflictions, judgements, misfortunes, to me who enquire farther into them than their visible effects, they both appeare, and in event have ever proved the secret and dissembled favours of his affection. It is a singular piece of wisedome to apprehend truly, and without passion the workes of God, and so well to distinguish his justice from his mercy, as not to miscall those noble attributes. (*P*, 126)

The apparent fervency of the opening is, it transpires, only a lead-in for a reasoned theological statement; it is a "posed" passion that ultimately confirms the calm, controlling view.

On the other hand, despite that overall serenity, we remain persuaded of Browne's profound faith. His is not a theological treatise presented from the standpoint of a cold rationalist. It offers instead a touching self-portrait of a soul that has been plunged into doubts and fears, has joyed in mystery and paradox, and has meditated long on the nature of death. But it is a prose-poem by one no longer actively engaged in a disturbed search for spiritual truth, who is content instead with the religious philosophy he has evolved— rendering unto reason that which is reason's while yet rendering unto God that which is God's.

The Two Tables
in *Religio Medici*

Raymond B. Waddington

Let not the twelve, but the two Tables be thy Law.
  Sir Thomas Browne, *Christian Morals,* III.21

"Here—the Ten Commandments. She was a great believer in some of them."
  Joe Orton, *Loot* (1966)

In conscious reaction to an earlier tradition of impressionistic "appreciation," twentieth-century critics of *Religio Medici* have focused with increasing discrimination upon the interrelated issues of genre and style. While our comprehension necessarily remains imperfect, we have been instructed and enlightened by the dialogue among, on the one hand, those who perceive the genre as personal essay, spiritual autobiography, or meditation and, on the other, those who describe the style as Attic, baroque, "middle," epistolary, or Anglican.[1] Yet, for all the attention to these two issues, another fundamental matter, structure, comes close to being ignored.

Even scholars who acknowledge the importance of the bipartite structure in *Religio* do not always come to terms with it. Those who have done so most frequently offer a rationale based upon the scheme of the theological virtues. Part II commences with the assertion,

> Now for that other Vertue of Charity, without which Faith is a meer notion, and of no existence, I have ever endeavoured to nourish the mercifule disposition, and humane inclination I borrowed from my Parents, and regulate it to the written and prescribed Lawes of Charity. (*P,* 133)

Thus, it is explained, Browne retrospectively calls attention to his implicit

---

1. For a recent assessment of these views, see Anne Drury Hall, "Epistle, Meditation, and Sir Thomas Browne's *Religio Medici," Publications of the Modern Language Association* 96 (1979): 234–46.

scheme of division; if the subject of Part II is Charity, Part I must concern Faith and Hope. There are only two parts and not three because, since Faith cannot be separated from Hope, these two virtues inevitably conflate into one consideration.[2] Some readers, possibly troubled by the element of circular reasoning in the latter explanation, limit their descriptions to the two virtues directly named by Browne: the subject of Part I is Faith and that of Part II is Charity.[3]

I wish to raise a different possibility, however, and to suggest that the phrase "that other Vertue of Charity" contains a characteristic bit of word play. The "other Vertue" is not a different moral excellence to which he now turns for the first time. Since references to Charity are frequent in Part I, such a statement would be self-evidently contradictory. Rather, he addresses another aspect or quality (see *OED*, "virtue," II) of the virtue, moral excellence (*OED*, sv, I.3), upon which he has been reflecting throughout. Although our sense of the meaning of *charity* unfortunately has narrowed, the two aspects of the virtue to which Browne punningly alerts us are the traditionally accepted ones: "Man's love of God and his neighbours, commanded as the fulfilling of the Law, Matt. xxii. 37, 39" (*OED*, sv, b). The two branches of Charity, love of God and love of one's neighbors, were instilled in the memories of Protestant Englishmen by basic religious instruction. The *OED* cites the 1552 *Catechism* of Archbishop John Hamilton: "Quhate is cherite? It is lufe, quharby we lufe God for his awin saik . . . and our neichbour for Gods saik, or in God." The formulation varied little from Hamilton to Browne, writing eighty years later: "Now there is another part of charity, which is the Basis and Pillar of this, and that is the love of God, for whom wee love our neighbour: for this I thinke charity, to love God for himselfe, and our neighbour for God" (*P*, 159). Here, nearing the end of Part II, Browne reverts to its opening, explaining unmistakably his first teasing reference and asserting the relation between the two parts of Charity and the two parts of *Religio Medici*.

Like a set of parentheses, the two remarks provide a definitive context for understanding the discourse of Part II that they literally bracket; but, in elucidating the distinction between the two aspects of Charity which governs Browne's partition, figuratively the remarks also embrace and define the two parts. The two great commandments of Matthew 22:36–40, which Hamilton and Browne faithfully echo, constitute Christ's abridgement of the Ten Commandments into two. As James Ussher, Bishop of Armagh, marvels, "sith it was great cunning to contrive the whole will of God into

2. See Frank L. Huntley, *Sir Thomas Browne: A Biographical and Critical Study* (Ann Arbor, 1962), p. 107; Joan Webber, *The Eloquent "I": Style and Self in Seventeenth-Century Prose* (Madison, 1968), p. 161; and *P*, 49, n. 133.

3. See Leonard Nathanson, *The Strategy of Truth: A Study of Sir Thomas Browne* (Chicago, 1967), pp. 80–81; and John R. Mulder, *The Temple of the Mind* (New York, 1969), p. 158, n. 9.

Ten words, it must needs be more wonderfull to bring all into two."[4] Because Moses engraved the Ten Commandments upon two tables, the presumption arose that the disposition between tables conformed to the distinction in duties prescribed by the commandments, the first four pertaining to God and the last six to man. Christ's "two words," therefore, summarize the lessons of the Two Tables. Ussher expounds the belief catechistically:

> *What is the summe of the first?*
> Thou shalt love the Lord thy God with all thy heart, and with all thy Soule, and with'all thy strength, and with all thy minde, *Deutero.*6.5. *Mat.*22.37, 38. *Luke* 10.27
> *What is the summe of the second?*
> Thou shalt love thy Neighbour as thy selfe, *Luke* 19.19, *Matth.* 22.39 *Luke* 10.27
> *What is the summe of this summe?*
> Love, which consisteth in two heads (as we have heard) to wit the love of God, and of our neighbour, *Luk.* 10.27 I *Iohn* 5.2. I *Tim.* 1.4,5.[5]

When Browne speaks of regulating his natural inclination "to the written and prescribed Lawes of Charity," he alludes obviously to the Second Table of laws governing love for one's neighbor. The two parts of Browne's treatise are distinguished by the Two Tables.[6] *Religio Medici* is a meditation upon the Two Tables in which the two kinds of love there embodied not only supply the general subjects for the two parts but, as I shall demonstrate, the series of commandments upon each table also provides an implicit structure of argument within those parts.[7]

In a valuable, recent study of religious attitudes in Stuart England, J. Sears McGee has maintained that, rather than by looking for sharp doctrinal oppositions, we can discriminate Puritan from Anglican most sensitively by seeking differences of interpretation and emphasis in commonly shared

---

4. *A Body of Divinitie; or, The Svmme and Svbstance of Christian Religion* (London, 1645), p. 209. In the following analysis I shall take this exposition as a standard for comparison. It is a useful one because it is a full and suggestive commentary, appropriate to the time period of *Religio,* and because its author was greatly respected by Anglican and Puritan alike.

5. Ibid., pp. 208–9.

6. Huntley, *Sir Thomas Browne,* p. 107, suggests this possibility, among several others, as a general model for the dual structure. I wish to argue, however, that it is a particular model. The "Two Tables" designation for the Ten Commandments was ubiquitous. See, for example, the heading for Exodus 20 in the Geneva Bible.

7. For *Religio* as a meditation, see especially Nathanson, *The Strategy of Truth,* pp. 76–81, 93–99; and Hall, "Epistle," pp. 236–39. She observes, "But when a writer borrowed the meditation for literary purposes and gave up the clear stages of the formal meditation, he still had to deal with the problem of artistic shape . . . the problem in longer ones was to prevent them from turning into rambling soliloquies, lacking direction and emphasis" (p. 237). In *Religio* the form of the Two Tables supplies that needed shape.

beliefs. Using as his standard the Ten Commandments to which both Anglican and Puritan were absolutely committed as an article of faith, McGee discerns significant differences in treatment:

> Puritans tended to emphasize the duties of the First Table, whereas Anglicans tended to emphasize those of the Second. Further, the Puritans insisted upon an interpretation of the requirements of the First Table which the Anglicans rejected in favor of their own. These contrasting emphases and interpretations provide a key to the "bosom sins" which each set of partisans accused the other of committing, thereby demonstrating the falsity of their conversions and the unsoundness of their hopes of salvation.[8]

An unusually succinct statement of the Anglican position was preached by Thomas Pierce in a 1658 sermon: "the Second Table is the touchstone of our obedience to the First. Our chiefest duty towards God is our duty towards our neighbor."[9]

Scholars have described Browne's religious position as moderate, if sometimes idiosyncratic, Anglicanism, his commitment to toleration and irenicism giving him strong affinities with the latitudinarians and the Cambridge Platonists.[10] This religious profile largely determines his handling both of the Two Tables generally and of the individual commandments specifically. Meditating upon their personal significance for himself, Browne never names the commandments and branches by rote as would the catechumen; the familiar sequence of topics is taken for granted. Recognizably, however, the meditation upon them is an Anglican one. Browne typically seizes upon the aspect of a commandment that appeals to him, rather than giving a comprehensive exposition, and presents the commandment in positive form, visualizing how the duty may be fulfilled in daily life and not enumerating all of its violations. Part I of *Religio Medici* is more than twice as long as Part II, implicitly acknowledging the supreme importance of the First Table. Part II, however, is a far more systematic and direct application of the Second Table, contrasting with the looser, more selective, and more generalized exposition of the First Table in Part I. In short, the immediacy of Second Table duties and the remoteness of First Table duties are expressions of Browne's Anglicanism.

I

Although the transitions are elusive and the points of logical progression sometimes difficult to specify, the topics and ordering of Part I generally are

---

8. *The Godly Man in Stuart England: Anglicans, Puritans, and the Two Tables, 1620–1670* (New Haven, 1976), p. 70. The chronological span helpfully corresponds to that of Browne's maturity.

9. Quoted by McGee, ibid., p. 244.

10. See, particularly, Huntley, *Sir Thomas Browne*; Nathanson, *The Strategy of Truth*, pp. 116–41; and *P*, 23–32.

clear enough. *Religio Medici* begins with a definition of its author's religious faith as Christian, Protestant, and Anglican (sections 1–5). Browne states his aversion to religious controversy, explains his position on heresies, asserts his belief in the fundamental Christian mysteries, and states the relation between reason and faith (6–10). The second and most lengthy division presents his conception of God, who is comprehended through His attributes of wisdom and eternity (11–13). These attributes themselves are perceived through the traditional sources of revelation, the two books of Nature and Scripture (13–35). Studying causality in Nature reveals God's Providence, the manifestation of His two attributes (14–18); the subject of Providence leads to consideration of Fortune and other, related failures of Faith (19–20); that, in turn, leads to questions of belief in the Scriptures (21–25), in martyrs, miracles, and relics (26–29), and in the spirit world, both good and bad (30–33). Since man is the microcosm uniting the two realms of matter and spirit, Nature and Scripture, the succeeding unit takes up the situation and nature of man (34–42). This includes the inevitability of death (37–38, 40); but, since man's life span is determined by Providence (43), that occurrence must be happy. Browne then contemplates the four Last Things (44–52), the question of salvation (53–58), and his own spiritual state (59–60). The circular progression, thus, is from religion, to God, to God's works, to man as the microcosm of those works, to man's relationship to God—which is to say, his religion.

Generally speaking, all of these are First Table topics, properly dominated by the First Commandment, which was understood to epitomize all the others. John Hooper declares, "The first part of the first commandment containeth, as thou seest by the interpretation of Moses, the fountain and original of all true religion; and is as the foundation and root, from whence springeth all the other commandments; and is comprehended in these four words: knowledge of God: fear of God: faith in God: and loue of God."[11] To Ussher it commands "The having of a God; and herein Religion" and it requires the "knowing of God in himselfe, in his properties, and in his workes."[12] Browne, therefore, states his religious position as it is founded in his knowledge of God through contemplation of his mysteries, attributes, and works; he professes his faith in God (Part I, sections 9–10, 20) and affirms "I feare God, yet am not afraid of him" (*P,* 126), making the whole meditation an expression of his love for God.

Yet the conventionality of that general outline takes on greatly different contours if we juxtapose it to the contemporary debate about the interpretation of First Table duties. In McGee's reconstruction of that debate, the crucial issue emerges as a question of authority: obedience to God or obedience to man? In 1633 William Laud was appointed archbishop of Canterbury, climaxing more than a decade of steadily increasing power and

11. *A Declaration of the Ten Holy Commandments,* cap. 4, in *Early Writings,* ed. Samuel Carr, The Parker Society, 20 (Cambridge, 1943), p. 306.
12. Ussher, *A Body of Divinitie,* p. 214.

influence within the Church of England. Laud's campaign to restore "decency" and conformity to the Church culminated in the prescription of ceremonial observances for services and in the reissue of the *Book of Sports,* authorizing Sunday recreations, both acts that the Puritans saw as seriously infringing upon their efforts to obey the First Table laws. Puritan reactions against the Laudian "innovations" resulted in the concerted suppression of Puritan preachers, lecturers, and the abolition of the "Feoffees for Impropriations." Attempts by the Puritans to demonstrate their obedience to God in all First Table matters were thus manifested in three areas of human disobedience: "the opposition to ceremonial innovations, the defense of 'godly preaching' and lecturing, and the demand for precise observation of the Sabbath." Conversely, "The Anglican strategy of opposition to the puritan interpretation of Christian duties was, in effect, a detour around the First Table to the Second." McGee's analysis finds the Anglican rebuttal to rest upon two, central arguments:

> The first was that no man could consider himself anything other than damned if he were a rebel and a schismatic. To disobey the prince by rebellion and the Church of England by schism was the deadliest kind of sin and a conclusive sign of reprobation if it went unrepented. The second argument was that no man could have assurance of salvation if he were guilty of the sin of uncharitableness. One form of uncharitableness was the judging of others by calling them superstitious idolators, oppressors of Christian liberty, and the like.

More positively stated, the Anglicans believed that First Table duties were "entirely fulfilled by honest participation in the prescribed rituals and that puritan attacks upon those rituals were unjustified." Further, "the mark of a good Christian was avoidance of theological controversy and concentration upon Second Table duties; and finally, that an acceptable measure of perfection in those duties was attainable by using Christ as an exemplar."[13]

Through circumstantial evidence, we can fix the composition of *Religio Medici* within the period from December 1633 to October 1635,[14] precisely the span of time during which Laud was at the zenith of his power and during which Puritan response to his measures reached the most frenzied pitch of indignation. Both at the time that *Religio* was written and at the time that it was published—when the power advantage had shifted from Anglican to Puritan—the intensity of polarized feelings attaching to interpretation of the Two Tables established fields of meaning against which Browne deliberately charted his own course. James N. Wise has argued that implicitly *Religio* is "a piece of contemporary argumentation. The tolerance, skepticism, and charitableness of the persona—that self-image which permeates and unifies the work—conflicts with the climate of his times

13. McGee, *The Godly Man,* pp. 78, 106, 95.
14. See Huntley, *Sir Thomas Browne,* p. 91.

without Browne's needing to call attention to the fact."[15] I believe that, more than the persona per se, the Two Tables structure of *Religio* defines the dimension of the religious controversy; but Wise correctly responds to the gesture of both opposition and allegiance.

That gesture is asserted with the very first sentence as Browne concedes the circumstances of his life that might create the impression of irreligion. From the scandal of his profession and the course of his studies he continues to "the indifferency of my behaviour, and discourse in matters of Religion, neither violently defending one, nor with that common ardour and contention opposing another" (*P*, 61). Insofar as the last concession has received scrutiny, *indifferency* has been glossed as "impartial" or understood to mean negligence, even an outright admission of religious apathy: "His vaunted tolerance is really indifference: he doesn't want to be bothered and he doesn't want to bother us either."[16] Nothing could be further from the truth. By "the indifferency of [his] behaviour and discourse," Browne aligns himself with the doctrine of adiaphorism, which Patrick Collinson has described as "the cornerstone of Anglicanism."[17] Essentially, adiaphorism delineates the belief that "things indifferent," neither commanded nor forbidden by the Bible (ceremonies, for instance), are harmless in themselves and therefore should be performed if so authorized by the Church. Conversely, Puritans took the position—rather like Shylock examining his bond for mercy—that what is not in the Bible does not exist; for them "things indifferent" were an unwarranted intrusion by humans upon God's law. Humphrey Sydenham mocks the Puritan attitude:

> 'Tis true, some Ceremonies we retaine yet, as matters of *Indifferency*, and not of *Substance*, and these (forsooth) are so hainous, that they are *Thornes* in their sides, and prickles in their eyes; matter of *Ceremony*, is now matter of Conscience, and rather than subscribe, *Silence*, *Suspension*, *Imprisionment*, they venture on, and sometimes suffer too; where a *Brethren-Contribution* fats them, then al the Fortunes they were masters of before; and this (beloued) cannot be *zeale*, but *Schisme*.[18]

Browne's stance is the opposite of the noncommitment that the careless

15. *Sir Thomas Browne's "Religio Medici" and Two Seventeenth-Century Critics* (Columbia, Mo., 1972), p. 1. See also pp. 12, 179.

16. Stanley E. Fish, *Self-Consuming Artifacts: The Experience of Seventeenth-Century Literature* (Berkeley, 1972), p. 368.

17. *The Elizabethan Puritan Movement* (Berkeley, 1967), pp. 27–28. On this subject, see particularly Bernard J. Verkamp, *The Indifferent Mean: Adiaphorism in the English Reformation to 1554* (Athens, Ohio, and Detroit, 1977); John S. Coolidge, *The Pauline Renaissance in England* (Oxford, 1970), pp. 23–54; McGee, *The Godly Man*, pp. 83–88, 95–97, 236–43; also *OED*, "indifferent," 10.c. Nathanson, *The Strategy of Truth*, pp. 112–16, touches on "things indifferent" but makes no specific application to Browne.

18. "The Waters of Marah and Meriah" (1630), in *In God's Name*, ed. John Chandos (Indianapolis, 1971), p. 315.

modern reader attributes to him. Using the vocabulary of contemporary religious controversy, he sketches a shorthand definition that he fully amplifies in his pledge of loyalty to the Church of England and to the Thirty-nine Articles:

> whatsoever is beyond, as points indifferent, I observe according to the rules of my private reason, or the humor and fashion of my devotion, neither believing this, because *Luther* affirmed it, or disproving that because *Calvin* hath disavouched it. I condemne not all things in the Councell of *Trent,* nor approve all in the Synod of *Dort.* In briefe, where the Scripture is silent, the Church is my Text; where that speakes, 'tis but my Comment: where there is a joynt silence of both, I borrow not the rules of my Religion from *Rome* or *Geneva,* but the dictates of my owne reason. (*P,* 64)

It hardly seems necessary to enumerate the signatures of the Anglican *via media* in this declaration; but, for emphasis, we should underscore the importance assigned to reason, the equation of reason with the voice of the Church, and therefore the acceptance of the Church's authority in "points indifferent."[19]

Sydenham's attack upon Puritan anticeremonialism permits us to triangulate a habitual set of concerns in Anglican writing. The opposite of "indifferency" is misguided "zeal," a stock characterization of Puritan fanaticism well before Ben Jonson's Zeal-of-the-Land Busy. The point of intersection between the two attitudes occurs in the differing assessments of Charity, which is the motivational force behind the Anglican engagement to adiaphorism: "their indifferent mean was not nearly so much the work of rational legislation as it was the work of love—a 'bande and knott of charity.' "[20] If the retention and proliferation of ceremonies arose immediately from a charitable concern for the diverse human needs of the English people, however, the Puritans rejected this concern as pernicious and evil. John Preston typifies the opposing attitude in his exhortation, "Examine yourselves by this, for it is a sure rule, if you love the Lord you will hate that which is evill."[21] True Charity for Preston consists of hatred for those actions Sydenham would consider indifferent. It is no accident that Sydenham's conjunction of "indifferency" and "zeal" occurs in the context of a sermon upon Charity: *"If I giue my Body to be burned* (saith Saint *Paul*) *and haue not Charity, it profiteth me nothing, nay had I all faith, so that I could*

---

19. On the importance of reason to the Anglican position, see, for example, Huntley, *Sir Thomas Browne,* pp. 20–23; and their view of the Two Tables, see McGee, *The Godly Man,* p. 70.

20. Verkamp, *The Indifferent Mean,* pp. 165–73; quotation, p. 172.

21. From the fourth of his *Eighteen Sermons* (1630), in Chandos, ed., *In God's Name,* p. 297. See also Chandos's comparison of Preston and Sydenham, pp. 289–90.

remoue mountains, and haue not Charity, I am nothing."[22] Similarly, Browne's initial profession of indifference and toleration is completed by a predictable qualification, "neither doth herein my zeale so farre make me forget the generall charitie I owe unto humanity" (*P*, 61), and his full definition of the Anglican "indifferent mean" is complemented by his insistence that it is uncharitable to abuse the pope, to "whom as a temporall Prince, we owe the duty of good language" (*P*, 65). Browne is no closet Roman Catholic; rather, he tries to establish the principle of obedience to ecclesiastical authority with the most extreme of examples.

As Browne elaborates the definition of his religion in these first ten sections of Part I, his underlying strategy advances a coherent argument. Embracing the principle of Charity in one's life means accepting the temporal authority of the Church of England: "in Divinity I love to keepe the road, and though not in an implicite, yet an humble faith, follow the great wheele of the Church" (*P*, 66). This entails, naturally, an Anglican position upon ceremony and ritual: "I love to use the civility of my knee, my hat, and hand, with all those outward and sensible motions, which may expresse, or promote my invisible devotion. I should violate my owne arme rather than a Church, nor willingly deface the memory of Saint or Martyr" (*P*, 63). In keeping with his conciliatory stance, Browne does not advocate a strict, Laudian line; on the contested issue of prayers for the dead, for instance, he reluctantly condemns the practice. In general, he urges avoidance of controversy and charitable toleration of as many doctrinal and ceremonial differences as possible. These attitudes further two important ends. "For Anglicans outward civil peace and religious unity were sacred."[23] Browne thus is willing to overlook the external differences between Protestant and Catholic—"there is between us one common name and appellation, one faith, and necessary body of principles common to us both" (*P*, 62)—and leave "an honest possibility of a reconciliation, which . . . peaceable Spirits doe desire" (*P*, 64), although he admits the unlikeliness of this ever happening. Even the "allegorical description of *Hermes*" that he postulates as a definition of God (*P*, 71) requires interpretation as a partisan gesture. As a concept that extends in a tradition of Christian Neoplatonism from the *Corpus Hermetica* through Nicolas of Cusa, Marsilio Ficino, Rabelais, and the contemporary Cambridge Platonists, it serves to evoke the irenic princi-

---

22. In ibid., p. 313. This set of associations in Anglican apologetics survives well into the Restoration. Joseph Glanvill, for example, writes in *Catholicke Charity Recommended* (1669): "Beware of Zeal about Opinions . . . this is a vitious, and dangerous excess, destructive to Christian Charity, and the publick weal, and order." For some background to the idea of religious zeal, see M. Thomas Hester, " 'Zeal' as Satire: The Decorum of Donne's *Satyres,"* *Genre* 10 (1977): 173–94.

23. McGee, *The Godly Man*, p. 245.

ples of such works as Cusanus's *De pace fidei* and Ficino's *De christiana religione*.[24]

Browne's plea for simultaneous obedience to the law of Charity and to the temporal authority of the Church could scarcely have been missed. Corresponding to the place "disobedience" holds in the Anglican lexicon, "Idolatry," McGee finds, "was the most comprehensive and evocative word in the puritan vocabulary of sin."[25] It is not surprising, then, that the pugnacious Alexander Ross discovered a virtual anthology of idolatries in these sections of *Religio:* praying in a Catholic church is active idolatry; pitying, rather than condemning, pilgrims and friars is a toleration of idolatry; weeping at religious processions condones idolatry; civility to the pope is not Charity but stupidity; and one should not "follow the great wheele of the Church" when the Church is wrong.[26] The contrast in belief could not be greater, nor the difference in First Table attitudes more neatly illustrated.

Through the middle of Part I of *Religio Medici,* the refutation of Puritan beliefs recedes from the surface. Seeking knowledge of God by consideration of his properties or attributes (sections 11–13) is a First Commandment topic, just as "Meditation on the Creatures of God" (14–18, 36–42) and "Meditation in the Word" (21–25) are recommended means of divine knowledge.[27] But the actual development of these sections intermingles the closely related issues of the Second and Third commandments, demonstrating the proposition that the First contains the seeds of all the others. Considerations of Providence and its false opposite Fortune are, for Ussher, Third Commandment matters, but witchcraft, magic, and "judiciall Astrology"—"consulting with Star-gazers," as Ussher puts it—come under the Second.[28]

What Browne chooses to include and to omit is in itself instructive. He is direct in his support of Anglican ceremonialism, but silent on the Puritans' assertion of their right to preach God's Word without governmental interference. It may be that he was uncomfortable with Laud's program of enforced conformity: "Persecution is a bad and indirect way to plant Religion; It hath beene the unhappy method of angry devotions, not onely to confirme honest Religion, but wicked Heresies, and extravagant opinions" (*P*, 93). Nonetheless, there are oblique indications of his points of

24. Occurrences of the circle metaphor are cited by Huntley, *Sir Thomas Browne,* pp. 108–9; Norman J. Endicott, ed., *The Prose of Sir Thomas Browne* (Garden City, N.Y., 1967), p. 543, n. 23; and C. A. Patrides, ed., *The Cambridge Platonists* (London, 1969), p. 36. For the relevance of the Continental tradition of religious toleration to the formation of the Anglican church, see Verkamp, *The Indifferent Mean,* pp. 136–43.

25. *The Godly Man,* p. 100.

26. See Ross, *Medicus Medicatus; or, The Physicians Religion Cured by a Lenitive or Gentle Potion* (London, 1645), pp. 2–10, 15; and Wise, *Sir Thomas Browne's "Religio Medici,"* pp. 122–68, especially 124–30. Wise quotes generously from Ross.

27. Ussher, *A Body of Divinitie,* pp. 215, 219.

28. Ibid., pp. 240, 229, respectively.

difference with the Puritans. He acknowledges mysteries, improbabilities, and disputed points in the Bible (Part I, section 22); his propensity in sections 45–46 to read it "mystically rather than literally" drew Ross's attack.[29] His digression upon the excess of books, "those swarms and millions of *Rhapsodies*" (*P,* 92) may take aim at the sermons, devotions, and commentaries of the "Saints"; he expresses his disbelief in the expectations of the millenarians (*P,* 93); and he asserts dryly, "neither can I properly terme all those that suffer in matters of Religion Martyrs" (*P,* 94). Indeed, although he admits no fear of death, he would not martyr himself in a dubious cause: "yet from the morall duty I owe to the Commandement of God, and the naturall respects that I tender unto the conservation of my essence and being, I would not perish upon a Ceremony, Politick points, or indifferency" (*P,* 94–95). The commandment, of course, is the Sixth, against murder. Again, the Anglican method of obeying the First Table through the Second counters the Puritan belief in obedience to one's concept of God at whatever cost.

Nor does Browne directly confront the hotly disputed issue of observing the Sabbath. The Fourth Commandment generated a larger body of commentary and controversy than any other single Scriptural text;[30] and Charles I's decision to reissue the *Book of Sports* in 1633 tempered to steel the Puritan determination to observe the Sabbath as strictly as possible. Unlike his silence on preaching the Word, however, Browne's direct omission of this issue indicates not avoidance but a firm, if tacit, approval of the Anglican position. As we have seen, consideration of God's wisdom and eternity coalesces in apprehension of the workings of Providence, His benevolent order manifested through human time in a plan that can be understood fully only from an eternal perspective. When Browne's focus shifts to man as the epitome of God's works, he reflects on time, eternity, and Providence in man's life, recognizing the inevitability of death (Part I, sections 37–38), the determination of his life span by Providence (43–44), and the possibility of spiritual immortality. This train of thought leads to recognition of another order of human time: "every man hath a double Horoscope, one of his humanity, his birth; another of his Christianity, his baptisme, and from this doe I compute or calculate my Nativitie" (*P,* 116).

In this section Browne meditates upon his life in the Church that was founded through the institution of the sacraments by Christ's Passion. Reflecting upon his Savior's death, he is led to consider his own death, his

29. Ross, *Medicus Medicatus,* pp. 51–53; and Wise, *Sir Thomas Browne's "Religio Medici,"* pp. 150–54.

30. See Boyd M. Barry, *Process of Speech: Puritan Religious Writings and "Paradise Lost"* (Baltimore, 1976), p. 62. For the Sabbatarian controversy, consult pp. 62–101; McGee, *The Godly Man,* pp. 77–89, 180–82; and Patrick Collinson, "The Beginnings of English Sabbatarianism," in *Studies in Church History,* ed. C. W. Dugmore and Charles Duggan (London, 1964), 1:207–21.

state of spiritual preparation for it, and the need to imitate Christ in his own daily life:

> the way to be immortall is to die daily, nor can I thinke I have the true Theory of death, when I contemplate a skull ... I have therefore enlarged that common *Memento mori,* into a more Christian memorandum, *Memento quatuor novissima,* those foure inevitable points of us all, Death, Judgement, Heaven, and Hell. (*P,* 116)

Working through the Last Things, Browne comes to a conviction of God's mercy (Part I, section 53) and of the necessity of salvation through Christ (54), who alone is capable of redeeming man's mixed nature (55). Man is Chiron, at once half-beast and physician to the gods. Like John Donne, Browne perceives "both *Adams* met in me": "and thus was I dead before I was alive; though my grave be *England,* my dying place was Paradise, and *Eve* miscarried of mee before she conceiv'd of *Cain*" (*P,* 132). The belief that God is obeyed by undertaking an *imitatio Christi* to develop the better side of man's mixed nature marks the Anglican accent in both Donne and Browne;[31] and this sequence of *Religio* may be illuminated by comparison with another notable Anglican poet.

George Herbert concludes "The Church" with a suite of five eschatological poems—"Death," "Dooms-day," "Judgement," "Heaven," and "Love (III)"—corresponding closely to Browne's examination of the end of man's life in the Church. Whereas Browne treats hell as a symbolic, and nonterrifying, place, Herbert simply omits it. As Browne's meditation upon the Last Things is stimulated by thinking about the meaning of baptism, so Herbert's is completed with a consideration of the Eucharist. Their Anglican faith in the priority of the incarnate Word over the Puritan's preached Word leads them to find the meaning of their lives, and their salvation, in the great example set by Christ. Equally Anglican is their shared view that attaining salvation by imitating Christ is not difficult but easy, if man will only allow it to be so.[32] Browne complains that "whilst the mercies of God doth promise us heaven, our conceits and opinions exclude us from that place" (*P,* 130); and the gracious "host" of Herbert's poem gently makes it evident that only man's willfullness denies him the feast. The concept of "Love," Christian charity, is supremely and perfectly embodied in the actions celebrated in the sacraments; and man need only freely accept and embody them in his own life.

Meditations upon the meaning of the sacraments and upon one's role within the Church are Fourth Commandment topics.[33] In considering the Last Things of man's life, however, Browne completes his Sabbath duties in another sense. In the passages to which Ross objected for their "mystical" interpretation of Scripture, Browne shifts from the life of man to the life of

31. Compare McGee, *The Godly Man,* pp. 107–13.
32. Ibid., pp. 110–13.
33. Ussher, *A Body of Divinitie,* pp. 249–50.

the world, alluding first to the six days of Creation (Part I, section 45) and then to the six-thousand-year span of history. In so doing, he implicitly relies upon the one-thousand-year "Day of the Lord" (Psalms 90:4) to evoke a familiar scheme of time, the typological correlation between the week of Creation and the week of human history. According to Augustine,

> the sixth is now in progress, and will end in the coming of the exalted Saviour to judgement. What answers to the seventh day is the rest of the saints,—not in this life, but in another, where the rich man saw Lazarus at rest while he was tormented in hell; where there is no evening, because there is no decay. On the sixth day, in Genesis, man is formed after the image of God; in the sixth period of the world there is the clear discovery of our transformation in the renewing of our mind, according to the image of Him who created us.[34]

In contemplating Judgment Day (Part I, sections 47–48), which completes the last day of work in the week of history, and "the necessary Mansions of our restored selves" that lie beyond it, Browne looks ahead to the eternal Sabbath. As Hooper observes, "the sabbath hitherunto from the beginning of the world was and is a type and figure of the eternal and everlasting rest that is to come."[35] By meditating upon the Eternal Sabbath and seeking to prepare himself for it before the sixth day runs out, Browne fulfills the central meaning of the Fourth Commandment. His refusal to mention the minutiae of the external forms of Sunday observance is a gesture of Anglican devotion and a reproof to the Puritan who keeps the letter of the day but misses its spirit.

In other ways, as well, the final sections of Part I return to the overtly partisan manner of its opening. The millenarians who believe that they can determine the exact time of the Second Coming exhibit both their madness and their impiety (section 46). Anglican opposition to Puritan views of election is forthright: "those who doe confine the Church of God, either to particular Nations, Churches, or Families, have made it farre narrower than our Saviour ever meant it" (*P*, 129). Such sectarian beliefs as those held by the atomists and familists are condemned as a breach of Charity (section 56). For Browne the state of election is unknowable by man; "I hold no infallible warrant from my owne sense to confirme me in the certainty thereof" (*P*, 131), he says, turning—with a fine irony—one of the Puritans' code words back upon them.[36] He objects to those "who pretend unto salvation," and the Puritan concept of the "brethren," a closed shop of the

34. *Contra Faustinum,* in *Works,* ed. Marcus Dods (Edinburgh, 1892), 5:208–9. For this tradition, see Raymond B. Waddington, "The Death of Adam: Vision and Voice in Books XI and XII of *Paradise Lost,*" *Modern Philology* 70 (1972): 16–17.

35. *Declaration of the Ten Holy Commandments,* p. 339. For this conception, see Michael Lieb, "Holy Rest: A Reading of *Paradise Lost,*" *ELH: Journal of English Literary History* 39 (1972): 238–44.

36. For the implications of *warrant,* see McGee, *The Godly Man,* pp. 85–88, 124–28.

recognizably elect, fills him with dismay: "That name and compellation of *little Flocke,* doth not comfort but deject my devotion" (*P,* 131).[37] The very last section of Part I hurls Anglican belief into the teeth of the opposition. "Insolent zeales that doe decry good workes and rely onely upon faith, take not away merit: for depending upon the efficacy of their faith, they enforce the condition of God, and in a more sophisticall way doe seeme to challenge Heaven" (*P,* 132). Faith in God, as Browne has argued throughout, is best manifested through the works of Charity. Alluding to Christ's parable about the grain of faith that can remove mountains (Matthew 17:20), he undoubtedly understands it, as did Sydenham, through St. Paul's clarification: "and though I have all faith, so that I could remove mountains, and have not charity, I am nothing" (1 Corinthians 13:2).

II

Since no one has ever doubted that the subject of Part II of *Religio* is Charity, the task here is the easier one. The concern with the Commandments is far more overt than in Part I; in fifteen sections they are mentioned directly three times (sections 1, 4, 5). It remains to be shown that Browne's consideration of the Second Table commandments, while not completely systematic and never comprehensive, is yet more punctilious and straightforward in its progression than is the discussion of the First Table commandments in Part I. Finally, it will be argued that this, too, is a characteristically Anglican exposition, emphasizing the importance of both material and spiritual charity, extending spiritual charity to the brotherhood of man and not just the brotherhood of saints, and perceiving these Second Table acts of Charity as the satisfaction of the First Table duties.[38] The examination of spiritual charity greatly outweighs that of material charity, not only because the nature of spiritual charity was crucial but also as a silent refutation of the Puritan belief that Anglicans stressed material to the neglect of spiritual charity.

Part II commences with one of Browne's most hyperbolic, and quotable, assertions of tolerance: "I have no antipathy, or rather Idio-syncrasie, in dyet, humour, ayre, any thing" (*P,* 133). The rhetorical purpose of the amusing enumeration that follows is to throw into relief what he *cannot* tolerate. "If there be any among those common objects of hatred I doe contemne and laugh at, it is that great enemy of reason, vertue and religion, the multitude, . . . one great beast, & a monstrosity more prodigious than Hydra" (*P,* 134). This conjunction of seemingly "whitmanesque" confession and "traditionally conservative" attitude has misled at least one sensi-

---

37. Endicott, *Prose of Sir Thomas Browne,* p. 552, n. 159, notes the Puritan usage of "little Flocke." McGee, *The Godly Man,* pp. 171–89, discusses the exclusive view of brotherhood.

38. See McGee, *The Godly Man,* pp. 189–234, 247–48.

tive, modern reader to mistake its function.[39] Browne's "multitude," containing "Mechanicks" and "a rabble even amongst the Gentry," is defined by belief, not social class; it subverts the natural political order on principle:

> Let us speake like Politicians, there is a Nobility without Heraldry, a naturall dignity,whereby one man is ranked with another, another Filed before him, according to the quality of his desert, and preheminence of his good parts. Though the corruption of these times, and the byas of present practise wheele another way, thus it was in the first and primitive Common-wealths, and is yet in the integrity and Cradle of well-ordered polities, till corruption getteth ground. (*P*, 134)

Speaking like a politician, Browne addresses the most crucial of contemporary Fifth Commandment issues. Ussher thus interprets "the meaning and scope" of this commandment: "That the equality of mens persons and places in whatsoever estate, Natural, Civill, or Ecclesiasticall, and with whatsoever relation to us, be duely acknowledged and respected." Particularly at stake in the 1630s was the inflammable question of subjects' obedience to "All Civill Magistrates, whether they be Supreame, as Emperors and Kings, or inferior Governours under them." The sins of such subjects are tersely summed up by Ussher under two points: "1. Disobedience, and Rebellion. 2. Refusing and repining to pay dues."[40] At the time *Religio* was written, the second, taxation, dominated the nation's consciousness; but, by the time *Religio* was published, the first had replaced it.

Having dealt with the overwhelming question, Browne proceeds in section 2 of Part II to a more general explanation of the motives governing human charity. Although he asserts again his "indifferent temper," the true religious purpose of Charity is obedience to God: "I give no almes to satisfie the hunger of my Brother, but to fulfill and accomplish the Will and Command of my God" (*P*, 135). This second beginning to Part II designates the conventional division of the Second Table between the Fifth Commandment, which alone concerns "special duties to special persons," and the last four, "those that generally concerne all men, either in their life, chastity, goods, or good name."[41] The remainder of section 2 also seems introductory, standing as an oblique meditation upon the general meaning of the Sixth and Seventh commandments, which, as a subset, legislate the sanctity of the human body in distinction from the succeeding injunctions to respect man's possessions and reputation. Browne's musings upon physiognomy and chiromancy lead to a recognition that every man is an individual and to a celebration of the image of God in man.

Sections 3 through 8, with side glances at other commandments, present an extended consideration of the Sixth Commandment. Browne is not

---

39. See Webber, *The Eloquent "I,"* pp. 164–65.
40. *A Body of Divinitie*, pp. 256, 265, 267, respectively.
41. Ibid., p. 255.

unconventional in regarding spiritual charity as equal in importance to material charity (*P*, 137), but his exposition of spiritual charity pointedly repudiates the Puritan tendency to reserve the virtue for like-minded "Saints" or "Brethren": "I cannot fall out or contemne a man for an errour, or conceive why a difference in opinion should divide an affection: for controversies . . . if they meete with discreet and peaceable natures, doe not infringe the Lawes of Charity" (*P*, 138). As Browne's imagery makes plain, "angry, wrathfull and loathsome speeches against our brother"[42] are contrary to the Sixth Commandment, constituting verbal assassination: "For by a word wee wound a thousand, and at one blow assassine the honour of a Nation" (*P*, 140). " 'Tis the generall complaint of these times," he observes, "that charity growes cold; which I perceive most verified in those which most doe manifest the fires and flames of zeale" (*P*, 141). Ironically, since "Charity begins at home," such uncharitable behavior is only self-destructive: "*Non occides*, is the Commandement of God, yet scarse observed by any man; for I perceive every man is his own *Atropos*" (*P*, 141).

Sections 5 and 6 explore the topic of friendship, climaxing in what may be biographical revelation:

> I hope I do not breake the fifth Commandement, if I conceive I may love my friend before the nearest of my bloud, even those to whom I owe the principles of life; I never yet cast a true affection on a Woman, but I have loved my Friend as I do vertue, my soule, my God. (*P*, 142–43)

Alexander Ross hastened to assure Browne that he was indeed violating the Fifth Commandment.[43] But, whether the friend is real or symbolic, the sentence declares total fidelity to the positive duty of the Sixth. As Christ had exhorted, Browne loves his neighbor as himself,[44] loving him spiritually and finding "the true object, not onely of friendship but charity" (*P*, 143). He loves God through loving his neighbor, God's own image.[45] As with Donne, "the Toll of a passing Bell" stirs his awareness of the brotherhood of man within the Church and he extends the charity of his prayers even to enemies. Browne concludes by recognizing that it is a charitable duty to hate, not one's neighbor, but one's own vices (section 7), rejoicing in his avoidance of pride, particularly "a mortall enemy to Charity" (*P*, 146).

The Seventh Commandment, whether from temperamental or from political reasons, gets short shrift in Browne's litany. Section 7 includes in passing a denial that lechery appeals to him, and the selective, highly abstract, and figurative presentation of this commandment in section 9 is consistent with that denial. Browne's professed desire to "procreate like trees" and "perpetuate the world without this triviall and vulgar way of

42. Ibid., p. 273.
43. *Medicus Medicatus*, pp. 170–71.
44. Matthew 19:19; also Ussher, *A Body of Divinitie*, pp. 210, 268.
45. Ussher, *A Body of Divinitie*, pp. 270, 276.

coition" (*P*, 148) was as risible to his contemporaries as it is us today; nonetheless, its meaning as an assertion of chastity, the essence of the commandment,[46] is unequivocal. Browne's modulation from appreciation of feminine beauty, to delight in music, to the meaning of harmony as an intimation of divine order and as the pattern of the soul is similarly oblique but does not stray from the point.[47] Not only does this modulation implicitly assert Browne's own temperance, it also expounds the meaning of chastity through an established metaphor. The audience of a masque presented at Ludlow Castle about the time Browne wrote this would have comprehended the correspondences between chastity, music, and spiritual harmony.

One of the aids to obeying the Seventh Commandment is "Labour in our Vocation,"[48] by which means Browne bridges to the next commandment. As a physician he desires that the entire world may remain in temper; he labors in his lawful calling out of charity, not out of love for money.[49] The theme of harmony continues, however, as Browne reflects upon the harmony of his own disposition (section 10). He is wary, nonetheless, of the possibility of distemper within himself, admitting—as the Tenth Commandment instructs[50]—his heritage of Original Sin: " 'Tis I that doe infect my selfe, the man without a Navell yet lives in me" (*P*, 152). In accordance with the Eighth, he must moderate his concupiscence and avoid covetousness.[51] Scrutinizing "the Microcosme of mine owne frame" in section 11, he looks at himself through the Ninth Commandment. The reverse of bearing false witness is a positive commitment to "the conservation of truth," especially in reference to fame and reputation, one's own as well as one's neighbor's.[52] Browne mistrusts the judgment of the world: "Men that look upon my outside, perusing onely my condition, and fortunes, do erre in my altitude; for I am above *Atlas* his shoulders" (*P*, 153). The commandment advises him "to look more to the inward, then the outward man" and "to give a true testimony of himselfe" by "modest acknowledging that which is good in us,"[53] so Browne enumerates what is good in him—both generally, "There is surely a peece of Divinity in us" (*P*, 153), and individually. Still affirming his fulfillment of the Eighth Commandment,[54] he protests that he has no love of money, no worldly ambition, and that he is content with what Providence has ordained for him.

46. Ibid., p. 277.
47. For a sermon extensively expounding the values Anglicans attached to music, see Sydenham, "The Well-Tuned Cymball" (1630), in Chandos, ed., *In God's Name*, pp. 319–27.
48. Ussher, *A Body of Divinitie*, p. 285.
49. Ibid., pp. 288–93.
50. Ibid., p. 325.
51. Ibid., pp. 289–91.
52. Ibid., pp. 307, 313–14.
53. Ibid., pp. 320, 321.
54. Ibid., pp. 288–89, 291.

Indeed, he is so willing to leave this world that he prays each night as if he were to "sleepe unto the resurrection" (*P*, 157).

Section 13 is devoted to the Tenth Commandment. After his lengthy presentation of spiritual charity, Browne here takes up the less controversial matter of material charity. He first denies that he is covetous, regarding avarice as a form of madness. He believes that every man can be charitable, whatever his worldly means. "I have a private method which others observe not, I take the opportunity of my selfe to do good, I borrow occasion of charity from mine owne necessities, and supply the wants of others, when I am in most neede my selfe" (*P*, 158). Even so, material and spiritual charity are equally important: "I cannot behold a Beggar without relieving his necessities with my purse, or his soule with my prayers" (*P*, 159). The entire action of Charity is a fulfillment of the First Table through the Second. *"Hee that giveth to the poore lendeth to the Lord;* there is more Rhetorick in that one sentence than in a Library of Sermons" (*P*, 158–59). The relation between the tables is stated even more directly in section 14, "for this I thinke charity, to love God for himselfe, and our neighbour for God" (*P*, 159), after which the meditation concludes with a serenely Anglican formulation: "Blesse mee in this life with but the peace of my conscience, command of my affections, the love of thy selfe and my dearest friends, and I shall be happy enough to pity *Cæsar*" (*P*, 160–61). Peace, obedience, love of God, and love of neighbor. As the angel Michael teaches Milton's Adam, "Love, / By name to come call'd Charity" is "the soul" of all virtues. Browne's meditation upon the Two Tables proves his wholehearted agreement. As he wrote in *Christian Morals, "Moses* broke the Tables without breaking of the Law; but where Charity is broke, the Law it self is shattered, which cannot be whole without Love, which is the fulfilling of it" (*P*, 422). Browne and Milton would part company, however, in the definition and application of Charity; and in *Religio Medici* emphases such as those upon "peace" and "obedience" signal Browne's firm alliance to the Church of England.

The preceding analysis neglects much of what we value in Sir Thomas Browne. It says very little about style, the projection of self, the range and play of mind, curious learning, or philosophical currents. It does do two things. First, it refutes the common view of *Religio* as an amorphous, repetitive, essayistic ramble, arbitrarily divided into two parts, by attempting to show that the Two Tables, while admittedly flexible vertebrae, supply a structure of topics and themes that ought to be recognizable to any reader sufficiently beguiled by Browne's title to open the book. Second, by locating Browne's handling of the Two Tables within the context of contemporary religious and political controversy, it answers those critics who find Browne flawed by lack of intellectual toughness, by nonengagement with the real world, or by the ease of his affirmations. Browne's contemporary critics Digby and Ross were wrong in most particulars but right in their general assumption that Browne was engaging in religious controversy. Certainly, when Browne prepared the authorized, 1643 edition of *Religio* for publication, he did not tone down the controversial dimension, but augmented it with the preface and the four added sections.[55] A part of our failure as readers is attributable to the loss of a vocabulary. The slogans of any controversy die with their cause; and "indifferent," for instance, now seems the most indifferent of words. But the recent past has taught us that within a partisan context even the flourishing of flowers or the length of a person's hair can be a provocative and inflammatory gesture. So the effort at recovery must be made. This is not to reduce Browne to the significance of the pamphleteers preserved from oblivion by the diligence of George Thomason, only to maintain that we must first apprehend what is contemporary in Browne before we can really comprehend what is universal.

55. The implications of the preface are noted by Patrides (*P*, 24); those of the four sections added to Part I, by Hall in "Epistle," p. 246, n. 25.

Religio Medici
in the English Revolution

Michael Wilding

I

Commentator after commentator has accepted Browne's statement "To the Reader," which prefaces the authorized edition of *Religio Medici* (1643), that the work was written "about seven yeares past" and thus has read it as a product of the 1630s, as a late metaphysical meditation. Yet in this very stress on times past—and he repeats his assertion, "it was set downe many yeares past"—Browne is emphasizing times present, the time of publication, the time of his readers. In stressing how things may have changed, how "there might be many things therein plausible unto my passed apprehension, which are not agreeable unto my present selfe," he is inviting a comparison between times past and times present, and any such comparison in 1643 inevitably invoked the circumstances of revolution and civil war.

There is no doubt about the 1640s context: the preface, as C. A. Patrides has pointed out, "supplies both the immediate context and the degree of personal involvement" (*P, 24*): "the name of his Majesty defamed, the honour of Parliament depraved, the writings of both depravedly, anticipatively, counterfeitly imprinted." And Browne's complaint about the "tyranny" of the press is the expression of a definite, partisan position in the political conflict. It followed Charles I's proclamation at the beginning of the revolutionary period, in February 1639: "For whereas the Print is the King's in all Kingdoms, these seditious Men have taken upon them to print what they please, though we forbid it."[1] A supporter of the king and of Archbishop William Laud might lament the "tyranny" of the press, but the press, together with the pulpit and the petition, was one of the puritans' main weapons of propaganda. For the puritans, separatists, and radicals, the

---

1. William Haller, *Liberty and Reformation in the Puritan Revolution* (New York, 1955), p. 9.

"tyranny" had been the censorship and licensing of the press by Charles and Laud. "In 1637, by decree of Star Chamber, the number of authorised printers in London was reduced to twenty, and savage corporal penalties were denounced against illegal printing."[2] The breakdown in censorship after 1640 was a liberation: "Nothing gave more resounding emphasis to the overthrow of Laud's power in the state than the collapse of his power over the press."[3]

Browne appropriated the outraged note of "tyranny" for new purposes. Under the guise of complaint, he took the opportunity to reissue "a full and intended copy of that Peece, which was most imperfectly and surreptitiously published before." The unauthorized edition had appeared in December 1642, a year from which George Thomason collected some 2,134 publications, "the highest total in any year up to the Restoration," Perez Zagorin remarks, "a fact that sufficiently demonstrates the accelerated preoccupation with political-ecclesiastical issues in the first stages of the revolution's progress."[4]

To situate *Religio Medici* in the context of the pamphlet war at the time of its publication, rather than in the mid-1630s when it was hypothetically composed, is to realize its ideological significance, to see Browne's participation in the sociopolitical debate of the English revolution. The changes between the 1642 and 1643 editions provide ready access to politically sensitive passages. As Simon Wilkin pointed out, "In all the manuscript copies are to be found, without exception, those passages of the surreptitious edition which have been omitted in that of 1643, but not one of the numerous additions nor of the most important alterations it contains."[5]

Jean-Jacques Denonain calculated that Browne made more than 650 changes from the 1642 to the 1643 edition.[6] Some of the changes involved a word or phrase, some involved additional passages, and four entire new sections (8, 28, 43, 56) were added in Part I. The first of the four added sections occurs early: "That Heresies should arise we have the prophecy of Christ, but that old ones should be abolished wee hold no prediction." Browne is not concerned with the nature of particular heresies, but with their multiplication:

> even in Doctrines hereticall there will be super-heresies, and Arians not onely divided from their Church, but also among themselves: for heads that are disposed unto Schisme and complexionally propense to innovation, are naturally indisposed for a community, nor will ever be confined unto the order or œconomy of one body; and therefore when

2. Christopher Hill, *The Century of Revolution, 1603–1714* (Edinburgh, 1961), pp. 98–99.
3. Haller, *Liberty and Reformation*, p. 33.
4. *The Court and the Country: The Beginning of the English Revolution* (New York, 1970), p. 204.
5. *The Works of Sir Thomas Browne*, ed. Simon Wilkin (London, 1846), 2:vi–vii.
6. *Religio Medici*, ed. Jean-Jacques Denonain (Cambridge, 1953), p. xxvii.

> they separate from others they knit but loosely among themselves; nor contented with a generall breach or dichotomie with their church, do subdivide and mince themselves almost into Atomes. (*P*, 68–69)

Innovation was the contemporary term for revolution (*revolution* retained the sense of returning to the same point), and *separate* alludes to the separatists, those who wished to separate from the Church of England rather than work for Puritan reforms within the Church. The language has its political specificities. Historians are agreed that the proliferation of sects did not occur until the impeachment of Laud on 18 December 1640. "Until 1641 separatism was numerically insignificant and without much influence upon religious life," Zagorin wrote, but, as Brian Manning stated, "during 1641 the separatists increased dramatically in numbers and influence."[7] Both cite a report from Thomas Knyvett, dated 17 January 1641, on Browne's hometown: "Conventicles every night in Norwich, as publicly known as the sermons in the daytime, and they say much more frequented." Browne's correction of the 1642 text here is not the restoration of a passage that had been "by transcription successively corrupted untill it arrived in a most depraved copy at the presse" ("To the Reader") but a new observation written for the 1643 edition. The destructiveness of sectarian schism is Browne's theme in this added section, as it is in another entirely new section (56) added in 1643, which concludes:

> 'Tis true we all hold there is a number of Elect and many to be saved, yet take our opinions together, and from the confusion thereof there will be no such things as salvation, nor shall any one be saved; for first the Church of *Rome* condemneth us, wee likewise them, the Sub-reformists and Sectaries sentence the Doctrine of our Church as damnable, the Atomist, or Familist reprobates all these, and all these them againe. Thus whilst the mercies of God doth promise us heaven, our conceits and opinions exclude us from that place. There must be therefore more than one Saint *Peter,* particular Churches and Sects usurpe the gates of heaven, and turne the key against each other, and thus we goe to heaven against each others wills, conceits and opinions, and with as much uncharity as ignorance, doe erre I feare in points, not onely of our owne, but on[e] anothers salvation. (*P,* 130)

Wilkin quotes *Gurney's Observations:* "The spirit of charity which pervades this section is truly characteristick of its author."[8] But the whole passage is characteristic of Browne's university-educated, elitist contempt for the "ignorance" of the clashing sects, for the "vulgarity of those judgements" stressed in the opening line of the section, for the social implications of the theological beliefs of the radical sects. As Christopher Hill remarks, "in the early 1640s attitudes towards the lower-class heresy of Familism were

---

7. Zagorin, *The Court and the Country,* p. 232, and Brian Manning, *The English People and the English Revolution,* rev. ed. (Harmondsworth, 1978), p. 51.
	8. *The Works of Sir Thomas Browne,* 2:82.

almost the test of radicalism."[9] For the theological positions had their political implications:

> The Family of Love and the Grindletonians had taught that prelapsarian perfection could be attained in this life. But before the 1640s such doctrines had been kept underground. Now nothing could be suppressed. Plebeian materialist scepticism and anticlericalism could express themselves freely, and fused with theological antinomianism. The result was a rejection of clerical control of religious and moral life.[10]

Browne's distaste for the sects is characteristic of the whole of *Religio Medici*. It is there from the beginning, appearing as early as section 6 of Part I:

> I could never divide my selfe from any man upon the difference of an opinion, or be angry with his judgement for not agreeing with mee in that, from which perhaps within a few dayes I should dissent my selfe: I have no Genius to disputes in Religion. (*P*, 65)

The addition in 1643 of *love to* and *I hope . . . not* (italicized in the quotation following) are additions of emphasis that underline the message of happy conformity to the establishment church:

> In Philosophy where truth seemes double-faced, there is no man more paradoxicall then my self; but in Divinity I *love to* keepe the road, and though not in an implicite, yet an humble faith, follow the great wheele of the Church, by which I move, not reserving any proper poles or motion from the epicycle of my own braine; by this meanes I leave no gap for Heresies, Schismes, or Errors, of which at present, *I hope* I shall *not* injure Truth, to say, I have no taint or tincture. (*P*, 66)

The pacific note has often been remarked upon. But in the context of the book's publication, it is a tendentious peacefulness. The implication is that all would be well if heretics and schismatics and dissenters would stop being troublesome and disturbing the peace. Browne's peaceableness is the peaceableness of the conservative who is satisfied with the arrangement of society—an arrangement suiting his own class. All *other* opinions that disturb this peace are heretical, schismatic, dissident. And it is the peaceability of the elitist who argues that disputes in religion are not for everyone, not for the ignorant, not for those with "inconsiderate zeale":

> Every man is not a proper Champion for Truth, nor fit to take up the Gantlet in the cause of Veritie: Many from the ignorance of these Maximes, and an inconsiderate zeale unto Truth, have too rashly charged the troopes of error, and remaine as Trophees unto the enemies of Truth: A man may be in as just possession of Truth as of a City, and yet bee forced to surrender; tis therefore farre better to enjoy her with peace, than to hazzard her on a battell. (*P*, 65–66)

9. *The World Turned Upside Down*, rev. ed. (Harmondsworth, 1975), pp. 35–36.
10. Ibid., p. 166.

Browne singles out certain aspects of sectarian beliefs for specific rejection. Of the "Heresies, Schisms, or Errors" that he is preserved from by following "the great wheele of the Church,"

> I must confesse my greener studies have been polluted with two or three, not any begotten in the latter Centuries, but old and obsolete, such as could never have been revived, but by such extravagant and irregular heads as mine. (*P,* 66)

Following on from this, he opens section 7 thus: "Now the first of mine was that of the Arabians, that the soules of men perished with their bodies, but should yet bee raised againe at the last day" (*P,* 67). But this was no "obsolete," obscure, or purely foreign heresy. Hill notes how "in the forties mortalism appeared above the surface. By 1644 it was alarming the House of Commons" and "in 1648 two Royalist newspapers declared that the mortalist heresy had been partly responsible for the revolutionary nature of the Civil War."[11] Not only was mortalism current, it was specifically associated with the emerging radical protestants. "Nomenclature varies, but the radical tendency of the heresy, whose best-known spokesman was a Leveller leader, is clear."[12]

Similarly, Browne's anti-millenarianism and skepticism about Antichrist indicate his consistent opposition to the world view of the radical sects. Although millenarian beliefs were not confined to the radicals, their expression increasingly implied a revolutionary component. Joseph Mede's *Key of the Revelation* (1627) had not appeared in English translation under Laud, but "a translation was ordered to be printed in 1643 by a committee of the House of Commons."[13] Browne's skepticism about the possibility of millenarian prediction is associated with his sad amazement at the propensity of Christianity to produce sects:

> And herein I must accuse those of my own Religion; for there is not any of such a fugitive faith, such an unstable beliefe, as a Christian; none that do so oft transforme themselves, not unto severall shapes of Christianity and of the same Species, but unto more unnaturall and contrary formes, of Jew and Mohametan, that from the name of Saviour can condescend to the bare terme of Prophet; and from an old beliefe that he is come, fall to a new expectation of his comming: It is the promise of Christ to make us all one flock; but how and when this union shall be, is as obscure to me as the last day. (*P,* 93)

He returns to the theme later, stressing the impossibility of predicting the end of the world:

> Now to determine the day and yeare of this inevitable time, is not onely

---

11. *Milton and the English Revolution* (London, 1977), pp. 318, 321.
12. Ibid., p. 319.
13. Hill, *The World Turned Upside Down,* pp. 95–96; also his *Antichrist in Seventeenth-Century England* (London, 1971), pp. 27–28.

convincible and statute madnesse, but also manifest impiety; How shall we interpret *Elias* 6000. yeares . . .?

it hath not onely mocked the predictions of sundry Astrologers in ages past, but the prophecies of many melancholy heads in these present, who neither understanding reasonably things past or present, pretend a knowledge of things to come, heads ordained onely to manifest the incredible effects of melancholy, and to fulfill old prophecies, rather than be the authors of new. "In those dayes there shall come warres and rumours of warres", to me seemes no prophesie, but a constant truth, in all times verified since it was pronounced: There shall bee signes in the Moone and Starres, how comes he then like a theefe in the night, when he gives an item of his comming? That common signe drawne from the revelation of Antichrist is as obscure as any; in our common compute he hath beene come these many yeares, but for my owne part to speake freely, I am halfe of opinion that Antichrist is the Philosophers stone in Divinity, for the discovery and invention whereof, though there be prescribed rules, and probable inductions, yet hath hardly any man attained the perfect discovery thereof. That generall opinion that the world growes neere its end, hath possessed all ages past as neerely as ours. (*P*, 118–19)

The assurance of the 1642 text that "no man" had "attained the perfect discovery" of Antichrist was typically softened in 1643 to "hardly any man." As W. A. Greenhill remarked of the alterations, Browne "took the opportunity of modifying various positive and strongly worded propositions by the substitution of less dogmatic expressions."[14] But Browne's overall skepticism about the Antichrist remained unchanged from 1642 to 1643. He never calls the pope Antichrist, he assures us, and he declares that "that opinion, that Antichrist should be borne of the Tribe of *Dan* by conjunction with the Devill, is ridiculous, and a conceit fitter for a Rabbin than a Christian" (*P*, 65, 98). This skepticism is not without its political implications. Hill, in his study *Antichrist in the Seventeenth Century*, points out that "after Laud's rise to dominance the English church no longer proclaimed the Pope to be the Antichrist. No vernacular translation of the seminal works on Revelation and Daniel by Brightman, Mede, Pareus or Alsted was published in England until after the meeting of the Long Parliament." The emergence of Antichrist, identified with the great Beast of Revelation, indicated the world was in its last days. The destruction of Antichrist would mark the beginning of Christ's thousand-year rule. "The time-tables of Napier, Brightman, Mede, Archer put the rule of Christ on earth in the near future. This gave a utopian perspective for political action." The correct identification of Antichrist developed a political urgency. "Johann Hilten, a fifteenth-century prophet popular among protestants, had predicted the end of the world for 1651. John Swan in 1635 noted that some gave 1657

14. *Religio Medici: A Facsimile of the First Edition*, ed. W. A. Greenhill (London, 1883), p. xxvi.

for the date, though he was not himself convinced." *Religio Medici* appeared amidst a flood of millenarian speculations. Sixteen forty-one saw the publication of *A Revelation of Mr Brightman's Revelation* ... , *Brightman's Predictions and Prophecies, Napier's Narration,* and John Archer's *Personall Reign of Christ upon Earth,* among others, and these were followed in 1642 by a summary of Johann Alsted's work, *The World's Proceeding Woes,* by Francis Potter's *An Interpretation of the Number 666,* and by Joseph Mede's *The Apostasy of the Latter Times.*[15] Grotius was told that eighty such treatises had appeared in England by 1649.[16] This was the context in which Browne derided computations of the end of the world as decisively as he did the identifications of Antichrist.

Browne's three references to Antichrist are in both the 1642 and the 1643 texts. And he deals with millenarian predictions in section 43, one of those added in 1643:

> the whole world, whose solid and well composed substance must not expect the duration and period of its constitution, when all things are compleated in it, its age is accomplished, and the last and generall fever may as naturally destroy it before six thousand, as me before forty. (*P,* 114)

As it now stands, *Religio Medici* displays a seeming contradiction that is the expression of Browne's conservative consistency: the millenium cannot be predicted, yet is said to be due in A. D. 2000, in other words, six thousand years after the generally accepted date of creation in circa 4000 B.C. (*P,* 118). But even this is uncertain: "our ends are as obscure as our beginnings," Browne continues. He tentatively accepts a date for the millenium well into the future, but stresses that even that cannot be relied upon; the implicit point is that those specific predictions that the millenium is about to begin err both according to traditional belief and in being specific about the unknowable. Browne's anti-millenarianism, seen in its sociopolitical context, suggests a conservative's worry over the transformation of the millenarian expectations among the sects into radical activism.

II

The second part of *Religio Medici* deals with "that other Vertue of Charity," and its first section develops into a denunciation of the "multitude." This hostility to mass action, directly following the rejection of the beliefs of the radical sects, establishes Browne's firm, antipopulist stance:

> If there be any among those common objects of hatred I doe contemne and laugh at, it is that great enemy of reason, vertue and religion, the multitude, that numerous piece of monstrosity, which taken asunder

15. Hill, *Antichrist,* pp. 37, 163, 111.
16. Christopher Hill, *Puritanism and Revolution* (London, 1958), p. 325.

seeme men, and the reasonable creatures of God; but confused together, make but one great beast, & a monstrosity more prodigious than Hydra; it is no breach of Charity to call these fooles, it is the stile all holy Writers have afforded them, set downe by *Solomon* in canonicall Scripture, and a point of our faith to beleeve so. (*P*, 134)

Browne's condemnation certainly had a long tradition behind it. C. A. Patrides, discussing "the beast with many heads," cites examples ranging through such writers as Barnaby Rich, Shakespeare, Lancelot Andrewes, Arthur Warwick, and Pierre Charron.[17] But, in the context of the book's publication, Browne's condemnation attained a new pertinence. J. S. Morrill says of 1640–1641, "It is unclear whether rioting and violence were more extensive than hitherto, but most gentlemen certainly *believed* that they were. Disruption, often with an overt class bias, was certainly widespread."[18] Discussing "the many-headed monster," Christopher Hill remarks that Browne was "thoroughly orthodox in thinking it was 'no breach of charity' to call the multitude fools"; but, Hill stresses, "this contemptuous attitude thinly concealed the fears of the propertied class."[19]

Brian Manning's study *The English People and the English Revolution* has documented the increasing involvement of the multitude in direct action, from the huge crowds that welcomed the release by the Long Parliament of Prynne, Burton, and Bastwick, onward. Fifteen thousand people signed the "root and branch" petition in November 1640; twenty to thirty thousand signed a petition demanding justice against the earl of Strafford, and it was delivered by a multitude of ten thousand. A crowd of five to fifteen thousand assembled at Westminster on 3 May 1641, demanding Strafford's execution; the multitude threatened the houses of the Spanish, French, and Portuguese ambassadors, and the Queen Mother was driven from England. The closing days of December 1641 were marked by sustained riots and demonstrations at Westminster, preventing the bishops from taking their seats in the House of Lords, and on 10 January 1642 Charles fled from London.

The mass demonstrations and marches on Parliament with petitions continued through 1642. Nor was the activity confined to London. Norfolk fishermen cast down salt-marsh enclosures, and rioting against royalists and papist property owners occurred on a large scale in Essex and Suffolk. The houses of the countess of Rivers at St. Osyth in Essex and at Long Melford in Suffolk, of Sir Francis Mannock at Stoke-by-Nayland in Suffolk, and of Sir John Lucas near Colchester were attacked and sacked.[20]

17. "'The Beast with Many Heads': Renaissance Views on the Multitude," *Shakespeare Quarterly* 16 (1965): 241–46.

18. *The Revolt of the Provinces: Conservatives and Radicals in the English Civil War, 1630–1650* (London, 1976), p. 34.

19. *Change and Continuity in Seventeenth-Century England* (London, 1974), pp. 186, 189.

20. Manning, *The English People*, pp. 141, 189, 205, 182, 190–91.

It was in this climate of direct action by the multitude that *Religio Medici*, with its attacks on the multitude, appeared. Hill points out that "Charles I in his Declaration of 23 October 1642 played on social anxieties by speaking of 'endeavours . . . to raise an implacable malice and hatred between the gentry and commonalty of the kingdom . . . insomuch as the highways and villages have not been safe for gentlemen to pass through without violence or affront.' "[21] One of Browne's resonant additions to the 1643 edition that might seem to be simply the philosophic play of metaphysical wit takes on a more specific paranoia in this context:

> 'Tis not onely the mischiefe of diseases, and the villanie of poysons that make an end of us, we vainly accuse the fury of Gunnes, and the new inventions of death; 'tis in the power of every hand to destroy us, and wee are beholding unto every one wee meete hee doth not kill us. (*P*, 115)

The passage had a particular relevance for a society divided by class hostilities and, after Charles raised his standard in August 1642, embroiled in civil war.

Edward Dowden and Joan Bennett both argue that in detecting "a rabble even amongst the Gentry" (*P*, 134) Browne showed that his antipathy for the multitude was "not a class-feeling," the multitude was not "any particular class of men."[22] Contemporary accounts of the crowds that assembled on 3 May 1641 at Westminster demanding the execution of Strafford "were agreed that the crowds comprised 'for the most part men of good fashion'; 'many of them captains of the City and men of eminent rank'; 'many thousand of the most substantial of the citizens'; 'citizens of very good account, some worth £30,000, some £40,000.' "[23] The following day "the well-to-do demonstrators . . . sent their servants"; this "rabble amongst the Gentry" remained involved.

Browne's inclusion of "gentry" in the rabble, then, rather than demonstrating his lack of class feeling, can be seen as expressing a specific sociopolitical position, a reaction against the multitude that parliamentarians were suspected of manipulating. Though Browne includes gentry in his rabble, it is quite clear that his distaste and contempt for the multitude is a distaste for the style of the plebeians, the mechanics, the "ignorant": "a sort of Plebeian heads, . . . men in the same Levell with Mechanickes" (*P*, 134). He cannot assert the wisdom of God without sneering at the ignorance of the "vulgar," the crowd: "The advantage I have of the vulgar, with the content and happinesse I conceive therein, is an ample recompence for all my endeavours, in what part of knowledg soever" (*P*, 74). In 1643 he added to this passage a further ten lines on God's wisdom, "his most beauteous

---

21. *Change and Continuity,* p. 196.

22. Dowden, *Puritan and Anglican* (London, 1900), p. 53, and Bennett, *Sir Thomas Browne* (Cambridge, 1962), p. 99.

23. Manning, *The English People,* p. 25.

attribute." He also toned down his elitism in that famous assertion of the value of intellectual inquiry, a passage arguing for the religious value of scientific investigation while at the same time condemning yet again the vulgar, the rude, the rustic:

> The wisedome of God receives small honour from those vulgar heads, that rudely stare about and with a grosse rusticity admire his workes; those highly magnifie him whose judicious enquiry into his acts, and deliberate research into his creatures, returne the duty of a devout and learned admiration. (*P*, 75)

In 1642 "small honour" had been "no honour," and "those highly magnifie him" had been "those onely magnifie him." The contempt for the unlettered remains in the 1643 version, but its finality, its intransigence, is slightly modified. (It was always there with Browne, and we can find it again in *Pseudodoxia Epidemica.*)

The literary tradition gave the weight of traditional authority to class prejudice and allowed contemporary events to be alluded to without any dangerous specificity, avoiding reprisal under the cover of generality. But just because there was a literary tradition we should not forget that opposite opinions were also expressed—and increasingly so at this time. In 1641, interpreting Revelation 19:6, *A Glimpse of Sion's Glory* proclaimed that "The Voice, of Jesus Christ reigning in his Church, comes first from the multitude, the common people";[24] and in April 1642 Milton's *Apology against a Pamphlet called a Modest Confutation of the Animadversion of the Remonstrant against Smectymnuus* "commended parliament for its considerable reception . . . of the petitions even of its humblest citizens."[25]

Browne's rejection of the millenarian interpretations of his time is part of his rejection of any idea of the poor establishing God's kingdom on earth. "The poor existed as objects of the charity of the rich, Browne and many others tell us: but this charity must be reasonable, socially responsible. The assumption, sharply contrasting with early protestant hopes, is that poverty will continue."[26] The poor exist to be the object of charity for the rich; they are part of the social hierarchy. Browne wrote:

> Let us speake like Politicians, there is a Nobility without Heraldry, a naturall dignity, whereby one man is ranked with another, another Filed before him, according to the quality of his desert, and preheminence of his good parts. (*P*, 134)

Browne presents this social hierarchy as part of the natural order of things, "for there is in this Universe a Staire, or manifest Scale of creatures, rising not disorderly, or in confusion, but with a comely method and

---

24. Stuart Prall, ed., *The Puritan Revolution: A Documentary History* (New York, 1968), p. 87.
25. Haller, *Liberty and Reformation*, p. 25.
26. Christopher Hill, *Society and Puritanism in Pre-Revolutionary England,* rev. ed. (London, 1969), p. 281.

proportion" (*P*, 101). These may well be "time-honoured commonplaces," as Patrides remarks (*P*, 26–27), but Browne reasserts them with a credo that suggests their contemporary urgency. "I beleeve there shall never be an Anarchy in Heaven, but as there are Hierarchies amongst the Angels, so shall there be degrees of priority amongst the Saints" (*P*, 131). It is "the corruption of these times" that has disturbed the orderly hierarchy of the "first and primitive Common-wealths," but the hierarchical principle

> is yet in the integrity and Cradle of well-ordered polities, till corruption getteth ground, ruder desires labouring after that which wiser considerations contemn, every one having a liberty to amasse & heape up riches, and they a license or faculty to doe or purchase any thing. (*P*, 134–35)

The 1643 preface opened with a reflection on the "times wherein I have lived to behold . . . the name of his Majesty defamed, the honour of Parliament depraved." The context was spelled out by which the reader could interpret "the corruption of these times" in section 1 of Part II as referring to the events of the 1640s.

With this reading of *Religio Medici*'s hostility to the radical sects and to the multitude, it is worth reconsidering Browne's much-proclaimed toleration. W. K. Jordan claims "the noble latitudinarianism and moderation which were being raised as the reply to bigotry are everywhere manifest in Browne's writing."[27] But Browne's toleration of Roman Catholics is but part of his intolerance for the sectarians and his contempt for the multitude. It is all of a piece with his acceptance of Laudian ceremony and of the hierarchical, authoritarian social meanings of that policy.

> In the forms of worship, stress was laid on the revival of hieratic ritual and visual ornament, in ways which had not been seen for over sixty years. Communion tables were put back in the east end of churches, and protected by altar rails; the erection of organs and stained-glass windows was encouraged; the clergy were ordered to use the surplice and the laity to kneel at the altar rails to receive the sacrament.[28]

Browne proclaims his ceremonialism and explains the social uses of it:

> I am, I confesse, naturally inclined to that, which misguided zeale termes superstition . . . at my devotion I love to use the civility of my knee, my hat, and hand, with all those outward and sensible motions, which may expresse, or promote my invisible devotion. I should violate my owne arme rather then a Church, nor willingly deface the memory of Saint or Martyr. At the sight of a Crosse or Crucifix I can dispence with my hat, but scarce with the thought or memory of my Saviour; I cannot laugh at but rather pity the fruitless journeys of Pilgrims, or

---

27. *The Development of Religious Toleration in England* (Cambridge, Mass., 1936), 2:447.

28. Lawrence Stone, *The Causes of the English Revolution, 1529–1642* (London, 1972), p. 119.

contemne the miserable condition of Friers; for though misplaced in circumstance, there is something in it of devotion: I could never heare the *Ave Marie* Bell without an elevation. . . . There are questionlesse both in Greek, Roman, and African Churches, solemnities, and ceremonies, whereof the wiser zeales doe make a Christian use, and stand condemned by us; not as evill in themselves, but as allurements and baits of superstitions to those vulgar heads that looke asquint on the face of truth, and those unstable judgements that cannot consist in the narrow point and centre of vertue without a reele or stagger to the circumference. (*P*, 63–64)

Ceremonials, then, are baits for the ignorant vulgar. But the ignorant vulgar were less attracted to the images of social control than was Browne. Hill remarks on "the popular iconoclasm which broke out whenever opportunity offered: in the late 1630s and 40s altar rails were pulled down, altars desecrated, statues on tombs destroyed, ecclesiastical documents burnt, pigs and horses baptized."[29] The 1642 text contained a much more specific reference to this iconoclasm with its vocabulary of explicitly physical violence and its specific reference to the so breakable "church window," which in 1643 became simply "church": "I should cut off my arm, rather than violate a Church window, then deface or demolish the memory of a Saint or Martyr." The 1643 text allows the possibility of physical violence within its more abstract expression, but its language is not as unavoidably physical as the 1642 "cut off" and "demolish."

It may be that Browne wanted to avoid validating iconoclasm by giving expression to it; or it may be that by removing the specific terminology, he is allowing the reader to believe that he is speaking merely metaphorically, not referring to specific incidents. On 22 February 1641 "the Cathedral Blades of Norwich" rushed to the defense of the cathedral, believing "the Apprentices . . . would have pulled down their Organs."[30] Norwich Cathedral was in fact ransacked three years later, its windows broken, monuments torn up, icons smashed. The puritan feeling was there, and Browne may have cautiously preferred not to antagonize it; he did not remove the passage altogether, he simply made its unavoidable physicality ambiguously metaphorical. But the changes did not alter the basic standpoint, the reverence for the church building. It is in pointed contrast to the radical sectarian view we find in George Fox's revelation of 1646: "it was opened in me, 'That God, who made the world, did not dwell in temples made with hands' ";[31] or in *Paradise Lost* where the "upright heart and pure" is asserted as preferred before all temples (I, 18). "His people were his temple, and he dwelt in them," as Fox put it.

Browne's comments on church music have to be seen in this politically

---

29. *The World Turned Upside Down*, p. 29.

30. Frank L. Huntley, *Sir Thomas Browne: A Biographical and Critical Study* (Ann Arbor, 1962), p. 27.

31. *Journal* (Leeds, 1836), 1:89.

charged context. Indeed Browne's tone becomes combative against those who "declaime against all Church musicke" (*P,* 149). "All" had been "our" in 1642, and the number of other detailed changes in this passage suggest the political sensitivity of the topic. For it was highly sensitive. "Choral singing and the playing of organs in church were the work of Antichrist, introduced by the Pope in the significant year 666," according to Henry Burton in a sermon preached before the House of Commons and published in 1641 as *Englands Bondage and Hope of Deliverance,* and to William Thomas in a speech to Parliament in June 1641.[32] Against this radical puritan position Browne asserts that

> Whatsoever is harmonically composed, delights in harmony; which makes me much distrust the symmetry of those heads which declaime against all Church musicke. For my selfe, not only from my obedience but my particular genius, I doe imbrace it. (*P,* 149)

"From my obedience" replaces "for my Catholike obedience" of 1642, lest "Catholike" should be interpreted as papist, and the implication of Laudian enforcement followed grudgingly that might be deduced from "I am obliged to maintain it" in 1642 is replaced by "I doe imbrace it." It is one of the rare occasions that Browne's emendations make the 1643 text more challenging, more combative; and the reference a couple of lines further on to "my Maker" in 1642 is changed to "the first Composer," asserting the divinity of church music.

Not only is Browne inclined toward tolerance of ceremonial and various Roman Catholic practices such as "the prayer for the dead; whereunto I was inclined from some charitable inducements" ([*P,* 67–68]; 1642: "enclined by an excesse of charity"). Negatively, the puritan stress upon the centrality of preaching finds no echo in his work:

> those usuall Satyrs, and invectives of the Pulpit may perchance produce a good effect on the vulgar, whose eares are opener to Rhetorick then Logick, yet doe they in no wise confirme the faith of wiser beleevers, who know that a good cause needs not to be patron'd by a passion, but can sustaine it selfe upon a temperate dispute. (*P,* 65)

Preaching for Browne is identified with "those popular scurrilities and opprobrious scoffes of the Bishop of *Rome,* whom as a temporall Prince, we owe the duty of good language" (*P,* 65). The radical implications of encouraging disrespect for authority disturb him; implicitly he endorses the bishops' opposition to preaching. In September 1641 the Commons passed a motion, made by Cromwell, voting "general permission to the people of any parish to 'set up a Lecture' and maintain a preacher at their own charge 'to preach every Lords Day, where there is no Preaching; and to preach One [week-]Day in every Week, where there is no weekly Lecture.' "[33] But

32. Hill, *Antichrist,* p. 75.
33. Haller, *Liberty and Reformation,* pp. 24–25, 360.

preaching is no part of the *Religio Medici;* in fact, it is a significant absence. The toleration for Roman Catholicism in a context of widespread fears of popish plots, as documented by Manning,[34] similarly forms part of a hostility to radical, sectarian puritanism.

To place the components of Browne's "toleration" against the grievances expressed in the "root and branch" petition presented to Parliament on 11 December 1640 is to see his conservative, oppositional stance. The signatories complained, among other things, of

> 7. . . . the want of preaching ministers in very many places both of England and Wales . . .
> 9. The hindering of godly books to be printed . . . the restraint of reprinting books formerly licensed, without relicensing.
> 11. The growth of Popery . . .
> 13. . . . the prelates here in England, by themselves or their disciples, plead and maintain that the Pope is not Antichrist, and that the Church of Rome is a true Church . . .
> 14. The great conformity and likeness both continued and increased of our church to the Church of Rome, in vestures, postures, ceremonies and administrations . . .
> 15. The standing up at *Gloria Patri* and at the reading of the Gospel, praying towards the East, the bowing at the name of Jesus, the bowing to the altar towards the East, cross in baptism, the kneeling at the Communion.[35]

III

This reading is a preliminary attempt to situate *Religio Medici* in the context of the English revolution, in the context in which it was published and first read. Browne's claim, which he perhaps too emphatically repeats, that the work was composed many years before publication in 1642, may be true; it may be that the work was begun many years earlier and progressively added to. Certainly the work was added to between the "unauthorized" editions of 1642 and the authorized edition of 1643, with passages that relate to contemporary social upheavals; and contemporary readers could not have read references to "the present antipathies between the two extreames" (*P,* 64) without thinking of the antipathies between Charles I and Parliament. *Religio Medici* is not a work that puts forward an explicit or positive political position; but negatively, in its rejection of sectarianism, mass action, millenarianism, the multitude, and any manifestations of plebeian puritan activism, it is possible to locate the work in a cautious, conservative, law-and-order context. Under the guise of religious apology and intellectual speculation, through "wit," a political picture is presented. The attacks on the sects and the multitude are the iconography, the shared

34. *The English People,* pp. 33 ff.
35. Prall, ed., *The Puritan Revolution,* pp. 98–99.

language, of the emerging conservative party of law and order that provided the basis of the royalist movement,[36] but that was careful enough not to be too explicitly assertive. Who knew what forces might eventually dominate? I am not arguing that this is the only or the total meaning of *Religio Medici;* it is in part a covert meaning, but it is not an esoteric one. I have drawn my historical evidence from the standard historians of the period—Haller, Hill, Manning, Morrill, Stone, Zagorin—for Browne embodies a recognized, mainstream political response to the documented political circumstances and events of his time. In part, no doubt, this is why *Religio Medici*, apart from the eight extant manuscript copies—none in Browne's hand—went through five editions between 1642 and 1645 and, after an interval of eleven years, another three editions between 1656 and 1659.[37] But this is less to deny or reduce its spiritual meanings than to suggest political uses to which spiritual insights can be attached.[38]

36. Compare Stone, *Causes of the English Revolution*, p. 141.

37. *Religio Medici*, ed. Denonain, pp. ix–xxi, and Geoffrey Keynes, *A Bibliography of Sir Thomas Browne, Kt, M. D.* (Cambridge, 1924), pp. 9–14.

38. I am grateful to Christopher Bentley, Christopher Hill, and C. A. Patrides for their help with this paper.

Browne and Paul Nash:
The Genesis of Form

Philip Brockbank

A tricentenary is a time for resurrection and for the celebration of continuing life. Over the past three hundred years Sir Thomas Browne's
reputation has had many celebrants. Some, like Johnson and Coleridge,
have written under the spell of the old verbal witchcraft, but others have
commended the "warm and generous human sympathy" that makes *Religio
Medici* "one of the first great utterances on behalf of religious toleration."[1]
The very amplitude of Geoffrey Keynes's *Bibliography of Sir Thomas Browne*
might seem to allow Browne's claim that "there is no man's minde of such
discordant and jarring a temper to which a tuneable disposition may not
strike a harmony" (*P,* 151). But Browne's name has been on the *Index,* and
Stanley Fish has recently told us that "His vaunted tolerance is really
indifference: he doesn't want to be bothered and he doesn't want to bother
us either."[2] Browne, says Fish, "insists everywhere on the essential
homogeneity of whatever is discretely perceived." It is so; for it is a hazard of
human thought that our generalizing capacities are at odds with our powers
of discrimination; and in ways that Fish has generously helped us to
understand, the structure of Browne's thought is intimately related to that
of his prose, and to our consciousness of the world. "Lord deliver me from
my selfe, is a part of my Letany, and the first voyce of my retired imagina-
tions. There is no man alone, because every man is a *Microcosme,* and carries
the whole world about him"(*P,* 152). Disengagement from the self, even
the solicitous and sorrowing self—the one that does want to be bothered—
seems often in Browne's art to be an aspiring impulse of the "retired
imagination."

Writing at a time when men of fierce conviction (including Milton) were
seeking to change the world, Browne invites us to be content with, and to

1. Jeremiah S. Finch, *Sir Thomas Browne* (New York, 1950), p. 10.
2. *Self-Consuming Artifacts: The Experience of Seventeenth-Century Literature*
(Berkeley, 1972), p. 368.

marvel at, the world as it is. We are asked to re-create, in a contemplative rapture, those ordering processes that first brought the world into being. In a diminished perspective we may see Browne as a cultivated bourgeois, the professional physician who, because of his acknowledged place in society, is ready to conform to the old allegiances, less anxious to change the human world than to sustain it. His prose could be said to afford solace to an educated reader of the middle station, neither ambitious for the extravagant, or magnanimous, life of the patrician landowner, nor preoccupied with the ordeals of the poor; for "Statists that labour to contrive a Common-wealth without poverty, take away the object of charity" (*P,* 159). In an ampler perspective, however, Browne's work is poised between the millenial hopes of the early seventeenth century, when war and revolution seemed to so many to promise a triumphal reentry into the kingdom of God upon earth, and the optimistic theodicies of the late seventeenth century, which prefaced the Enlightenment and the age of tolerance. Is Browne's tolerance really indifference, or does it manifest a will to keep a therapeutic distance from the contending energies that were bringing about the destruction of Christendom in the Europe and the England of his time? I do not believe this question can be resolved, but I am enough of a Brownean to feel that it should be revolved. Questions of commitment and tolerance are still of urgent interest to us. In an effort to cross the space between Browne's century and our own, and hoping a little to upstage Stanley Fish's account of "The Bad Physician," I am invoking the responses of Paul Nash, the English war artist, abstract landscape painter, and occasional engraver.

Almost exactly fifty years ago Nash was invited by Desmond Flowers of Cassell's publishing house to illustrate a book of his own choice; he alighted on *Hydriotaphia* and *The Garden of Cyrus.* The volume, an acclaimed masterpiece of book production, scrupulously edited by Nash's friend John Carter, appeared in 1932. If we are susceptible to economic explanations of the functions of imaginative art, we might "place" the prose and the prints without feeling an obligation to look closely at either. We may feel that one minor master was recognizing that his talents were in tune with those of another and that together they could appeal to an elite market of subscribers. But those who at the time made much of the work were not, in Arnold's terms, barbarians or philistines, but "aliens." They were those who, like Carter himself, Herbert Read, and Antony Bertram (who wrote the earliest and still the fullest account of the enterprise[3]), realized that Nash had found in Browne a new impetus and direction to his own major work.

The illustrations offer us an opportunity to keep pace with the analogues between two modes of art and two historical moments of perception. I shall suggest, in the rough geometry of my own argument, that there is a parallel between seventeenth- and twentieth-century experiences of violence in Europe, and a convergence of Nash's interest in the processes of creation

3. *Paul Nash: The Portrait of an Artist* (London, 1955), pp. 194–201.

upon Browne's. Nash did not, as far as I know, attend directly (as Brecht did) to the wars of the seventeenth century, and there is no reason to believe that Browne, in his art as distinct from his life, was specifically recoiling from the Cromwellian soldiery described by his patient, Bishop Joseph Hall, as "drinking and tobacconing" in Norwich Cathedral, "as freely as if it had turned alehouse."[4] But Nash, after his months in the Ypres salient, could be expected to respond with more than usual intensity to the very first sentence that Browne addressed to his reading public: "Certainly that man were greedy of life, who should desire to live when all the world were at an end; and he must needs be very impatient, who would repine at death in the society of all things that suffer under it" (*P*, 59). Much of the revolving symmetry of Browne's art is meant to recall us to our place in the community of mortality: "We vainly accuse the fury of Gunnes, and the new inventions of death; 'tis in the power of every hand to destroy us, and wee are beholding unto every one wee meete hee doth not kill us" (*P*, 115). In the later works that Nash chose to illustrate, however, what Nash saw in Browne was a common preoccupation with the generation of form out of void, of order out of decay, of life out of death. Where Brecht, visiting the seventeenth century in *Mother Courage,* was preoccupied with survival—even mere survival—Nash, turning to Browne, recovered from the seventeenth century that confidence in the processes of generation that was later proclaimed in his final paintings.

By 1924 Nash had produced for the Nonesuch Press a series of illustrations to Genesis.[5] The twelve small wood engravings are known by titles suggested by the text—"The Creation of the Firmament," "Vegetation," "Cattle and Creeping Things," "The Sun and the Moon"—but they could all be glossed from *Religio Medici:* "God being all things is contrary unto nothing out of which were made all things, and so nothing became something, and *Omneity* informed *Nullity* into an essence" (*P*, 105). Nash might have been more pleased than dismayed by Fish's observation that O, N, and E hide unity in Browne's triplet of grand concluding words. He begins the illustrations of Genesis with "The Void," and, working with his engraver's tool, mimicking the art of God, he elicits light from darkness and persuades it to assume commanding geometric forms. In the self-created history of Nash's own art, it is not difficult to perceive in "The Face of the Waters" and "The Division of Light from Darkness" those clarifications of sea and wave geometry already to be found in "Night Tide" and other Dymchurch paintings.[6] But, more strikingly, the title and the emergent forms of "Void" take us back to the great oil painting of the same name, made out of Nash's

---

4. Cited in Finch, *Sir Thomas Browne,* p. 127.

5. The preparatory drawings are reproduced in Margot Eates, *Paul Nash: The Master of the Image* (London, 1973), pls. 36–37; three of the engravings are in Andrew Causey, *Paul Nash* (Oxford, 1980), pls. 155, 156, 273.

6. See Causey, *Paul Nash,* pls. 133, 138, 149, and Eates, *Paul Nash,* pls. 35, 40. For wave geometry, see also D'Arcy Wentworth Thompson, *On Growth and Form* (Cambridge, 1917), p. 236.

experience of Passchendaele, while the sloping blocks and pyramidal edges that break through the water in "The Dry Land Appearing" recall similar forms rising out of the shell craters in "The Menin Road."[7] Taken together, "The Division of Light" and "The Creation of the Firmament" are abstracted versions of forms found in "We are Making a New World."[8] In that ironic epigraph to desolation we may find the occasion for Nash's return both to Genesis and to Browne; for in the 1920s and the early 1930s Nash was endeavoring to transcend the irony. Like Otto Dix, his counterpart in the German trenches, Nash had been fascinated and moved to see vegetable life returning to the shattered earth of Flanders.[9] Yet the indefatigable exuberance of natural growth was not enough to satisfy an imagination that looked not only for renewed life but also for renewed order. Something, to borrow Eliot's image, might be made to grow out of the stony rubbish, but Nash the artist needed new prospects of form out of void. "Art is the perfection of Nature: Were the world now as it was the sixt day, there were yet a Chaos: Nature hath made one world, and Art another. In briefe, all things are artificiall, for nature is the Art of God" (*P*, 81). It is on the seventh day that God, the "skilfull Geometrician," resting from labor, looks upon "the beauteous structure of the world" and finds that it is good. Thus it came about that, six years after the publication of Nash's Genesis, a design analogous to that of "Vegetation" appeared as the frontispiece of *The Garden of Cyrus*.

While Nash was in France a book was published in England that happily affords another stepping stone from *The Garden of Cyrus* into the twentieth century. Sir D'Arcy Wentworth Thompson's *On Growth and Form* might have delighted Browne, both verbally and perceptually, attending as it does to tetrahedral and hexagonal symmetry, to asymmetry and anisotropy, the properties of corals, spicules, foraminifers, radiolarians, and the calycles of campanularian zoophytes. Nash owned the book and evidently knew it well enough for us to be able to speculate that, for example, one campanularian zoophyte prompted the shape of the vase in the second plate of *The Garden of Cyrus*.[10] Thompson is himself very aware of Browne's "quaint and beautiful account" of hexagonal and quincuncial symmetry, and a number of his observations on honeycombs, on the five-petaled flower, and on the asymmetry of leaves find a place in this latter-day Book of Genesis. Nash may even have been remembering *On Growth and Form* in his Genesis plate "Contemplation," which bears some resemblance to Thompson's determination of the pyramidal angles terminating what Browne calls the "three lozenges at the bottom of every cell" of the honeycomb.[11] Thompson's

7. Eates, *Paul Nash*, pls. 16, 36d, 19.

8. Ibid., pls. 36b, 36c, 16.

9. See the letter printed in Causey, *Paul Nash*, p. 67 and pl. 69.

10. See Thompson, *On Growth and Form*, p. 237, fig. 72A; but Nash may have owned such a vase (see Causey, *Paul Nash*, pl. 162: "Dahlias").

11. Thompson, *On Growth and Form*, p. 330; Eates, *Paul Nash*, pl. 37e; Browne, *P*, 355.

book, in itself and in its choice of epigraphs from Thomas Aquinas and from the president of the British Association, registers confidence at once in the mechanical sciences of the late nineteenth century and in the Thomist doctrines of an ordered creation. Browne warned Nicholas Bacon to expect "no mathematicall truths" from *The Garden of Cyrus,* but his insights into the geometry of nature and into the energies of generative growth have a lasting validity, and for Nash in 1931 they were crucial.

Nash studied Browne's text carefully and had an exact command of it. While he rarely renders a report or an image literally, he not only reacts to local effects but also encourages a reader's scattered perceptions to coalesce into new orders; and he contrives to create in collotype and watercolor a visual equivalent to the prolific allusiveness and the aphoristic immediacies of Browne's style. "Nature hath furnished one part of the Earth," says Browne, "and man another," and "a large part of the earth is still in the Urne unto us" (*P,* 267). The simplicities become equivocations as we reflect upon them, and Nash's frontispiece (Figure 1) is answeringly poised between emphatic yet uncertain divisions—between earth and air, light and dark, this side and that side of a window, underground and overground, seen and unseen, now and then, and known and unknown. On one side of the wall a white shadow is cast by an invisible urn. For Nash, the opening paragraph of *Hydriotaphia* is haunted by a recollection of *The Garden of Cyrus:* "Life it self is but the shadow of death, and souls departed but the shadows of the living: All things fall under this name. The Sunne it self is but the dark *simulachrum,* and light but the shadow of God" (*P,* 376).

A smaller figure in the text shows a skeleton with a conspicuous skull lying under the sea, which Browne, alluding to the Deluge, calls "the smartest grave" (*P,* 268). Thales, we are told later, thought "that water was the originall of all things" and therefore "most equal to submit into the principle of putrefaction, and conclude in a moist relentment." Like Eliot, Nash in his "death by water" keeps in touch with *The Tempest,* "Of his bones are coral made," but his fish forms, corals, and shells have their consorts in *On Growth and Form,*[12] and the conjunctions of death and life call the second book of the volume back into the first.

To perceive the general movement of Nash's thirty designs it is useful to recall his own titles for the fourteen full plates of the series. After the frontispiece they are: "Tokens," "Buried Urne," "Funeral Pyre," "Mansions of the Dead," "Ghosts," "Sorrow," "Vegetable Creation," "Poisonous Plantations," "The Quincunx artificially considered," "The Quincunx naturally considered" (two plates), "The Quincunx mystically considered," and "The Order of Five." Seven, it may be said, are for the book of death, and seven are for the correspondent book of life; taking multiple hints from the text, each group offers intimations of the other.

12. *On Growth and Form,* p. 325.

Figure 1. "Frontispiece"

Figure 2. "Tokens"

Figure 3. "Buried Urne"

Figure 4. "Funeral Pyre"

Figure 5. "Mansions of the Dead"

Figure 6. "Ghosts"

Figure 7. "Sorrow"

Figure 8. "Vegetable Creation"

Figure 9. "Poisonous Plantations"

Figure 10. "The Quincunx artificially considered"

Figure 11. "The Quincunx naturally considered" (1)

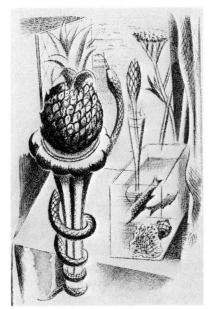

Figure 12. "The Quincunx
naturally considered" (2)

Figure 13. "The Quincunx
mystically considered"

Figure 14. "The Order of Five"

"Tokens" (Figure 2) is a gathering of life relics mostly culled from Chapter II, "Combes, Plates like Boxes, fastened with Iron pins, and handsomely overwrought like the necks or bridges of Musicall Instruments, long brasse plates overwrought like the handles of neat implements, brazen nippers to pull away hair" (*P,* 280). Instead of the "golden Bees" of the text, Nash offers two bird ornaments, perhaps alluding to the "mysticall figures of Peacocks, Doves and Cocks" called the "hinting imagery of the Resurrection; which is the life of the grave, and sweetens our habitations in the Land of Moles and Pismires" (*P,* 290). An earlier image of resurrection provides the end piece to Chapter I, showing two ascending forms—a phoenix (very like a cock) and a rising serpent—against a sun, with stepped rocks climbing in the background. Nash's "Tokens" remain objects in a sepulcher, exposed to the archaeologist's inquiring eye. But they cast uncertain shadows, both actual and symbolic. We are left to wonder where the light breaking in upon the rich earth and the sand comes from, to discover the living worms moving in harmony with the relics and artifacts of the dead.

In the third plate, "Buried Urne" (Figure 3), a large and a small urn are housed together in another society of death, conceiving "some satisfaction to be neighbours in the grave, to lye Urne by Urne, and touch but in their names" (*P,* 289). In the large family urn, "the Ashes of their nearest friends and kindred might successively be received . . . while their collateral memorials lay in *minor* vessels about them." Oak leaves and flowers survive to tell of old honors and habits that Browne reports ("The *Romans* affected the Rose, the Greeks *Amaranthus* and myrtle"[*P,* 299]), and under the soil a darkened area of the larger urn may allude to "the *Homerical* Urne of *Patroclus*" covered in "a purple piece of silk" (*P,* 285). The first of several clear allusions to the heroic dead is to be found in the decussated wreath touching the smaller urn, its form echoed by a natural root on the right. "Bay leaves," we are told in *Hydriotaphia,* "were found green in the Tomb of *S. Humbert,*" but Nash is anticipating the "Triumphal Oval, and Civicall Crowns of Laurel, Oake, and Myrtle" (*P,* 335) that were pleated after the quincuncial order. Both in this plate and in the design preceding it (of one ring upon a finger bone and another upon a root of "Quich, or Dogsgrass"), the earth is felt to be "the mother Element," and Nash's smaller urn is one of "the common form with necks . . . a proper figure, making our last bed with our first; nor much unlike the Urnes of our Nativity, while we lay in the nether part of the Earth, and inward vault of our Microcosme" (*P,* 284).

In the next plate (Figure 4) Nash attends to the element of fire: "What the Sun compoundeth, fire analyseth, not transmuteth. That devouring agent leaves almost allwayes a morsell for the Earth, whereof all things are but a colonie; and which, if time permits, the mother Element will have in their primitive masse again" (*P,* 293). "Funeral Pyres" interlards five layers of logs on a platform, making a quincuncial box; in characteristic play with perspective, Nash's flames reach behind a temple, with cypress tree, which might otherwise have been supposed distant; the fire-reflecting clouds disengage from the smoke and fragment into multiplying bird forms and birds. The morsel that Browne's fire leaves for the earth is a monumental hand—another glance at the quincunx.

Flying and ascending forms released from boxes into cloud and air compose the fifth plate, "The Mansions of the Dead" (Figure 5). It is usually considered in relation to a passage in Chapter IV: "Before *Plato* could speak, the soul had wings in *Homer,* which fell not, but flew out of the body into the mansions of the dead" (*P,* 298). But it also recollects Browne's observation in the previous chapter that *"Plato*'s historian of the other world, lies twelve dayes incorrupted, while his soul was viewing the large stations of the dead" (*P,* 291). The design was an important one in Nash's development, yielding the oil painting *Aerial Composition* a year later.[13] In a letter to Hartley Ramsden in 1941 Nash supposes himself to have misinterpreted Browne, who "must have been thinking of tombs *under the earth* when he wrote of 'The Soul Visiting the Mansions of the Dead.' "[14] The allusion in Chapter III, however, is to Plato's story of Er, the son of Armenius, whose corpse remained intact until his soul returned from visiting the openings "of heaven and earth" that receive departed souls after judgment (*Republic* X. 614B). In Chapter IV the glance at Homer takes us on to *Phaedrus* 248, where "souls are fain and eager to behold the plain of truth." "Whatsoever soul has followed in the train of a god, and discerned something of truth," says Socrates, "shall be kept from sorrow until a new revolution shall begin. . . . but meeting with some mischance comes to be burdened with a load of forgetfulness and wrongdoing, and because of that burden sheds her wings and falls to the earth." The flying forms of Nash, however, are not clearly souls; they are insects, and their flight from eggs, or rather in eggs, to a death-transcending order anticipates Browne's reflection in Chapter III of *The Garden of Cyrus* that "The Æquivocall production of things under undiscerned principles makes a large part of generation" (*P,* 351). Nash is pursuing the minimal conditions of generation and makes a covert connection between the high life in Plato and the low life of putrefaction. "If they be sterill or untimely cast," says Browne, of "the seeds of Caterpillars or Cankers . . . their production is often a Fly, which we have observed from corrupted and mouldred Egges, both of Hens and Fishes" (*P,* 351). Andrew Causey shows how Nash's pictorial imagery over a range of his paintings frees the soul from the body like a bird from its cage.[15] In the present sequence, a figure three pages before "Mansions of the Dead" is of the boxed dead, a skeleton in a coffin, making Browne's point that "Teeth, bones, and hair, give the most lasting defiance to corruption" (*P,* 295). The boxed-in dead give place to eggs floating in a space that appears to be

13. Causey, *Paul Nash,* pls. 266, 267.
14. Bertram, *Paul Nash,* pp. 195–96; Causey, *Paul Nash,* p. 224.
15. Causey, *Paul Nash,* pp. 224–25.

amplified and liberated by the lattices of cages and egg-boxes rather than contained by them.

Nash's vision of the Platonic winged soul is more abstract both in thought and in design than is the next plate, "Ghosts" (Figure 6), which faces in the text a speculation that "Ghosts were but Images and shadows of the soul, received in higher mansions, according to the ancient division of body, soul, and image or *simulachrum* of them both" (*P,* 303). Scholars have found in the design a personal iconography. A figure of the artist himself descends into a submarine Hades presided over by a sibyl who recalls the *"Sybilla"* who tells Aeneas in Virgil that "the thin habit of spirits was beyond the force of weapons." At the same time the sibyl alludes to Sybil Fountain, a woman once loved by Nash and the subject of two earlier paintings.[16] Browne muses upon men who "set up the Deity of *Morta,* and fruitlessly adored Divinities without ears" (*P,* 302); at some distance from his earless sibyl, Nash insinuates the earless primitive figure of a god. Among the marine forms are the living jellyfish, one ascending in flowing splendor, the other cryptically waiting at the head of the steps. The mode is surreal, dreamlike, inviting interpretation by one of Browne's "Oneirocritical masters," but its phallic and fluid forms must be allowed to make their own claims on our unconscious—a humanoid worm makes its way along the ground, and hand-winged clouds pass in the marine air. Browne's text, however, is hospitable to the metamorphosed dead tree trunk that dominates the foreground and to the wreath form that seems to dissolve on the surface beside it. Nash may remind us, too, that Thales thought "water was the originall of all things" and that Browne speaks of the womb as well as of the obscurities of our awareness as the "inward vault of our Microcosme."

In antiquity, Browne tells us, "mourning without hope, they had an happy fraud against excessive lamentation, by a common opinion that deep sorrow disturbed their ghosts" (*P,* 300). In the final plate of *Hydriotaphia,* "Sorrow" (Figure 7), three beribboned ruined columns diminish into the middle distance, composing the remains of a temple or of a sequence of cenotaphs: "The variety of Monuments hath often obscured true graves: and *Cenotaphs* confounded Sepulchres" (*P,* 290). A liberated soul hovers facing the sun, while from the sun quincuncial lines descend upon the wreath and upon a torn evergreen branch: "that the Funerall pyre consisted of sweet fuell, Cypresse, Firre, Larix, Yewe, and Trees perpetually verdant, lay silent expressions of their surviving hopes" (*P,* 299). A mask lying close to the branch may well be, as Causey supposes, a memory of Shelley's Platonizing metaphor, "the loathsome mask has fallen,"[17] and the figure in flight, like the soul in *Phaedrus,* in a contemplative ecstasy (out of the body) perceives (without eyes) a mathematical principle. Opposite the plate, however, Browne's text reflects upon the transience of human grief:

16. See Bertram, *Paul Nash,* p. 197; for the paintings, see Causey, *Paul Nash,* pl. 17: "Vision at Evening," and Eates, *Paul Nash,* pl. 1a: "Our Lady of Inspiration."
17. Causey, *Paul Nash,* p. 226.

Darknesse and light divide the course of time, and oblivion shares with memory, a great part even of our living beings; we slightly remember our felicities, and the smartest stroaks of affliction leave but short smart upon us. Sense endureth no extremities, and sorrows destroy us or themselves. To weep into stones are fables. Afflictions induce callosities, miseries are slippery, or fall like snow upon us, which notwithstanding is no unhappy stupidity. To be ignorant of evils to come, and forgetful of evils past, is a mercifull provision in nature, whereby we digest the mixture of our few and evil dayes, and our delivered senses not relapsing into cutting remembrances, our sorrows are not kept raw by the edge of repetitions. (*P*, 311)

Nash's own language of light and darkness plays allusively upon Browne's, both in "Ghosts" and in "Sorrow," to quiet and transmute the pain of the past. The figure flying out of *Hydriotaphia* may again be Nash himself, addressing himself to the geometries of the sun, leaving the cenotaphs of the honored dead. "Let them not therefore complaine of immaturitie that die about thirty, they fall but like the whole world, whose solid and well composed substance must not expect the duration and period of its constitution"(*P*, 114).

Of the remaining small figures in the text, one tells that in antiquity "Juglers shewed tricks with Skeletons" (*P*, 289), that "it is hard to be deceived in the distinction of *Negro*'s sculls" (*P*, 296), and perhaps that, with the assistance of Dürer and Thompson, skulls can be geometrically analyzed.[18] In a literal rendering of the pyramids, Nash abstains from setting them incongruously upon an undulating flux, as he had in "The Pyramids of the Sea" (1912). Toward the end Nash offers us a tree and an open grave with an urn, to remind us that "old families last not three oaks" (*P*, 309); an imposed circle within a square shows us that "Circles and right lines limit and close all bodies, and the mortall right-lined circle, must conclude and shut up all."[19] But Nash's oak takes from *The Garden of Cyrus* "a commodious radiation" in its growth and a "due expansion" of its branches "for shadow or delight" (*P*, 365); the grave perspectives yield the quincuncial lattice; and the letter within a circle inscribed on the trunk is not "O The character of death" only, but also an anticipation of the Hebrew character *He* in *The Garden of Cyrus*, the "Seal," says Browne, of "the mother of the Life and Fountain of souls in Cabalisticall Technology" (*P*, 382).[20] The tail piece of *Hydriotaphia* is a quincunicial lozenge with ambiguously interre-

18. Thompson, *On Growth and Form*, pp. 740–43.
19. See also Browne's account of Plato's treatment of the circles and right lines of the soul in *The Garden of Cyrus* IV (*P*, 378); for an interesting account of Conrad's understanding of them, see W. Bonney, *Thorns and Arabesques* (Baltimore, 1980), pp. 200–201.
20. Where, in his attempt to order the generative cycle, Browne adduces the fifth Hebrew letter *He* (quoted by Nash in his headpiece to *The Garden of Cyrus* V as ה); Joyce's "cabalistic technology," in a similar attempt, turns the fifth letter *E* on its side as a *siglum* for Earwicker in *Finnegans Wake*.

lated domains of earth, air, and water; Nash inscribed the word *FINIS* here himself, while at the end of *The Garden of Cyrus* he leaves it to the printer.

The sense of awakened life when we turn to the frontispiece of *The Garden of Cyrus*, "Vegetable Creation" (Figure 8), and to the first page of the text is electrifying. A design that grows out of the Genesis wood engraving "Vegetation" is irradiated by Nash's readiness to share Browne's satisfaction with the colors of the natural world: "And therefore providence hath arched and paved the great house of the world, with colours of mediocrity, that is, blew and green, above and below the sight, moderately terminating the *acies* of the eye" (*P*, 373).

The next plate, "Poisonous Plantations" (Figure 9), finds death in the living world, reflecting the life found earlier in the world of the dead. "Some," Browne tells Nicholas Bacon, "commendably affected Plantations of venemous Vegetables" (*P*, 320), and in Chapter I we find that "King *Attalus* lives for his poysonous plantations of *Aconites*, Henbane, Hellebore, and plants hardly admitted within the walls of Paradise" (*P*, 328). Nash shows us a vase, vial, and hourglass on a windowsill, with a selection of toxic plants, including some of the most elegantly shaped—cuckoopint, deadly nightshade, and foxglove. The vial may allude to Browne the physician: "The greatest Balsames do lie enveloped in the bodies of most powerfull Corrosives; I say moreover, and I ground upon experience, that poysons containe within themselves their owne Antidote, and that which preserves them from the venom of themselves" (*P*, 152). Nash's design is a complex of unduloid and quincuncial forms, both natural and artificial, persisting into the optical perspectives of the garden outside the window. A strange seed box and eye form upon the vase (or calyx) may be observing with Browne that "It is no wonder that this Quincuncial order was first and still affected as gratefull unto the Eye: For all things are seen Quincuncially" (*P*, 376).

The next five plates, significantly, are devoted to the "Quincunx" or "Order of Five." In "The Quincunx artificially considered" (Figure 10), the bust of a Caesar broods, with eyes noticeably closed, in a ruined building, over nets and a fisherman's basket by a moonlit sea. The "figured pavement of the ancients," the lattice window, the nets, and once again the "Civicall Crown" all have their counterparts in the text (*P*, 334–36). Nash finds his unity of design in the geometry of light playing upon the reticulated surface of the water. Where a tree trunk is haunted by a human trunk in "Ghosts," a natural rock trunk rises from this sea, with an ambiguously natural or artificial stepped pyramid echoing the steps of the house or temple. The closed eyes suggest both the transience of the sublunar world and a timeless act of contemplation, to be recalled by Nash's last figure in the book.

The first of the pair called "The Quincunx naturally considered" (Figure 11) selects seven of the many forms that exemplify nature's delight in the quincunx—the teasel, sunflower, fern, catkin, pinecone, oak leaf, and acorn. The ascendant teasel flourishes also in Browne's prose: "he that considereth that fabrick so regularly palisadoed, and stemm'd with flowers of the royall colour; in the house of the solitary maggot, may find the Seraglio of *Solomon*" (*P,* 344). But the design is dominated by the "ordination there is in the favaginous Sockets, and Lozenge seeds of the noble flower of the Sunne. Wherein in Lozenge figured boxes nature shuts up the seeds, and balsame which is about them" (*P,* 345–46). Nash's sunflower leaves are flamelike and already intimate the energy and dominion of his late studies of the sunflower and the sun, while his perception of the flower finds a single image for Browne's affirmation of order and of life; it "doth neatly declare how nature Geometrizeth, and observeth order in all things" (*P,* 356), and it recalls from *Hydriotaphia* that "Life is a pure flame, and we live by an invisible Sun within us" (*P,* 313). Later in the text Nash finds related images for Browne's observations about "the solisesquious and Sun-following plants." The convolvulus, it is said, "observes both motions of the Sunne, while the flower twists Æquinoctially from the left hand to the right, according to the daily revolution; The stalk twineth ecliptically from the right to the left, according to the annual conversion" (*P,* 367). Nash sets his rotating convolvulus alongside an exuberant figure of the "large roots . . . of Mandrakes" (*P,* 369) under the geometric radiations of the sun.

The second plate of the "Quincunx naturally considered" (Figure 12) and the last plate, "The Order of Five" (Figure 14), are decorative displays of quincuncial forms (pineapples, snakes, fish, fircones; leaves, starfish, seed boxes, and flowers) that take a free and relaxed pleasure in "the delights, commodities, mysteries, with other concernments of this order"—they are, in Browne's phrase, "additionall ampliations" (*P,* 364). "The Quincunx mystically considered" (Figure 13), however, raises directly a question that the volume otherwise holds at arm's length. What did Nash's interest in the geometry of natural form owe to the European art movements of his time? Nash was acquainted with Henry Nevinson's work, for example, and was sometimes influenced by it. His illustrations to *King Lear*[21] recall Nevinson in their treatment of marching armies, and the severe geometry of nature that Lear confronts in the storm, like the human world in Nash's rendering of the play, is hard and oppressive. The geometry of light and dark in "The Void" and "The Menin Road," however, appears to owe as much to battle experience as to the pressure of a theory of form; shell bursts and sunlight breaking through smoke invite a treatment that solidifies rigorous forms of earth and sky.[22] "The Quincunx mystically considered" is a more refined and lyrical abstraction whose forms are redispositions at once of Nash's own "Quincunx naturally considered" and of Picasso's "Poised Objects" (1928).[23] The optics of Browne's prose play a part:

21. *Shakespeare's The Tragedie of King Lear* (London, 1927).
22. See Causey, *Paul Nash,* pp. 76–80, which includes two Vorticist engravings of shell bursts.
23. See ibid., pp. 231–32.

> For making the angle of incidence equal to that of reflexion, the visuall raye returneth Quincuncially, and after the form of a V, and the line of reflexion being continued unto the place of vision, there ariseth a semi-decussation, which makes the object seen in a perpendicular unto it self, and as farre below the reflectent, as it is from above. (*P*, 376)

But the effects are not optical only; for reflections (and echoes) are "not only verified in the way of sence, but in animall and intellectual receptions. Things entring upon the intellect by a Pyramid from without, and thence into the memory by another from within" (*P*, 377). Glancing at the distortions "ill placed in the Mathematicks of some brains," the text passes to Egyptian philosophy and tells us that "the genial spirits of both worlds, do trace their way in ascending and descending Pyramids, mystically apprehended in the Letter X" (*P*, 377). What Browne, Nash, and Picasso have in common is a keen awareness of the creativity of perception. We carry within us the forms that are without us. Creation exists only on the day it is contemplated and perceived, on the seventh day; and on that day we perceive that "All things began in order, so shall they end, and so they begin again; according to the ordainer of order and mysticall Mathematicks of the City of Heaven" (*P*, 387).

Making play with his skepticism and his fideism, Browne tells us in a felicitous pre-Keplerian conceit that he likes to "follow the great wheele of the Church, by which I move, not reserving any proper poles or motion from the epicycle of my own braine" (*P*, 66). He contrives to allow to his own individuality (his "numerical self," as he calls it) a lively freedom of movement within a comprehensive cycle. That cycle, however, as it reaches us in *Hydriotaphia, The Garden of Cyrus,* and much of *Religio Medici,* is not the "great wheele of the Church" but the generative cycle; it is within this cycle that Browne most characteristically seeks to bring our thoughts to rest. He looked forward to Giambattista Vico along much the same sight lines as Joyce was to look back at him, within a tradition that claims, as Stuart Hampshire puts it, "that the story of the human race can only in part be told as a progress, as of a man growing up from childhood to maturity to old age and decay; it must also be told as an overlapping of great circles, like the circles of the seasons."[24]

Browne's circling revolutionary thought, however, depends neither upon a naive response to seasonal rhythm nor upon a sophisticated interpretation of history. It finds its impetus in what we might call the epicycles of the language. A sentence in Browne is apt to turn back upon itself in tenor and cadence, leaving only just enough momentum to carry the reader to the next. The flux of words owes more to the principle of plenitude than to the dialectics of discourse. It invites wonder, delight, celebration, commemoration, astonishment, amazement, and admiration—rarely consecutive thought. Yet an austere intelligence is at work, too, with a keen sense of the

---

24. G. Tagliacozzo and D. P. Venene, eds., *Vico's Science of Humanity* (Baltimore, 1976), p. 323.

dependence of life upon structure. The affinities with Leibniz cannot be lightly set aside, but Browne's distinction is in the territory of words. It is in words that he makes manifest the prolific variety of the world. Like Vico, but as a maker, not as a theorist, he finds unity for mankind in the poetic evocations of a language that flows into the present from a remote past. He is an archaeologist of words and perpetually startles us with his discoveries:

> Physicians are not without the use of this decussation in severall operations, in ligatures and union of dissolved continuities. Mechanicks make use hereof in forcipall Organs, and Instruments of Incision; wherein who can but magnifie the power of decussation, inservient to contrary ends, solution and consolidation, union, and division, illustrable from *Aristotle* in the old *Nucifragium* or Nutcracker, and the Instruments of Evulsion, compression or incision; which consisting of two *Vectes* or armes, converted towards each other, the innitency and stresse being made upon the *hypomachlion* or fulciment in the decussation and greater compression is made by the union of two impulsors. (*P*, 338–39)

Browne's verbal effects are not merely verbal. Even here, at their most extravagant, they are in touch with the craft and dexterity of surgery. Elsewhere, they keep track of the natural world, and readers with imperfect experience of it may be surprised, for example, by the "noble scent" of the "Goat-Beetle," the "dentall sockets and eggs in the Sea Hedgehogge," and "the Mathematicks of the neatest Retiary Spider" (*P*, 352, 354).

Nash's wit and playfulness acknowledge Browne's but do not consistently emulate them—Browne's scissors, for example, rest quietly in the illustrated text alongside a reticulated mummy. What Nash hears and sees in *Hydriotaphia* and *The Garden of Cyrus*—the great energies and orders of generative creation—will find a climax in his own art in the late landscapes of the sunflower and the vernal equinox. While Browne and Nash keep in their work a certain distance from the human scene, yet each in his own way "made use of Musick to excite or quiet the affections of their friends, according to different harmonies" (*P*, 300). If the stresses and distresses of the world are not to bring us again to the void familiar to Nash, "the field of Golgotha and dead men's skulls," Browne's "tuneable disposition" has much to commend it. If his sense of the splendors and ironies of human endeavor within the great circle of mortality can help us to keep going for another three hundred years, so much the better. The point is not, to get to the end; the point is, not to get to the end.

The Garden of Cyrus
As Prophecy

Frank L. Huntley

"Prophecy" in seventeenth-century England usually involved scriptural interpretation and in consequence sermonizing; it did not mean divinely inspired prediction. Browne is said to have possessed certain stochastic powers,[1] but we have no instance of his actually foretelling an event. Biographers are fond of mentioning his half-wish to die on his birthday (he did) and his expressed horror (unaware that his own skull was to be "lost" for some forty years) of a human skull being turned into a drinking goblet. Browne was not interested in prophecy that pretends to foretell with exact dates and details. He looked askance on all forms of divination such as hepatoscopy, *sortes Vergilianae,* geomancy, rhabdomancy, belomancy, necromancy, and chiromancy, though he lingered over the fateful sign in the palm of his own hand (it turned out to be not true). He was also skeptical of dreams as signs of future events. "The revelations of Heaven are conveyed by new impressions, and the immediate illumination of the soul," Browne had written, whereas it is the devil who has "endeavoured the opinion of the Deity, by the delusion of Dreams, and the discovery of things to come in sleep" (*K,* 2:66–67). The pagan Greeks were particularly foolish to believe anything coming from the oracle of Apollo at Delphi. On this subject Browne's "Miscellany Tract" begins: "Men looked upon ancient oracles as natural, artificial, demoniacal, or all" (*K,* 3:95–102). Repeating the essential pattern a dozen or so years later, Browne ended the subtitle of *The Garden of Cyrus* with: ". . . artificially, naturally, [and] mystically considered," where God, not the devil, commands.

I

Real prophecy, as opposed to divination, is a discovery, a vision, and a revelation of a profound truth that requires an act of faith. Springing from

---

1. The Reverend John Whitefoot's funeral sermon for Browne, alluded to by Dr. Johnson (*P,* 505). Once more I am grateful to John Huntley, my best critic.

the prototype of the Book of Revelation, the tradition has been carried on in literature by Dante, by Sidney when he hailed the poet once more as *vates,* by Spenser and Milton, and later by Blake and Shelley. In England its development was aided by the over eighty-five theological commentaries on the Book of Revelation published in the first half of the seventeenth century, especially by the more literary explanations of David Paré ("Pareus"), Joseph Mede, and Henry More. The literary characteristics will be postponed for a moment in order to note here that prophecy usually arises from an occasion of doubt or anguish and that it must have a clear statement of the "truth" that has been revealed. John of Patmos wrote during the Roman persecution, and the truth he saw comes in the last chapter when Jesus says: "And, behold, I come quickly; and my reward is with me, to give every man according as his work shall be [compare Matthew 16:27]. I am Alpha and Omega, the beginning and the end, the first and the last" (22:12–13). The Old Testament prophets writing during the Babylonian captivity envisioned the return to Jerusalem and the rebuilding of the temple.

The vision that Browne believed and set down in *The Garden of Cyrus* comes on the final page: "All things began in order, so shall they end, and so shall they begin again; according to the ordainer of order and mystical Mathematicks of the City of Heaven" (*P,* 387). The prophecy may be interpreted on two levels. First, personally, it could mean that God ordains the hour of each man's birth and of each man's death, and that through Jesus Christ men shall live again. Since Browne was writing during the protectorate, some might interpret the prophecy as foretelling the return of Charles II and the reestablishment of the Anglican church. I do not believe, however, that Browne, the quiet and scholarly physician in East Anglia, was that politically minded. Rather, the prophecy, in the second place, has cosmic dimensions: God created the universe and all that is in it; on the day of His judgment and Christ's Second Coming, this universe will be destroyed; then will begin the new era of perfect order in heaven.

That *The Garden* is a more religious and millenarian document than has been hitherto recognized may be initially suggested by asking the simple question, "Why Cyrus?" There is very little in this work about the hanging gardens of Babylon. Browne confesses that they may have been begun by Nebuchadnezzar, the despised royal predecessor of Cyrus at Babylon. Then he adds laconically that Cyrus "so nobly [beautified them] that he was also thought to be the authour thereof" (*P,* 327). Except for a brief denial of relevance (*P,* 369), this is the last we hear of Cyrus, barely into the first pages of Browne's book. Of course Browne had read his Herodotus and Xenophon, but he also knew that Cyrus is mentioned in the Bible by the writer of 2 Chronicles and by Jeremiah, Ezra, Daniel, and Isaiah as the king who led the children of Israel out of captivity and back to Jerusalem. The story is told in 2 Chronicles 36:22–23:

Now in the first year of Cyrus king of Persia, that the word of the Lord spoken by the mouth of Jeremiah [29:10] might be accomplished, the Lord stirred up the spirit of Cyrus king of Persia, that he made a proclamation throughout all his kingdom, and put it also in writing, saying, Thus saith Cyrus king of Persia: All the kingdoms of the earth hath the Lord God of heaven given me: and he hath charged me to build him a house in Jerusalem, which is in Judah.

Ezra, repeating the proclamation, describes the gathering of the Jews to return to their holy city and the beginning of the rebuilding of the temple (5:13). Isaiah takes up the happy theme: "[Cyrus, saith the Lord], is my shepherd, and shall perform all my pleasure; even saying to Jerusalem, Thou shalt be built, and to the temple, Thy foundation shall be laid" (44:28). "Thus saith the Lord to his anointed, to Cyrus, whose right hand I have holden, to subdue nations before him . . . to open before him the two-leaved gates; and the gates shall not be shut" (45:1). Thus by the very choice of a title, *The Garden of Cyrus,* Browne indirectly invokes the prophetic voices of the Old Testament.[2]

II

Did Browne have an occasion for prophecy? Since *The Garden of Cyrus* is a painstakingly detailed work that the accidental unearthing of the Walsingham urns interrupted (*P,* 264), it is probable that Browne was making notes and writing it for at least two years before it was registered on 9 March 1657/58.[3] For him this was a period of dissolution, anguish, perhaps despair. The Puritan revolution had already spent itself. Anglicans feared that with no consecration of new bishops for so many years the apostolic succession in England was close to extinction. Weary of experiments, they yearned for the ancient rites, particularly since they had been worshiping "underground" since 1 November 1655, when Cromwell had banned *The Book of Common Prayer.* A distressful picture comes to us in the diary of one of Browne's correspondents at the time, John Evelyn. "The Protector Oliver," wrote Evelyn on 26 February 1656/57, "now affecting king-ship, is petitioned to take the Title on him by all his new-made sycophant Lords, &c. but dares not for fear of the Phanaticks, not thoroughly purged out of his Rebell Army."[4] On 8 August 1657 Evelyn bemoaned "the folly of a sort of enthusiasts and desperate Men, pretending to set up the kingdom of Christ with the sword. To this pass was this age arrived when we had no King in Israel." Evelyn described a surreptitious Anglican service held on

2. In the same tract Browne writes that although Croesus failed to understand the warning the oracle gave him against the Medes and the Persians, he might have had "no small assistance from the Prophecy of Daniel . . . of Jeremiah and Isaiah, wherein he might reade the name of Cyrus who should restore the Captivity of the Jews, and must, therefore, be the great Monarch of all those Nations" (*P,* 98).

3. *Transactions of the Stationers' Register, 1640–1708,* ed. G. E. B. Eyre and C. R. Rivington (London, 1913), 2:168.

4. *The Diary of John Evelyn,* ed. E. S. deBeer (Oxford, 1955), 3:203.

Christmas Day 1657 in London. A Reverend Mr. Gunning had finished his sermon on the prophet Micah 7:2: "The good man is perished out of the earth; and there is none upright among men; they all lie in wait for blood; they hunt every man his brother with a net." During the Holy Eucharist that followed, Cromwell's soldiers invaded the chapel and took every communicant off to prison to be questioned; Evelyn was released, others were detained. "A sad day! The Church now in dens and caves of the earth," commented Evelyn on 23 March 1657/58, the very month *The Garden of Cyrus* was registered.

Withdrawn from politics, Browne had suffered nevertheless throughout the Great Rebellion. He had witnessed Norwich Cathedral desecrated by a detachment of the Parliamentary army and its whole interior destroyed.[5] In September 1656, as physician and friend, he had watched his own bishop, Joseph Hall, die, an exile from that very church. In 1656, also, he attended Robert Loveday, terminally ill from tuberculosis, and by the example of the young man's life and death privately advised his friend Sir John Pettus how to behave during "the torrent of vitious Times" (*P*, 410). The times were rife with prophecies by conjurers, diviners, astrologers, and almanacmakers. Among the more interesting of these was "Arise" (Rhys) Evans, a Welshman whose books included *A Voice from Heaven to the Commonwealth of England* (1652), *The Bloody Vision of John Farly Interpreted* (1653), *The Declaration of Arise Evans Counceling the Lord Protector and the Government* (1654), and *The Voice of King Charles the Father to King Charles the Son* (1655).[6] These and dozens more, especially those by such Puritans as Thomas Brightman, Nicholas Smith, and Gerrard Winstanley, often rested their prophecies on visions, inner voices, and spiritual awakenings, methods that Browne would have deemed irrational while he was composing *The Garden of Cyrus*.[7]

All his life he was obsessed by time and eternity. *The Garden* is actually his last major work, one that he might well have inscribed "*FINIS*." In many respects it returns to his first book, the *Religio Medici*. There, contemplating "those foure inevitable points of us all, Death, Judgement, Heaven, and Hell" (*P*, 116), Browne had declared that it would be mad and impious "to

---

5. See the description of this event by Hall in my *Bishop Joseph Hall (1574–1656): A Biographical and Critical Study* (Cambridge, 1979), p. 138.

6. Robert Loveday, a patient of Browne's in 1656, writing to his brother, describes "Arise" Evans: "I am acquainted with a Welsh Prophet here, one E. which seldom dreames without a Revelation, or sleeps without a Vision as he calls them, who tells the world of a sudden return of Monarchy to its old bias, and has been so saucy to petition our Grand Councel to bring Charles Stuart to his English Throne, and threatens their disobedience with an utter destruction. . . . For my part I read [his books] for nought but sport, but he is not half so much laugh'd at as he was at first" (*Letters* [1662], pp. 172–73). I have no doubt that the prophecies of "Arise" Evans had been a topic of conversation between the patient and Dr. Browne.

7. In "Miscellany Tract No. XII" (*K*, 3:103–8) Browne makes wild fun of a political prophecy sent to him by a friend for his consideration, titled "Concerning the Future State of Several Nations."

determine the day and yeare of this inevitable time" (*P,* 118). In 1658 he was of the same mind, a reason for prefacing *The Garden* with *Hydriotaphia*'s " 'Tis too late to be ambitious. The great mutations of the world are acted, or time may be too short for our designs" (*P,* 309). Nowhere in Browne do I discover the optimistic belief of Joachim da Fiore, of John Foxe's *Book of Martyrs,* and of some seventeenth-century Puritan prophets that the "era of Grace" would be enacted here on earth.[8] Browne retained not only his melancholic view that human history was swiftly nearing its end but also his joyful faith that the kingdom of heaven would follow: "For then indeed men shall rise out of the earth: the graves shall shoot up their concealed seeds, and in that great Autumn, men shall spring up, and awake from their Chaos again."[9] Cyrus of Persia rebuilt the historical Old Jerusalem, but the New Jerusalem will come when history and nature cease. According to St. John, the New Jerusalem will have "no need of the sun, neither of the moon to shine in it; for the glory of God [will] lighten it, and the Lamb [will] be the light thereof" (Revelation 21:23).

III

That *The Garden of Cyrus* prophesies the end of temporal disorder in God's good time may best be demonstrated by its built-in literary traits, which, though not shared by all prophetic prose writers, are common to many. Among the often overlapping ingredients of the genre, in the order of their increasing impact upon the reader, are synchronism, typology, pictorialization, discursiveness, numerology, and multiplicity.[10] In their combination, they make *The Garden* quite different from anything Browne had written before.

First of all, prophecy cannot escape synchronism, in which historically separate moments of time converge, collapse, and reassemble in a design of love beyond mortal comprehension. The prophet sees all things at once; he is privy to an eternal present. For a Protestant Christian, synchronism rests also on Augustinian psychology, wherein the three powers of the soul (memory, understanding, and will) act simultaneously and not, as St.

8. For the Joachimist philosophy of history, see C. A. Patrides, *"The Grand Design of God": The Literary Form of the Christian View of History* (London, 1972), pp. 30–32; for the Puritan prophetic view related to it, see T. Wilson Hayes, *Winstanley the Digger: A Literary Analysis of Radical Ideas in the English Revolution* (Cambridge, Mass., 1979), pp. 43–45, and John R. Knott, Jr., *The Sword of the Spirit: Puritan Responses to the Bible* (Chicago, 1980), chap. 4.

9. *Pseudodoxia Epidemica VI, i* (*K,* 2:399).

10. Readers of Joseph A. Wittreich, Jr., *Visionary Poetics: Milton's Tradition and His Legacy* (San Marino, Calif., 1979), will recognize how much I owe, in this section of my argument, to him. I have expressed my gratitude to him in conversation and am happy to do so again, in writing.

Thomas Aquinas analyzed the process, sequentially.[11] In the Gospel according to St. John, Jesus pleads with God to glorify him "with the glory I had with thee before the world was" (17:5). Browne at the age of thirty had been struck with the mixture of tenses in Christ's saying, "Before Abraham was, I am" (John 8:58), which reminded him that "*Eve* miscarried of mee before she conceiv'd of *Cain*" (*P*, 132).

Time in *The Garden of Cyrus* moves from ancient Egyptian lore, to Browne's own garden, back to Eden, forward to Moses, forward to Daniel at Belshazzar's feast, and back again to the third day of Creation. With no difficulty Browne speculates on the existence of quincuncial planting before the Flood, then after Noah had planted his vineyards, and then back to the garden of Eden if God had set the Tree of Knowledge in its center (*P*, 332–33).

Itself akin to synchronism, typology is a more easily recognizable ingredient of prophecy. The analogical method found precursors of the New Testament throughout the Old, a system that allowed Christians to make the whole Bible their own and not merely that part written after the coming of Christ. St. Paul's statement, for example, that Christ is the second Adam (1 Corinthians 15:22) shows how inseparable typology is from prophecy in that the type demands fulfillment, Adam being the type and Christ the antitype. What of the future? "But every man in his own order," St. Paul continues, "Christ the firstfruits; afterward they that are Christ's at his coming." Over half of the verses in the Book of Revelation quote or allude to verses in the Old Testament. St. John starts in the present, goes back to the type, and then leaps forward to the Apocalypse. So Browne in *The Garden of Cyrus* begins with antitypes, that is, man-made things ("artificial"), such as the orchards planted by man in the quincuncial pattern after the sixth day of Creation; these artificial designs have their type in the world after the third day of Creation ("natural"); then nature as type becomes the antitype for the actual type in the eternal mind of God ("mystical"). Browne must begin with orchards, rhomboidal arches, latticework, and coins because we cannot recognize the type until the antitype is before us. All typology is ex post facto.

The Old Testament was thoroughly familiar to Browne since he had worked on its chronology for Book VII of *Pseudodoxia Epidemica*. In *The Garden*, Browne cites the Pentateuch, believed to have been written by Moses, a great "prophet" (Deuteronomy 34:10), and also Ezekiel, Daniel, Jonah, Nehemiah, and Jeremiah, all of whom had nourished the subsequent typological interpretation of Scripture's unity. In Ezekiel (48:10), for example, Browne finds the ancient Hebrew custom of anointing the head of the high priest in the form of a *chi* (X) to be a gesture that "could not escape a typical thought of Christ" (*P*, 330). "The greatest mystery of Religion is

11. Louis L. Martz, *The Paradise Within: Studies in Vaughan, Traherne, and Milton* (New Haven, 1964), pp. 22–23.

expressed by adumbration," he continues, "and in the noblest part of Jewish Types, we find the Cherubims shadowing the Mercy-seat" (*P,* 376).

Browne's typology does not rely exclusively upon Scripture but mainly upon facts in botany, literature, history, and myth. Typology depends upon the belief that history reveals not accident but God's continuing divine purpose for mankind, which man may obstruct but cannot stop.[12] Thus, what the prophet declares through typology is, in the reader's mind, likely to happen; if the present was foreordained in the past, then the same present will project a similarly shaped future.

More significant than typology for the prophetic dimension of *The Garden of Cyrus* is its pictorialization. The prophet "shows" his truth, like Michael in the futuristic Book XI of *Paradise Lost,* making Adam and Eve observe before they are invited to hear. The Book of Revelation proceeds through pictures of sealed scrolls, angels, dragons, trumpets, and candlesticks. Prophetic poets like Dante and Milton give birth to artists like Gustave Doré; the narrative of Spenser's *Faerie Queene* is a series of vignettes; and Blake's engravings say as much as his prophetic poems do. Browne was fond of the graphic arts and was interested in the pictorial writing of ancient Egypt, which consisted of hieroglyphs that were supposed to have been available to Moses from the four-hundred-year Jewish habitation of that land. So in *The Garden of Cyrus* Browne expressed himself like this: "he that considereth the plain crosse upon the head of the Owl in the Laterane Obelisk, or the crosse erected upon a pitcher diffusing streams of water into two basins, with sprinkling branches in them, and all described upon a two-foot Altar, as in the Hieroglyphicks of the brazen Table of *Bembus,* will hardly decline all thought of Christian signality in them" (*P,* 330). Again, "If Ægyptian Philosophy may obtain, the scale of influences was thus desposed, and the genial spirits of both worlds, do trace their way in ascending and descending Pyramids, mystically apprehended in the Letter X, and the open Bill and stradling Legges of a Stork, which was imitated by that Character"(*P,* 377).

The visually minded reader of Chapter III of *The Garden* peers into a botanist's notebook containing laboratory sketches of hundreds of plants. Phrases like "It may be observed," "It is easily observable," or "Therein one may see" abound on practically every page. Harold Fisch wrote of Browne, "There are no strict barriers—as in Bacon—dividing Divinity from Natural Philosophy, for once Nature is seen as a Temple and the Scientist as a Priest, the religious attitude may coincide with the most scrupulous attention to the tasks of observation and research."[13] In addition to five-petaled flowers are pictures of crucigerous crowns, handled crosses, medals, beds, nets, magnified mouths of bees, cut jewels, battle formations, butterfly wings, building stones, and constellations in the sky—all presented for us to *see* the

12. Patrides, *"The Grand Design of God,"* pp. 6–9.
13. *Jerusalem and Albion: The Hebraic Factor in Seventeenth-Century Literature* (London, 1969), pp. 208–9.

central decussation or crossing of lines in the Greek letter *chi* (Χ). Such pictures, Browne would conclude, "afford delightful Truths, confirmable by sense and ocular Observation, which seems to me the surest path, to trace the Labyrinth of Truth" (*P*, 386).

A prophet, however, cannot depend upon pictures alone to carry his "story"; the piece of writing must start somewhere, have a kind of middle, and then end. Yet many a seventeenth-century vision apparently cannot be set down in a simple linear order. Prophecies are often discursive and full of digressions, the narrative map looking like the tracks made by the children of Israel wandering for forty years in the desert while all along God had a plan for them. Describing the quincunx in fuchsia and other flowers, Browne adds, "where by the way, he that observeth the rudimental spring of seeds . . ." (*P*, 347); this reminds him of the plastic principle and off he goes into four pages on generation, "queries which might enlarge but must conclude this digression" (*P*, 352). Again, he finds the reticulate design in "the inward parts of man" (*P*, 358) but is soon talking of the digestive system of cows and even the contrasting colors of fur on various other animals. Although Chapters IV and V bear the running title "The Quincunx Mystically Considered," the fourth chapter returns to quincunxes in man-made objects, a subject supposedly exhausted in Chapters I and II. Even the "mystical" final chapter casually returns to the subject of Chapter III: "most blossomes of Trees and greatest number of Flowers consist of five leaves" (*P*, 380). Despite beginning the treatise with "the third day of Creation," Browne does not seem to be past that day twenty-five pages later (*P*, 350). His phrase "the Labyrinth of Truth" (*P*, 386) best describes the latter-day prophet's habit of discursiveness. Even to the prophets of old, God rarely spoke clearly and directly. "Verily thou art a God that hidest thyself, O God of Israel," complained Isaiah (45:15).

More obviously than by discursive obscurity, prophetic writing is characterized by numerology. As in the time of John of Patmos and England's seventeenth century, prophecy flourishes in a Platonic or Neoplatonic ambience.[14] Browne quotes Plato's most mathematical dialogue, the *Timaeus* (*P*, 378), and, drawing upon the Pythagorean brotherhood, uses geometry and numbers to illustrate the pattern of creation.[15] Squares, triangles, cones, rectangles, and rhomboids are scattered everywhere, and especially prominent is the circle, for "five-leaved flowers are commonly disposed circularly about the *Stylus;* according to the higher geometry of nature, dividing a circle by five *radii*" (*P*, 353–54).

For Browne, numbers are more important even than geometry, as in the

14. Tony Stoneburner, "Notes on Prophecy and Apocalypse in a Time of Anarchy and Revolution: A Trying Out," in *Literature in Revolution,* ed. George A. White and Charles Newman (Chicago, 1972), pp. 245–82.

15. *Timaeus* 36b–d. The edition Browne used was probably the one left in his library, that of 1617 with notes by Meursius *(Sales Catalogue* [London, 1710], p. 11, no. 106).

Book of Revelation the numbers 7, 3, 12, and 144,000 dominate. In *Pseudodoxia Epidemica* he had inveighed against the superstitious practice of predicting either happy or dire results from the conjunctions of particular numbers. Every number from one to ten, said Browne, has been used by very good authors "to advantage the present discourse in hand" (Book IV, Chapter XII). Yet who could count the instances of five in *The Garden of Cyrus?* And why count them?

To illustrate the inevitable order in the universe and in the mind that created it, Browne uses not only the number five, but also three, nine, and ten, the symbol of perfection. For example, the perfect quadrate is made by nine (*P*, 341). If we set down the first nine numbers in rows of three, we have the five points of the quincunx, four at each corner and one in the middle. The two *V*'s, Roman fives, joined at their apexes make *X*, Roman ten; the number five, "hanging in the center of nine . . . will make the decussated number" (*P*, 379), that is, the figure of the cross, the Greek *chi* standing for Christ. Furthermore, all four of the central straight lines in the quadrate, that is, the two diagonals plus the vertical and the horizontal, yield as the sum of their terminals the "perfect number," ten, God: starting at the diagonal at number one and moving to the right we see that $1 + 9 = 10$, $2 + 8 = 10$, $3 + 7 = 10$, and $6 + 4 = 10$. For Browne, as for many others in the Renaissance, any attempt to read God's will requires close attention to the mathematics that fill God's universe.

The perfect quadrate showing the five points of the quincunx.

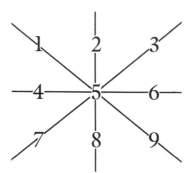

Finally, besides the synchronism, the typology, the pictorial symbols, the digressions, and the numerology, prophetic writing is often characterized by an excess, a multiplicity, as though the prophet, believing God is speaking through him, imitates the very extravagance of God's creation. In *The Garden of Cyrus,* the impression of multiplicity comes partly from the style: a nutcracker is "an instrument of Evulsion, compression or incision; which consisting of two Vectes or armes, converted towards each other, the innitency and stresse being made upon the *hypomachlion* or fulciment in the

decussation and greater compression is made by the union of two im-
pulsors" (*P*, 338–39). Even Browne can write more simply than that.

Excess abides also in Browne's irrelevances and in his habit of saying that
he will omit something and going right ahead to describe it in great detail. A
long account of animal and fish entrails ends: "We have not found them so
to answer our figure" (*P*, 359). "We shall decline the old themes," he says
(*P*, 329), but he does not. "We shall not call in the Hebrew Tenupha" (*P*,
338), but he does. "To omit the position of squared stones" (*P*, 334), "to
omit many other analogies" (ibid.), "to omit the ancient Cornopeion or
goatnet" (*P*, 336), "Not to urge the thwart enclosures" (*P*, 346), "We shall
not prie into it" (*P*, 337)—these are typical phrases. Despite the promises to
skip subjects, Browne incorporates them all as his examples burgeon into
the hundreds.

In a familiar passage, Coleridge described the sheer proliferation that
struck him when he came to the end of *The Garden of Cyrus:* "Quincunxes in
Heaven above, Quincunxes in Earth below, & Quincunxes in the water
beneath the Earth; Quincunxes in Deity, Quincunxes in the mind of men,
Quincunxes in bones, in optic nerves, in Roots of Trees, in leaves, in petals,
in everything!"[16] In raising natural man to his spiritual state, the prophet
turns the world upside down and makes him, as it were, act out his
antipodes.[17] As in the earlier chapters it is impossible to count the visual
instances of five, so in the latter part we are overwhelmed by the number of
"Why's?" Why did Christ feed five thousand persons with five loaves of
bread? Why did David have five pebbles in his pouch? Why did the ancients
mix five or three but not four parts of water with their wine? Why should
only a five-year-old ox be an acceptable sacrifice to Jupiter? Why? Why?
Why? (compare *P*, 383–86). The answers are not amenable to reason; man
can only wonder. But there it is, laid out in a panoply intended to overbur-
den the mind. Through his compulsion to speak, the prophet makes us
surrender to the weight, measure, and mass of the evidence.

Browne ends his piece fighting off sleep. One has to be wide awake in
order to prophesy, and that is why on the final page, again, Browne rejects
dreams, in which, unless you are a Jacob or a Daniel or an oneirocritic like
Joseph, the preoccupations of the day make "cables of cobwebs" (*P*, 387).
Even Jeremiah was aware of charlatans: "Let not your prophets and your
diviners, that be in the midst of you, deceive you, neither hearken to your
dreams which ye cause to be dreamed. For they prophesy falsely unto you in
my name; I have not sent them, saith the Lord" (29:8–9).

To summarize, given the general definition of prophecy as opposed to
divination, the contemporary interest in the Book of Revelation, and the
association of the name *Cyrus* with the Old Testament prophets; given the

16. *Coleridge on the Seventeenth Century,* ed. Roberta F. Brinkley (Durham, N.C.,
1955), p. 449.
17. See Christopher Hill, *The World Turned Upside Down* (London, 1972), the
title drawn primarily from Acts 17:6.

occasion of disorder at the time of writing and Browne's eschatological habit of mind; and given, especially, the six literary traits of the work itself, with its reiterated emblem of Christ, I conclude that *The Garden of Cyrus* is indeed prophecy, veiled, of course, but nevertheless a recognizable piece of seventeenth-century prophetic writing.[18] As a deeply committed Christian botanist and scholar, Browne could hope in 1658 that in God's time and by God's method order would be restored even though this might require the millenium. Casually he refers in *The Garden of Cyrus* to the Book of Revelation in a sentence whose diction is strikingly like that of his own prophecy: "For the form of *Babylon* the first City was square, and so shall be the last, according to the description of the holy City in the Apocalypse" (Revelation 21:16; *P,* 340). Even mitigating the seriousness of the whole with characteristic play, a measure of his objectivity, Browne proclaims with quiet certitude: "All things began in order, so shall they end, and so shall they begin again; according to the ordainer of order and mystical Mathematicks of the City of Heaven."

18. For millenarian prophecy in general, see Norman Cohn, *The Pursuit of the Millenium* (London, 1957). During England's unrest in the 1650s such millenarians as the "ranters" and the "diggers" set the tone. Before them were "prophets" like Heinrich Alsted (1627), whose work was translated by William Burton as *The Beloved City* (1643), Thomas Goodwin's *A Glimpse of Syon's Glory* (1641), John Archer's *Personal Reign of Christ* (1641), and so forth. The Anglican visionary, Evans, evidently a bit "crack't," called himself Merlin. Browne's refusal to speak as being "moved by the Spirit," his rejection of dreams, his carefully gathered evidence, and his sometimes whimsical yet quiet tone make *The Garden of Cyrus* a partial response to such "prophecies."

"Pitch beyond Ubiquity": Thought and Style in Sir Thomas Browne

D. W. Jefferson

All things are full of deity (*Jovis omnia plena*), so also in the little edifice of a chicken, and all its actions and operations, *Digitus Dei,* the finger of God, of the God of Nature, doth reveal himself.

These words are not by Sir Thomas Browne but occur in Martin Llewellyn's translation of William Harvey's *De generatione animalium,*[1] published a few years after the first edition of the *Pseudodoxia Epidemica.* They are akin to Browne's comments on the ancient error concerning the bear and its cubs. Men, said Browne, have vilified "the works of God, imputing that unto the tongue of a Beast, which is the strangest Artifice in all the acts of Nature"; later he uses the beautiful image of the "inward Phidias" (*K,* 2:173). This religious and imaginative sense of biological processes, expressing itself in a play of language, is characteristic of the period. Harvey's mind, of course, was much more purposively directed toward scientific discovery; but so far as the chicken and the egg were in question, Browne made some distinguished observations, and we have Joseph Needham's testimony that these represent "the first experiments in chemical embryology."[2] The researches of E. S. Merton have shown how seriously Browne was engaged with the conflicting theories of his time on subjects such as digestion, but also how in certain areas he was unable to respond fully to the work of Boyle and his contemporaries, who were of a later, more decisive phase of scientific thought. The literary form of the *Pseudodoxia Epidemica* did not give the best opportunity for systematic scientific inquiry, and, as Merton demonstrates, Browne's most interesting scientific ideas are scattered throughout the book and given no prominence.

Our concern here is mainly with the style and literary value of Browne's

1. *Anatomical Exercitations Concerning the Generation of Living Creatures,* trans. Martin Llewellyn (London, 1653), p. 310.
2. *A History of Embryology* (London, 1934), p. 120.

book, and certain distinctions can be made at the outset. Scientists like Harvey and Boyle address themselves to their specific tasks. They will not be read except by those who can summon the necessary interest in the technical problems, which are now a matter of history. The *Pseudodoxia Epidemica* as a work of literature is of interest to readers who are not necessarily curious about seventeenth-century science, though it makes a difference to students of literature that historians of science now take him so much more seriously. These distinctions must be made with caution. If Browne's observations on the sperm whale cast on the coast of Norfolk (*K*, 2:251–54) make an exceptionally good story, there is no lack of anecdotal value in the works of the great Royal Society men of the next age. Hooke describes the contrivance whereby he got himself stung by nettles while at the same time observing the process through the microscope;[3] Leeuwenhoek kept silkworms' eggs in a box which his wife, "who was always very warmly clad, constantly carried in her bosom."[4] Browne is by comparison less anecdotal. But from the literary point of view his book has the great advantage of being about traditional misconceptions concerning a wide variety of objects well known in nature or legend. The history of an error is for him the story of authorities in conflict, which would be entertaining to contemporaries brought up on such authorities and has value in the present age because of our interest in the history of ideas; though in the positivist atmosphere of the Victorian period Leslie Stephen, favorably inclined though he was to Browne as an artist, had only indulgent ridicule for these prescientific notions, which he referred to as a "stableful of hobbies" on which Browne was well equipped by temperament to ride "so as to amuse himself without loss of temper or dignity."[5] But more recently we have established the pervasiveness of such "prescientific" ideas during Browne's period and his serious contribution to the exposure of error. R. R. Cawley's learned essay, with its evidence of contemporary and much later concern with the unicorn, the viper, the kingfisher, the ostrich, the salamander, the swan's final song, and other themes with legendary associations, has set the record straight.[6] Browne's works could be useful in this respect and at the same time profit from the literary aspects of the tradition. His book requires of the reader no serious initiation into unfamiliar disciplines, except perhaps in several places where current scientific theories are brought into play; but these passages are brief. Here again a distinction is necessary. The *Pseudodoxia Epidemica* is often compared to the *Anatomy of Melancholy*, which also belongs to general literature, but there is no Democritus Junior here. Browne's plea in his

3. *Micrographia* . . . (London, 1665), p. 143.

4. *Select Works of Antony van Leeuwenhoek*, trans. Samuel Hoole (London, 1800), pp. 48–49.

5. *Hours in a Library*, rev. ed. (London, 1917), 1:252.

6. "The Timeliness of *Pseudodoxia Epidemica*," in Robert R. Cawley and George Vost, *Studies in Sir Thomas Browne* (Eugene, Ore., 1965), pp. 1–40.

address to the reader that "it was composed by snatches of time, as medical vacations, and the fruitless importunity of Uroscopy would permit" (*K*, 2:4) is about as far as he goes on the personal note. Hooke openly indulges his humor on the subject of the louse: "This is a Creature so officious, that 'twill be known to every one at one time or other, so busie, and so impudent, that it will be intruding it self in every one's company."[7] No biological phenomenon, no detail of anatomy or of sexual or excretory functioning in the lowliest things of nature moves Browne to depart from his exquisite reserve and decorum. But the decorum can operate in the interests of wit. In those places where the opportunity for wit is greatest, Browne takes the fullest advantage while still preserving a fastidiously distant manner. In general, his language has the effect of emphasizing the unity of his enterprise with the great humanist tradition. It is a grandiose and idiosyncratic gesture in the face of the changes that had to come: the development of new methodologies and a more practical level of discourse. The *Pseudodoxia Epidemica* is a literary monument of considerable impressiveness, and the literary historian is now in a better position to say in what sense this is true.

Book I supplies some pointers. In the first two chapters the early history of error is traced in the events of the Fall itself and the veritable rake's progress that immediately followed. Here Browne draws upon that extremely important tradition of commentary on Genesis discussed in Arnold Williams's *The Common Expositor*. Williams assigns the terminal date of 1633 to this tradition, so Browne may be seen as giving the final improvements and embellishments to modes of thinking that were soon to be superseded.[8] A characteristic of the tradition was strict devotion to the literal text, with immense thoroughness and resourcefulness in investigating every possibility of meaning and every difficulty caused by apparent inconsistencies in the inspired record. The combination of so much literalness with so much hermeneutical activity in a period so intellectually awake was inherently unstable, and it is easy to see the opportunities for wit that it presented to a mind like Browne's. On the questions, so often posed, relating to the precise nature of the first acts of sin, he composed a fine paragraph placing each question in its category:

> And therefore whether the Sin of our First Parents were the greatest of any since; whether the transgressions of Eve seducing did not exceed that of Adam seduced; or whether the resistibility of his Reason, did not equivalence the facility of her Seduction; we shall refer to the Schoolman.

He passes to similar questions that "we leave," in neatly ordered sequence, to the moralist, to the Talmudist, to the lawyer, and finally to God (*P*,

---

7. *Micrographia*, p. 211.
8. *The Common Expositor: An Account of the Commentaries on Genesis, 1527–1633* (Chapel Hill, N. C., 1948).

172–73). Man's proneness to error after the Fall is illustrated by a fact that, Browne claims, had not been noticed before: that of the six speeches uttered before the Flood, five are "most hainously injurious unto truth" (*K*, 2:21). Browne is at his best in his comments on Adam's plea that he hid himself from God, where he notes that Adam ignored God's omniscience and omnipresence: Adam's posterity "cannot but condemn the poverty of his conception, that thought to obscure himself from his Creator in the shade of the Garden, who had beheld him before in the darkness of his Chaos, and the great obscurity of Nothing." The paragraph ends with an even finer conceit. God's omnipresence is the delight of the blessed and the misery of the damned, whose sufferings are "desperate, and their afflictions without evasion; until they can get out of Trismegistus his Circle, that is, extend their wings above the Universe, and pitch beyond Ubiquity" (*K*, 2:21–22). Stanley E. Fish, in a critique of *Religio Medici,* refers to its "bastard scholasticism,"[9] while Walter Pater used the phrase "the poetry of scholasticism"[10] with reference to Browne. After Browne, scholastic wit tends to be found especially in satirical parody. In passages like these, though with no overtly subversive intention, the degree of license suggests that the use of such terms in serious discourse has been stretched to its limits. The sense of being poised on the furthermost edge of an era is part of the experience of reading Browne.

In another remarkable passage Browne demonstrates that Satan in the Book of Job excels Cain in truthfulness and that the father of lies would never be so foolish as to try to deceive God. So, "at the last day, when our offences shall be drawn into accompt, the subtility of that Inquisitor shall not present unto God a bundle of calumnies or confutable accusations, but will discreetly offer up unto his Omnisciency, a true and undeniable list of our transgressions" (*K*, 2:24). Error is a theme offering great scope for rhetoric, and the chapter ends with a daunting vision: "It is therefore no wonder that we have been erroneous ever since. And being now at the greatest distance from the beginning of Error, are almost lost in its dissemination, whose waies are boundless, and confess no circumscription" (*K*, 2:25). As for "the people," to whom Browne devotes the next chapter, they are "ready with open arms, to receive the encroachments of Error." They are "a confusion of knaves and fools, and a farriginous concurrence of all conditions, tempers, sexes and ages" (*P*, 174).

Having begun with theology, Book I concludes with it also, with the last two chapters being devoted to the instrumentality of Satan. Satan propagates monstrosities of error, which are condemned in an ominous display of scholastic language, often near to parody. Atheism is based on such errors,

For to desire there were no God, were plainly to unwish their own

9. *Self-Consuming Artifacts: The Experience of Seventeenth-Century Literature* (Berkeley, 1972), p. 355.
10. *Appreciations with an Essay on Style* (London, 1890), p. 159.

being; which must needs be annihilated in the substraction of that essence which substantially supporteth them, and restrains them from regression into nothing, and if, as some contend, no creature can desire his own annihilation, that Nothing is not appetible, and not to be at all, is worse than to be in the miserablest condition of something. (*K*, 2:64).

The fertility of Satan's invention and man's unlimited propensity to folly stimulate Browne's ingenuity. But the Adversary, with all his efforts, has failed to do one thing: to destroy the Scriptures. Their "longevity" and the "providence of that spirit which ever waketh over" them have preserved them. And here there is a surprising stroke of style, and one of those images that introduce sudden contrast into Browne's prose: "this is a stone too big for Satan's mouth, and a bit indeed Oblivion cannot swallow" (*K*, 2:70).

As for the technical aspects of erroneous thinking, all Browne has to offer is a brief discussion in Chapter 4 of a few traditional logical fallacies, which are relevant enough, however, to some of the vulgar errors treated in later books. The difference between this and the extraordinarily vigorous and penetrating criticism of the inveterate weaknesses of the human mind, and the wonderful sense of its possibilities, in the *Novum Organum* (wonderful in spite of Bacon's failure to arrive at the relevant methodology for science) could hardly be greater. Yet in his career of tireless observation and experiment, and in his generous collaboration with others, Browne would seem to be in some ways the exemplary Baconian, while Bacon himself is disappointing in these respects. Contradiction and idiosyncrasy seem characteristic of great men of this time. Browne's idiosyncrasy in Book I is a marked attachment to theological ideas that have virtually no relevance to his project, and with which he makes extravagant play. Theological reasons, in defiance of the Baconian principle, are offered in his rejection of specific errors, as in the passage already cited about the bear. He has presented the evidence of Aldrovandus, who had seen a perfectly formed cub just taken from its mother; but final causes must also be considered. He concludes with an explanation of the error. Cubs are born covered with a membrane that obscures their shape (*K*, 2:173). This is a good example of the neat structure of his chapters and of the way in which he combines experimental proof with eloquence in arguing theological points.

To return to Book I, Browne's short account in Chapters 6 through 9 of ancient authorities, their mistakes and plagiarisms, is masterly. His extraordinary knowledge of writers is compressed into a pithy and varied survey, the breadth of reference controlled not by any systematic arrangement of topics but by the unfailing sharpness of his interest in details and their connections. Here is a sentence rounding off a statement about Oppian, a characteristic testimonial, in language that brings together plainness and elegance and also some latinized terms with a total effect that imposes itself:

So that abating the annual mutation of sexes in the Hyaena, the single sex of the Rhinoceros, the Antipathy between the two Drums of a

Lamb and a Wolfe's skin, the informity of Cubs, the Venation of Centaures, the copulation of the Murena and the Viper, with some others, he may be read with great delight and profit. (*K*, 2:57)

Book III, which treats of errors relating to the biological world, contains many passages reminiscent of the commentaries on Genesis. In arguing against the ancient tradition that "the young Vipers force their way through the bowels of their Dam, or that the female Viper in the act of generation bites off the head of the male," Browne makes good use of the tradition whereby the facts of nature were to be reconciled with the literal statements of Scripture. He urges that this would "overthrow and frustrate" the benediction of God, *Be fruitful and multiply,* since the animal would "perish by multiplication," and this would make the blessing a greater curse than the actual curse later pronounced after the Fall: *in sorrow shalt thou bring forth.* "This were to confound the maledictions of God" (*K*, 2:207–8). The same benediction, he finds, would be "infringed" by the existence of the phoenix, which also violates the scriptural text that plainly states that the animals went into the Ark, "two and two of all flesh." Not satisfied with this, he notes that, though Heliogabalus had the ambition to eat a phoenix, it would have been a vain design "to destroy any species, or mutilate the great accomplishment of six days." And this leads digressively to the conviction that, though man could by abstaining from sex destroy the race, this would never happen; by the same token, Cain could not, if there had been no other woman living, have killed Eve. "The providence of God would have resisted: for that would have imposed another creation upon him, and to have animated a second Rib of Adam." Sallies of this kind belong fittingly to the period when the exegetical tradition had gone as far as it could go and was due to be replaced by the safer and more limited disciplines advocated by Richard Simon or by Spinoza's historical approach.[11] In the same chapter, Browne estimates that, if the phoenix actually lived for a thousand years, in accordance with some versions of the legend, the one "now in nature" would be the "sixth from Creation, but in the middle of its years; and if the Rabbin's prophecie succeed, shall end its days not in its own but in the general flames, without all hope of reviviction" (*K*, 2:195–98). Browne's resourcefulness in extracting interest from the errors operates in all directions. The ancient idea that the beaver, "to escape the Hunter, bites off his testicles or stones," he sees as entirely without support so far as its literal truth is concerned, but as rich in moral implications:

> If therefore any affirm a wise man should demean himself like the Bever, who to escape with his life, contemneth the loss of his genitals, that is in case of extremity, not strictly to endeavour the preservation of all, but to sit down in the enjoyment of the greater good, though with the detriment and hazard of the lesser; we may hereby apprehend a real and useful Truth. (*K*, 2:167–68)

After some consideration of the tradition that "a man becomes hoarse or

11. *The Common Expositor,* p. 260.

dumb, if a Wolf have the advantage first to eye him," which he sees as based on the natural fears of travelers who suddenly encounter wolves, Browne digresses into a magnificent tribute to Christians who had no such fear: "But thus could not the mouths of worthy Martyrs be silenced, who being exposed not onely to the eyes, but the merciless teeth of Wolves, gave loud expressions of their faith, and their holy clamours were heard as high as Heaven" (*K*, 2:180). The chapter on the alleged bisexuality of the hare terminates with a well-rounded denunciation of man, with his unbridled sexual license. The animals have their different methods: "For some couple laterally or sidewise, as Worms: some circularly or by complication, as Serpents . . . Some aversly, as all Crustaceous Animals, Lobsters, Shrimps, and Crevises, and also Retromingents, as Panthers, Tygers, and Hares." Whatever they do, this is their law. Only man "hath in his own kind run thorow the Anomalies of venery; and been so bold, not only to act, but represent to view, the irregular ways of Lust" (*K*, 2:218–19).

But we must turn to places where Browne's involvement with current scientific discussion is illustrated. On the question of the ostrich and its reputation for digesting iron, Aldrovandus supplies the testimony of experiment: "I observed the Ostrich to swallow Iron, but yet to exclude it undigested again" (Browne's translation from Latin). In Browne's vocabulary, *exclude* is the word for both excretion and giving birth. Browne now considers the possibility that the iron, though not digested, is nevertheless changed by entering the stomach, and here his abstract terminology—"chilification," "attrition," "vitriolous humidity"—is dominant, but with moments of contrast: "So rusty Iron crammed down the throat of a Cock, will become terse and clear again in its gizzard." The next stage in the argument, and here Browne is in touch with contemporary thought on the subject, is the idea that animals swallow hard objects, not to be digested but as an aid to digesting other things. In this context, Browne offers one of his celebrated observations: "So Poultrey, and especially the Turkey, do of themselves take down stones: and we have found at one time in the gizzard of a Turkey no less than seven hundred." Though inclined himself toward the chemical theory, he is considering here the case for the physical approach, offering the possibility that the iron swallowed by ostriches may have a similar function to that of stones "taken down" but not digested by other birds—"that is, in some ways to supply the use of teeth, by commolition, grinding and compression of their proper aliment, upon the action of the strongly conformed muscles of the stomack." The discussion is enlivened by odd observations of animal behavior: "Thus dogs will eat grass, which they digest not: Thus Camels to make the water sapid, do raise the mud with their feet: Thus horses will knabble at walls, Pigeons delight in salt stones. Rats will gnaw Iron" (*K*, 2:234–37).

Piquantly juxtaposed with and in contrast to the ostrich is the chameleon, which is said to live on air. As with the bear and the ostrich, Browne begins by mentioning among the authorities a contemporary who testifies against the tradition, showing that the chameleon has normal eating habits. Again, he invokes "the wisdom of nature," which, "abhorring superfluities," does not provide organs that are not used. The chameleon has digestive organs. Similarly, since bats have teats we may infer that they suckle their young; but since other "flying animals" lack these parts we cannot expect from them a "viviparous exclusion, but either a generation of eggs, or some vermiparous separation." The tongue of the chameleon, Browne finds, is an argument "to overthrow this airy nutrication," because tongues are for taste and air is "ingustible, void of all sapidity." By means of this extreme refinement of diction, but in combination with agility of mind and delicate precision with details, Browne succeeds in conveying a curiosity truly scientific but also imaginative. Discussing later the reasons for the error, he refers to the chameleon's continual "hiation, or holding open its mouth," the "greatness of its lungs," and its difficulty in filling them through the nostrils. He also notes its "paucity of blood," which might have given the impression that air provided a sufficient maintenance. But, as he says, other animals that feed normally are also short of blood, and "we do not read of much blood that was drawn from Frogs by Mice, in that famous battel of Homer." This chapter is comparatively long, with more theoretical discussion than most of the others, and it is partly Browne's management of the finely spun vocabulary that quickens the elaborate and meticulous argument. As with the ostrich, he is engaged with theories of digestion, and also of nutrition and respiration, and this is one of the chapters to which Merton devotes most attention.[12]

In the chapter on the elephant the theme is anatomy. Browne derides the "gray-headed error" of those who say that the elephant lacks joints. Accounts ancient and modern of the flexible movements of elephants are brought in to support the argument, but it is only halfway through the chapter that Browne refers to the elephant available for inspection in London, whose movements and parts he has asked his son Edward to scrutinize carefully (*K*, 4:68). But, he says, and this gives one pause, in spite of this and other elephants seen and observed in modern times, ancient error is strong enough to survive. The absurd notion of a stiff-legged embryonic elephant is presented in his driest idiom:

> They [the adherents of the erroneous tradition] disturb the position of the young ones in the womb; which upon extension of legs is not easily conceivable; and contrary unto the general contrivance of Nature. Nor do they consider the impossible exclusion thereof, upon extension and rigour of legs. (*K*, 2:250)

The enhanced reputation in intellectual history that Browne now enjoys removes some of the difficulties in the way of a more satisfying literary estimate. The removal of prejudice, albeit of Leslie Stephen's good humored kind, makes it possible to read the *Pseudodoxia Epidemica* with a

---

12. E. S. Merton, "Sir Thomas Browne's Theories of Respiration and Combustion," *Osiris* 10 (1952).

different sort of attention and thus to appreciate more fully the felicity of the treatment. To place Browne effectively in literary history, it is helpful to meditate on the ways in which phases of change can stimulate not only the forces destined to become dominant but also those that will soon lose their strength, so that the individuality of the old may express itself, though for the last time, with unprecedented effect. The artist in whose work these manifestations are apparent will represent both sides of the development: the innovatory side activates the inherited elements that are brought to this late consummation. Browne's sensibility is that of the late Renaissance modified and sharpened by the new spirit. The *Pseudodoxia Epidemica* reveals more of his sensibility than would be expected of such a work, but we must turn to one of his other productions for illustrations of those aspects by which he is chiefly known. A general statement on Sir Thomas Browne would be incomplete without some discussion of a work in which the themes of death and Christian piety are central, and for our purpose *A Letter to a Friend* will suffice.

The Renaissance was remarkable for its great wealth of materials from a variety of traditions rather than for its capacity to control them, except in imaginative art where a Shakespeare or a Cervantes could thrive on diversity, absorb every sort of material, and mix the kinds with infinite virtuosity. In the intellectual disciplines there was to be much sorting, discarding, and separating of spheres of inquiry before a new phase of progress could be inaugurated. It is easier today, with our awareness of the persistence of astrology into the scientific era, and of Newton and the pipes of Pan, to see that these changes did not come about in an entirely neat and orderly fashion. But a strong propensity to mix the kinds in the intellectual sphere in an age that had received Bacon's message was a sign of a late Renaissance sensibility. As we have seen, Browne in the *Pseudodoxia Epidemica* elaborated the theological aspects of his theme with a pointed exaggeration of the Renaissance custom of viewing all knowledge in the light of universal truths and traditions. *Hydriotaphia* is a more extravagant example of the same habit and an especially splendid manifestation of "lateness"; but here the meditations on mortality almost entirely monopolize the interest. *A Letter to a Friend* belongs to a literary genre that does not need to commit itself to specific terms of reference, but it also has a mixed character and in its elusive way it expresses aspects of his mentality different from those we have noted. It purports to be a letter of condolence but soon becomes a learned physician's discourse on aspects of his young patient's sickness and death and on the frailties of the body generally, with much play of literary allusion and continual changes of tone. Only occasional passages, but they are very beautiful, approximate to the spirit one associates with condolence; approximate, because even here there is a distance and a poetic refinement, which might suggest to us that this piece was composed outside the immediate context of personal grief. In the later pages of the letter the theme changes, with the ease always possible in the epistolary genre, and the author addresses his friend in terms of religious exhortation, with some memorable moral sentences ("Tread softly and circumspectly in this funambulous and narrow Path of Goodness" [*P*, 407]). The mixing of levels of discourse in Browne can be a means of achieving subtle effects, and the question is whether, with all its learned allusiveness and extreme literary artifice, its air of making the young man's death an occasion for one curious and fanciful observation after another, *A Letter to a Friend* is not a much more tender work than it has usually been taken to be, but with a tenderness that prefers to be largely indirect. When Browne refers to the failure of friends to recognize the symptoms of approaching death, with allusions to "Plautus's sick complexion" and the "Hippocratical face," and recalls his own opinion at the time that "he was not like to behold a Grasshopper," tenderness would seem to have found a sufficient disguise; but the reflections that follow, not borrowed from Hippocrates, about the changes in physiognomy that precede death, are mysterious and moving. The patient "loses his own face":

> He maintained not his proper countenance, but looked like his Uncle, the Lines of whose Face lay deep and invisible in his healthful Visage before: for as from our beginning we run through variety of Looks, before we come to consistent and settled Faces; so before our End, by sick and languishing Alterations, we put on new Visages: and in our Retreat to Earth, may fall upon such Looks which from community of seminal Originals were before latent in us. (*P*, 392)

In the next paragraph, about the patient's vain attempt to benefit from a change of air, Browne introduces a strange series of recondite allusions, literary and medical, actually digressing to consider the advantages of migrant birds, and the personal theme would seem to be entirely lost. Then we come to this:

> Tho we could not have his Life, yet we missed not our desires in his soft Departure, which was scarce an Expiration; and his End not unlike his Beginning, when the salient Point scarce affords a sensible motion. (*P*, 393)

In the *Pseudodoxia Epidemica* an abundance of references to authorities was to be expected, because the theme was the history of error. In a composition like the *Letter*, the references are gratuitous, a matter of idiosyncrasy, as in Montaigne's essays. The Renaissance produced a paradoxical state of affairs whereby a huge inflation of literary materials synchronized with a growing self-awareness of the kind that must eventually lead to independence from authorities. Montaigne was fully conscious of this predicament:

> To receive so many, so strange, yea, and so great wits, it must needs follow . . . that a man's own wit, force, droops, and as it were diminishes itselfe to make roome for others. I might say that as plants are choked by over-much moisture, and lamps dammed with too much

oyle, so are the actions of the mind over-whelmed by over-abundance of matter and studie . . .

Even as birds flutter and skip from field to picke up corne, or any graine, and without tasting the same, carrie it in their bils, therewith to feed their little ones; so doe our pedants gleane and picke learning from bookes, and never lodge it further than their lips, only disgorge and cast it to the wind . . . Is not that which I doe in the greatest part of this composition, all one and selfe same thing?[13]

A modern reader would have no misgivings about the effect of this miscellaneous wealth. In both writers the use of allusions is a means of enhancing individuality, and no one cultivates allusion with more individual style than Browne.

If his style expresses an extraordinary absorption in reflection, we need to remind ourselves that Browne was also the busiest of men and eminently practical. He can be cool about all matters relating to the body, living or dead. His pragmatic comment on Egyptian mummies is characteristic, if surprising in this context: "The *Egyptian* mummies that I have seen, have had their Mouths open, and somewhat gaping, which affordeth a good opportunity to view and observe their Teeth wherein 'tis not easie to find any wanting or decayed" (*P,* 398). He gives no impression of planning his moment for feeling and eloquence. Speculating in his usual inquiring manner on the timing of tides, with reference to Pliny's "odd and remarkable Passage concerning the Death of Men and Animals upon the Recess or Ebb of the Sea," he follows with this breathtaking sentence:

However, certain it is he died in the dead and deep part of the Night, when *Nox* might be most apprehensibly said to be the Daughter of Chaos, the Mother of Sleep and Death, according to the old Genealogy; and so went out of this World about that hour when our blessed Saviour entred it, and about what time many conceive he will return again unto it. (*P,* 394)

Browne's work belongs to the period of literature coinciding with the final years of Charles I's reign, the Civil War, and the Commonwealth. To say that it is the period of Milton and other pamphleteers, and of Hobbes, is to emphasize Puritan polemic and philosophical protest and innovation. Of the poets, apart from Milton himself, the finest were Crashaw and Vaughan, heartbroken by the outrage done to the church, exiles from the political scene in one way or another, and Marvell, the poet apart from Milton who was most successful in adjusting imaginatively and intellectually to what was happening. Otherwise, it was a period in which the lesser poets followed in the wake of the greater, more innovatory Jacobeans: Donne and Ben Jonson. These poets are associated in our minds, as in several cases they were by appointment, with the court. One of the motifs of Charles's life and reign was that of withdrawal, avoidance of forces building up against

13. *Essays,* trans. John Florio, World's Classics ed. (London, 1910), 1:148.

him, and the cultivation of a way of life and a cultural environment secure from alien pressures. These poets, limited by lack of engagement with anything new, attached to traditional themes and skills, may please us sometimes with their refinement and freshness of feeling, but they are of minor importance as voices in a vanishing order. Is it an accident that Jeremy Taylor, in comparison with the Donne of the sermons, is so devoid of dialectical vigor and spiritual drama, so enclosed in this world of beautiful images and pious analogies? In assessing Browne's role in literary history we must relate him in some way to this configuration of developments. The unprecedented outpouring of dissident opinion after 1640 must have brought home to a royalist and Anglican sensibility the disconcerting strength of alien forces. But after Milton's scornful descriptions of Arminian and Catholic devotion, the *Religio Medici,* published only two years later, contributes a welcome note of ease, and also of tolerance of at least some religious phenomena that the writer does not agree with. "At a solemne Procession," Browne says, "I have wept abundantly, while my consorts, blinde with opposition and prejudice, have fallen into an accesse of scorne and laughter" (*P,* 63). In his later works where he meditates on religious themes there is a philosophical repose, an untroubled contemplation of eternity, which some modern readers, with the twentieth-century demand for intensity and involvement, find unsatisfying. But Browne was after all not professionally committed to open up these topics to their fullest extent, and his contemplative writings are only part of a total achievement in which the labors of a physician and the personal and collaborative efforts on behalf of science must have taken up most of his time. In the work for which he is best known he represents a sensibility that chooses not to relate itself to the turbulence of the age and that indeed can insulate itself from personal relationships. The *Letter* comes nearest of all his writings to expressing the feelings of one human being for another. What is expressed, in his unique manner and idiom, is a certain aloofness. But it is an aloofness that belongs only to his chosen sphere of imaginative creation. Otherwise his life was well filled with fruitful relationships. It is the aloofness of the artist who creates something that is highly wrought but not renewable, the product of a tradition in a very late stage, when its relation to changing reality has become such that it can find expression only in a very distilled and stylized form. Great value is achieved when the tradition can express itself, in the face of change, with so much eloquence.

Browne's Cosmos Imagined:
Nature, Man, and God
in *Pseudodoxia Epidemica*

Robin Robbins

I

"Literature written in the metonymic mode," observes David Lodge, "tends to disguise itself as nonliterature."[1] By the metonymic mode he understands the generating of a text by movement between objects that are contiguous, that are in literal reality linked or associated. This mode is characteristic of realistic prose, as opposed to poetry, which typically moves forward by finding similarities in objects otherwise not associated, by the use of metaphor and simile. These do appear in prose, of course, but to a much smaller extent. Metonymy and its related figure synecdoche (the substitution of attributes, adjuncts, or parts for whole things themselves) are usual figures in realistic prose, which (except in the case of isolated experiments in total realism, exceptions that prove their own unviability) does not attempt to present the whole of reality. Laurence Sterne demonstrated the self-defeating nature of such an aim even within the little world of Tristram Shandy. Not only does the writer choose or imagine merely a part of the universe, but even that part has to be presented in terms of chosen parts, the choice being dictated by necessity, by relevance to the writer's purpose. In the uses of these figures lie the differences between one prose writer's imaginative vision and another's, these differences being found in what is left out as well as in what is included.

The purpose of Lodge's book is to evolve a freshly productive method of analyzing modern fiction. Though *Pseudodoxia Epidemica,* Browne's most varied and substantial work, is neither modern nor fictive, a further observation by Lodge will serve to set it firmly within the field of creative literature, to reveal it, despite its encyclopedic scope, as something more than an

1. *The Modes of Modern Writing* (London, 1979), p. 93.

encyclopedia. It is, rather, the imaginative evocation of one man's world, into which we are drawn not simply by the factual interest of its ostensible subjects, regardless of the style in which they are presented, or by a merely decorative appeal in that style itself, but also by the cumulative details that build in our minds a replica of Browne's way of seeing and feeling about the total reality in which we live. As Lodge puts it, although much that is indisputably "literature" is characteristically metonymic, nevertheless, "at the highest level of generality at which we can apply the metaphor/metonymy distinction, literature itself is metaphoric and nonliterature metonymic. The literary text is always metaphoric in the sense that when we interpret it . . . we make it into a total metaphor: the text is the vehicle, the world is the tenor."[2]

Browne first expressed his world view in *Religio Medici,* where he assessed his standing with God and man after years of study and travel. The doctor's religion is an imaginative synthesis of his faith and his scientific learning: "there are two bookes from whence I collect my Divinity; besides that written one of God, another of his servant Nature, that universall and publik Manuscript, that lies expans'd unto the eyes of all" (*P,* 78–79). Not only is there no clash here for him between religion and scientific knowledge, but each infuses him with enthusiasm for the other: "Those strange and mysticall transmigrations that I have observed in Silkewormes, turn'd my Philosophy into Divinity. There is in these workes of nature, which seeme to puzle reason, something Divine, and hath more in it then the eye of a common spectator doth discover" (*P,* 110).

Browne is writing within a set of traditions that are neither simply Christian nor coldly scientific, nor even a dualistic conjunction of the two. The view commonly expressed in the Middle Ages that physical man is little more than food for worms was counteracted in the sixteenth century for medically educated men like Browne by great anatomical works such as that of Andreas Vesalius—finely illustrated volumes presenting the delicate complexities of the human frame, its skeleton, muscles, nerves, blood vessels, and vital and sensory organs. Many centuries earlier, Galen had eulogized the skill of the divine maker in his treatise on *The Usefulness of the Parts.* In *The Garden of Cyrus,* Browne's contemplation of the inward parts of man prompts him to extend "that Elegant expression of Scripture, Thou hast curiously embroydered me," with the figurative gloss, "thou has wrought me up after the finest way of texture, and as it were with a Needle" (*P,* 358). Hence the philosophy that furnishes Browne's divinity is ultimately drawn not just from the "universall and publik Manuscript" of nature but also from what in the Genesis account, and especially for the humanist, is the culminating product of God through nature, man himself. "I could never content my contemplation," says Browne in *Religio Medici,*

with those generall pieces of wonders, the flux and reflux of the sea, the

2. Ibid., p. 109.

encrease of Nile, the conversion of the Needle to the North, and have studied to match and parallel those in the more obvious and neglected pieces of Nature, which without further travell I can doe in the Cosmography of my selfe; wee carry with us the wonders, we seeke without us: There is all *Africa,* and her prodigies in us; we are that bold and adventurous piece of nature, which he that studies, wisely learnes in a *compendium,* what others labour at in a divided piece and endlesse volume. (*P,* 78)

Here man is on a par with the world, a cosmos himself containing miraculous continents. The book that Browne reads is the world: the world for him is a projection of man; consequently, a world-embracing book such as *Pseudodoxia Epidemica* is man, but not man as put together by a thousand contributors to a work of reference. It is man the microcosm as conceived by one mind, and thus it is Browne himself.

In *Religio Medici* he takes his doctrine of man the microcosm beyond the realm of physical nature:

For the world, I count it not an Inne, but an Hospitall, and a place, not to live, but to die in. The world that I regard is my selfe, it is the Microcosme of mine owne frame, that I cast mine eye on; for the other, I use it but like my Globe, and turne it round sometimes for my recreation. Men that look upon my outside, perusing onely my condition, and fortunes, do erre in my altitude; for I am above *Atlas* his shoulders. The earth is a point not onely in respect of the heavens above us, but of that heavenly and celestiall part within us: that masse of flesh that circumscribes me, limits not my mind: that surface that tells the heavens it hath an end, cannot perswade me I have any; I take my circle to be above three hundred and sixty, though the number of the Arke do measure my body, it comprehendeth not my minde: whilst I study to finde how I am a Microcosme or little world, I finde my selfe something more than the great. (*P,* 153)

Here is a species of transcendence, both of the limits of the external world and of the confines of the self. While Browne performs the humanist exercise of studying himself, he finds—the unexpectedness is important—that instead of becoming centrally obsessed by or imprisoned in the self, he is (like Marvell in "The Garden") liberated into a sphere without limits, discovering his share in that infinite other, the divine, of whose definition by "Hermes Trismegistus" he was so fond as to repeat it half a dozen times in his works: God is a sphere whose center is everywhere and circumference nowhere.

Something of this transcendence may be achieved by immersion in the cosmos of *Pseudodoxia,* which is the verbal embodiment of those experiences of the concentric worlds of God, nature, and man to which Browne refers in *Religio Medici.* In the earlier work he is principally concerned with religious belief, but what he says of his approach to problems of faith—"I love to lose my selfe in a mystery to pursue my reason to an *oh altitudo*" (*P,* 69; the text alluded to is Romans 11:33: "O the depth of the riches both of the wisdom and knowledge of God! how unsearchable are his judgments, and his ways past finding out")—may be perceived in *Pseudodoxia* in his quest for natural and historical truths. "I love to lose my selfe," in the sense not of getting lost but of discarding the mundanely inquisitive part of oneself (as Keats felt it, an irritable reaching after certainties) in order to achieve a visionary comprehension of the quality of the subject, its depth, its extension. Just as the emblems of two later works, *Hydriotaphia* and *The Garden of Cyrus,* are an urn and a quincuncial lozenge or network, so that of *Pseudodoxia* could well be the traditional representation of a labyrinth, the word Browne himself used to characterize his undertaking in his address to the reader. In threading this labyrinth with him, we may share the pleasure of the text, the pleasure of reading it coinciding with the pleasure of writing it, as Browne loses himself in exploration of "the America and untravelled parts of Truth" (*K*, 2:5), seeing with the clear eyes of the scholar and scientist, while motivated by admiration for and attraction to the variety and color of human and natural history, sensing like Blake that everything that lives is holy.

Our experience of literature that purports to represent reality may be enhanced by awareness that the mind of the writer is necessarily selecting from that reality. The pure scientist (or, for that matter, the sociologist) may do no more than sample, at least in the primary stage of investigation, passively watching for meaningful generalizations to emerge. The artist, by contrast, is purposively selecting according to his imagined pattern of life. Unsurprisingly, after the dual focus on God and man in *Religio Medici,* the organizing vision we see vividly at work in *Pseudodoxia* is that of a Christian humanist.

Despite the factual nature of Browne's inquiries into natural and civil history, religious faith provides both an overall framework and a driving force. Book I begins in the garden of Eden, Book VII concludes with speculation on the fate of sinful souls. Book I itself, on the historical, natural, philosophical, psychological, and literary causes of error, finds the "father cause" in "our first . . . forefathers," Adam and Eve, and concludes with the first contriver of error, the devil. Concern for truth in religious matters is often the prime mover in the choice of topics: in Book V, fourteen out of the twenty-three chapters on pictures are on subjects of interest to Jews and Christians; in Book VI, the early history of the world is considered largely in the light of biblical accounts; more than half of Book VII is concerned with Judeo-Christian topics such as the forbidden fruit, the Tower of Babel, the Three Kings, the laughter of Jesus, and Pope Joan. Most of the other subjects in *Pseudodoxia,* though not theological, admit of scriptural quotation, as well as the more obviously necessary use of secular authority, reasoning, and experiment.

Even more of a force for cohesion, however, is Browne's humanism. We have seen in *Religio Medici* how interconnected for him were divinity and natural philosophy, and how, furthermore, by centering both in himself, he transcended self, abolishing the boundary between self and other and imaginatively entering into the whole world as if it were comprehended within the nerve endings of his own fingertips. From beginning to end, *Pseudodoxia* is concerned with the weakness and the wonderfulness of man, not merely with Christian doctrine: Adam and Eve are presented as people, our real forebears, and close to us in their folly and illogicality; the concluding paragraph of the work echoes the idea of *Religio Medici* that "there is all *Africa,* and her prodigies in us":

> And yet, if as some Stoicks opinion, and Seneca himself disputeth, these unruly affections that make us sin such prodigies, and even sins themselves, be animals; there is an history of Africa and story of Snakes in these. And if the transanimation of Pythagoras or method thereof were true, that the souls of men transmigrated into species answering their former natures: some men must surely live over many Serpents, and cannot escape that very brood whose sire Satan entered. (*K*, 2:548)

Likewise the authors favored by the humanist tradition appear alongside, without displacing, the Christian view: the name of Plato is the ninth word in Browne's preface to the reader and appears within nine lines of the end of the work. Between these points, several dozen references (though many are not explicit) show how intimately Platonic assumptions are woven into Browne's ideas of the world.

Even more obviously, *Pseudodoxia* is centered on man: the central book of the seven (itself a mystical number, graphically represented in the candlestick of Exodus and Revelation), Book IV, is concerned with "many popular and received Tenents concerning Man." In the preceding Books II and III, as Browne progresses up the chain of being from minerals, through plants, to animals, before reaching man, in the order traditional in medieval encyclopedias, he constantly relates his subjects to man in their uses and dangers. For him "the whole world was made for man" (*P*, 148), and while he unconditionally champions truth, because any error, however harmless it may seem, is a derogation of God's wisdom and a victory for the devil, he never advocates knowledge for its own sake: all his investigations are to the glory of God (which may, of course, excuse his least relevant explorations), and for the benefit of man.

This homocentricity, along with the supposed elegant design of nature, provides that fascination which is defined by Rudolf Otto as a necessary part of the *mysterium tremendum,* the sense of holiness.[3] The other element necessary to the numinous, power, is evoked in *Pseudodoxia,* as in *Paradise Lost,* by the vastness of the world it presents. From the first man in Book I to the medieval and Renaissance history in the closing chapters of Book VII,

---

3. *The Idea of the Holy,* trans. John W. Harvey (Oxford, 1923; Harmondsworth, 1959), pp. 45–53.

Browne ventures into every period of the history of the world. He sets foot imaginatively in all the cultures known to him, ancient and modern: Jewish, Assyrian, Egyptian, Greek, Roman, African, European, Mogul, and American Indian. While pondering any particular subject we have at least at the back of our minds the immensity and complex diversity of the world, whether conceived of according to Jewish legend or according to modern scientific belief.

Within chapters themselves, even within sentences and phrases, this all-embracing activity of mind continues. In Book I, Chapter 5, "Of Credulity and Supinity," Browne takes as examples of credulity the ancient Athenians, who thought their race was literally born of the earth, and the learned Arabs Geber, Avicenna, and Almanzor, who could believe such alleged doctrines of Islam as that in paradise the pleasure of copulation would be prolonged to fifty years. To exemplify extreme skepticism, Browne uses the ancient Greek Zeno of Elea, and his metaphors for the difficulty of attaining to truth juxtapose a saying of Democritus and an allusion to the Book of Genesis: "Truth, which wise men say doth lye in a Well, is not recoverable, but by exantlation. It were some extenuation of the Curse, if *In sudore vultus tui* were confinable unto corporal exercitations, and there still remained a Paradise or unthorny place of knowledg" (*K,* 2:38). For the chapter's peroration on the state of learning, Browne employs the myth of Sisyphus to typify academic labor by those unsuited to it, then a metaphor drawn from building, and finally (like Cicero—*De officiis,* I, 31 [110]—whose argument underlies this passage) the Roman name of the goddess of wisdom to stand for her gift:

> Now as there are many great Wits to be condemned, who have neglected the increment of Arts, and the sedulous pursuit of knowledge; so are there not a few very much to be pitied, whose industry being not attended with natural parts, they have sweat to little purpose, and rolled the stone in vain. Which chiefly proceedeth from natural incapacity, and genial indisposition, at least, to those particulars whereunto they apply their endeavours. And this is one reason why, though Universities be full of men, they are oftentimes empty of learning: Why, as there are some men do much without learning, so others but little with it, and few that attain to any measure of it. For many heads that undertake it, were never squared, nor timber'd for it. There are not only particular men, but whole Nations indisposed for learning; whereunto is required, not only education, but a pregnant Minerva, and teeming Constitution. (*K,* 2:39–40)

The idea inherent in the building metaphor, that men are purposively designed, becomes explicit as Browne's thought moves to his God, and finally we are reminded of that cynical exploit of Diogenes, looking for a wise man in daylight: "if the world went on as God hath ordained it, and were every one imployed in points concordant to their Natures, Professions, Arts, and Commonwealths would rise up of themselves; nor needed we a Lanthorn to find a man in Athens" (*K,* 2:40).

Although the allusions and figures of speech quoted from this chapter are neither directly functional nor essential to the substance of the argument, they are relevant not only in their local effects as analogies but also in their wider associations with the classical and Arabic worlds of learning, the two peaks of pre-Renaissance scientific achievement known to Browne. The allusions to Genesis and the designs of God remind us of what Browne's first two chapters set forth comprehensively, that the Fall of Man was intellectual as well as moral, foolish as well as sinful, because Adam, who named and was master of all earthly creatures, became subordinate to them, a slave of the soil, gashed by briers, vulnerable to serpents, and unable to pass his universal knowledge to his successors.

II

Metonymic and synecdochic processes on a wide scale are to be seen in the movement of Browne's mind between larger and smaller aspects of particular subjects, making transitions that might puzzle the reader who expected narrow specificity of aim and execution. Chapter 17 of Book III is announced at its head as being "Of Hares." There is here an immediate discrepancy for the reader who (treating *Pseudodoxia* as he normally would a factual reference book) has methodically found this chapter through the table of contents, for there it is billed as treating the popular and received tenent "That Hares are both male and female." It turns out, indeed, that Browne does not mean to produce (or reproduce) a monograph on the hare. Instead, the one alleged characteristic of changeable or dual sex is selected, with the specific justification that it was used by Jewish rabbis and others to symbolize "unnatural venery and degenerous effemination." Yet after the first paragraph it also appears that not only is the treatment of the hare reduced to one aspect of the animal but in addition, far more than being a mere report of the anatomical evidence of Browne's own eyes, this aspect of one subject, hares, turns out to be part of another, to which it gives way for a substantial part of the chapter: sex changes and hermaphroditism in other animals and—of prime interest—in man.

The subject is enhanced by wide reference to other animals—horses, asses, dogs, foxes, pheasants, cocks, beavers, hyenas, cows, deer, worms, apes, porcupines, hedgehogs, cuttlefish, lobsters, shrimps, crayfish, panthers, and tigers—and to nonsexual transformations lower down the hierarchy of creation in caterpillars, silkworms, barley, wheat, corn, mint, basil, and turnips. This well-stocked and multifarious world is extended chronologically by reference to Nero's hermaphroditical horses and geographically with an allusion to a sixteenth-century example in Antwerp. But man almost takes over the chapter from the hare and all other animals, as Browne enumerates known sex changes from Tiresias and Empedocles down to his own day, compares the anatomy and development of boys and girls, considers the fairness of legal restrictions on the sex lives of human hermaphrodites, mentions the rabbinic hypothesis that Adam was androgynous, and adduces, from classical history, medicine, comedy, and mythology, examples of superfetation in women.

This colonization of the hare's chapter by man is strikingly demonstrated in its conclusion. Having cataloged the different postures in copulation proper to various other species, Browne frees his pen to expatiate cogently on the practices of his own species: "This is the constant Law of their Coition, this they observe and transgress not: onely the vitiosity of man hath acted the varieties hereof; nor content with a digression from sex or species, hath in his own kind run thorow the Anomalies of venery; and been so bold, not only to act, but represent to view, the irregular ways of Lust" (*K,* 2:218–19). Our attention is transferred, as twice before in the chapter, from animal to man, and, with the reference to pictorial representations, back in time to well-known classical instances, such as the bedchamber of Tiberius in Suetonius and that curious digression in Seneca's *Natural Questions* on the enjoyment of sodomy while surrounded by enlarging mirrors, and to modern Italy, where Giulio Romano notoriously realized in his own medium Pietro Aretino's licentious sonnets, the *Lussuriosi* or "Postures." The shift into a rhetorical, higher style culminates in the pronounced rhythm of the concluding phrase, "the irregular ways of Lust"—anapest, anapest, iamb—whose prominent location leaves it to echo in the memory almost as an antititle to the chapter: if the text concerns the actual normality of the supposedly abnormal lower animal, the subtext is the sexual varieties of man, who is supposedly the superior standard of all creatures.

This freedom of intellectual movement—what Basil Willey called "the inter-availability of all his worlds of experience"[4]—is frequently and happily exercised by Browne. The chapter on right and left in man (Book IV, Chapter 5) goes back in time to Jews, Persians, Greeks, Romans, and Amazons; down the chain of being to horses, bulls, mules, squirrels, apes, monkeys, parrots, dogs, hedgehogs, and frogs; out into the firmament as described by philosophers, poets, astronomers, and soothsayers (in Book VI, Chapter 7, on east and west, his attention moves in the opposite direction, from the firmament to man's body); as well as under our skin, into the veins, liver, spleen, heart, and brain. From the positions of the microcosm, man, the argument moves by analogy to other parts of the macrocosm, then to the macrocosm as a whole.

Another example of the transformation of an animal subject into a human one is Book III, Chapter 9, "Of the Deer." Again the table of contents informs us that a particular topic, the supposed longevity of deer, is to be selected, and characteristically the argument includes through association the question whether the life of man is shortened by sexual intercourse, and then the argument is further widened with reference to the ravages of syphilis and to types of old age such as Nestor.

Such antonomasia, the substitution of typical, legendary names for attri-

4. *The Seventeenth Century Background* (London, 1934; 1967), p. 44.

butes, was a convention imbibed by schoolboys from such authors as Terence, Cicero, and Ovid, and thence popular with seventeenth-century wits. But for Browne there is more to antonomasia than mere decoration or ingenuity: it enacts a belief expressed in *Religio Medici:*

> For as though there were a *Metempsuchosis,* and the soule of one man passed into another, opinions doe finde after certaine revolutions, men and mindes like those that first begat them. To see our selves againe wee neede not looke for *Platoes* yeare; every man is not onely himselfe; there have beene many *Diogenes,* and as many *Timons,* though but few of that name; men are lived over againe, the world is now as it was in ages past, there was none then, but there hath been some one since that parallels him, and is as it were his revived selfe. (*P,* 66–67)

This belief in the recurrence of vices is expressed again in *Pseudodoxia:* "There is a certain list of vices committed in all Ages, and declaimed against by all Authors, which will last as long as humane nature; which, digested into common places, may serve for any Theme, and never be out of date until Dooms-day" (*K,* 2:42). A twist is given to this doctrine at the end of *Pseudodoxia* (Book VII, Chapter 19):

> of sins heteroclital, and such as want either name or president, there is oft times a sin even in their histories. We desire no records of such enormities; sins should be accounted new, that so they may be esteemed monstrous. They omit of monstrosity as they fall from their rarity; for, men count it veniall to err with their forefathers, and foolishly conceive they divide a sin in its society. The pens of men may sufficiently expatiate without these singularities of villany; For, as they encrease the hatred of vice in some, so do they enlarge the theory of wickedness in all. And this is one thing that may make latter ages worse then were the former; For, the vicious examples of Ages past, poyson the curiosity of these present, affording a hint of sin unto seduceable spirits, and soliciting those unto the imitation of them, whose heads were never so perversly principled as to invent them. (*K,* 2:547)

All these passages demonstrate Browne's vivid sense of being related to his predecessors on earth; the effect of his use of antonomasia is to include in his present world the populations of the past.

In the discussion of necrophilia in Book VII, Chapter 19, the topic is brought out of the remote Egyptian embalming rooms and revived as a subject for seventeenth-century court poets such as John Cleveland with the observation that "from wits that say 'tis more then incontinency for Hylas to sport with Hecuba, and youth to flame in the frozen embraces of age, we require a name for this" (*K,* 2:546). The names universalize the supposed vice but also stylize it so that it can be contemplated. Browne keeps literary surgical gloves on and uses wit as a disinfectant in his concluding mock-gerontophiliac quip: "Surely, if such depravities there be yet alive, deformity need not despair; nor will the eldest hopes be ever superannuated, since death hath spurs, and carcasses have been courted" (*K,* 2:546). The stark reality of the final clause is all the more effective for being preceded by the distancing effect of three metonymies and a personification.

Browne's employment of literary devices may, with its fictions and figures of speech, seem paradoxical in the light of his explicit and decided strictures on imaginative literature as a source of false beliefs that long outlast childhood. In his preface he deplores the fact that minor misconceptions picked up in youth become firm prejudices in age: "such as are but acorns in our younger brows, grow Oaks in our elder heads" (*K*, 2:4). He is much concerned, like Milton, with the defects of conventional education. At Winchester he himself probably had not been required to read a single text, even of the classics, that could in any sense be called scientific, and the same was true of the B.A. course at Oxford, even though a good number of the students were to go on to read medicine after their M.A. At the end of Book I, Chapter 9, on authors who propagate error, specifically "Poets and Poetical Writers," he argues:

> Now however to make use of Fictions, Apologues, and Fables, be not unwarrantable, and the intent of these inventions might point at laudable ends; yet do they afford our junior capacities a frequent occasion of error, setling impressions in our tender memories, which our advanced judgments generally neglect to expunge. This way the vain and idle fictions of the Gentiles did first insinuate into the heads of Christians; and thus are they continued even unto our days. Our first and literary apprehensions being commonly instructed in Authors which handle nothing else; wherewith our memories being stuffed, our inventions become pedantick, and cannot avoid their allusions; driving at these as at the highest elegancies, which are but the frigidities of wit, and become not the genius of manly ingenuities. It were therefore no loss like that of Galen's Library, if these had found the same fate; and would in some way requite the neglect of solid Authors, if they were less pursued. For were a pregnant wit educated in ignorance hereof, receiving only impressions from realities; upon such solid foundations, it must surely raise more substantial superstructions, and fall upon very many excellent strains, which have been jusled off by their intrusions. (*K*, 2:62)

With this severe, adult view of the fallacious products of literary fancy, Browne would seem to have had no qualms about excluding the arts from education rather than trying to reconcile them with the sciences. Yet, not only does he illustrate and adorn his discussion with quotations from classical poets that are not strictly necessary on an informational level—these might be mere relics of taught habits—but we may sometimes detect something far deeper in his temperament, a nostalgia for the wide-eyed, passionate wonder of childhood, which fired his mind before the development of his critical faculties enjoined suspicion of emotional responses. His early discovery of the plant world in the shops around his city home, probably before he went away to Winchester at the age of eleven, is recalled in *Religio Medici:* "I know most of the Plants of my Country and of those about mee; yet me thinkes I do not know so many as when I did but know an hundred, and had scarcely ever Simpled further than Cheap-side" (*P*, 147). Here he digresses on the delight of effortless discovery, when wonder at the world's novelties sustained him entirely, before the burdensome realization of how much was to be known reduced him almost to despairing skepticism. A surviving, potentially intellectually disabling capacity for wonder is admitted to in *Pseudodoxia*, where it is with regret that he dispatches some fallacious beliefs in miraculous properties of the loadstone: "perhaps too greedy of Magnalities, we are apt to make but favourable experiments concerning welcom Truths, and such desired verities" (*K*, 2:106). It may be that he is speaking of a temptation he himself has felt but resisted when at the end of the same chapter he rejects "Moral, Mystical, Theological" discourses of the loadstone because "though honest minds do glorifie God hereby; yet do they most powerfully magnifie him, and are to be looked on with another eye, who demonstratively set forth its Magnalities; who not from postulated or precarious inferences, entreat a courteous assent; but from experiments and undeniable effects, enforce the wonder of its Maker" (*K*, 2:116–17).

Browne perceives that scientists and scholars need an emotional stimulus to pursue "the knowledge of things through all the corners of nature," so as not to defect by the way, and tire "within the sober circumference of Knowledg" (*K*, 2:38, 39). One of man's most powerful feelings, sustaining men throughout their lives and impelling some to brave death, is that commonly called religious, a feeling that there exists a greater than human power, both terrible and attractive. Even those who do not profess allegiance to the myths, moral codes, and institutions of Browne's religion may be drawn into the many-layered world whose holiness he imaginatively evokes by investing its physical actuality with grandeur and fascination, reproducing in his reader his own responses of awe and love.

Wandering in the America of Truth: *Pseudodoxia Epidemica* and the Essay Tradition

Ted-Larry Pebworth

I

Pseudodoxia Epidemica has often been relegated to the cabinet of literary curiosities, even by those who have responded favorably to it. Critics have tended to be apologetic for the book as a sui generis exercise in arcane scholarship, while historians of science have often seen its belletristic presentation and its individualistic authorial presence as obscuring its scientific worth.[1] Yet it was Sir Thomas Browne's own favorite among his several works, and he spent much of his free time in the twenty-six years following its original appearance in 1646 augmenting and revising it and overseeing its republication in edition after edition. Considering the book's apparent lack of a sense of inevitable form—in any of its editions and despite all Browne's care—such devotion and industry strike many readers as peculiar. But *Pseudodoxia Epidemica* is more than a quaint document in the history of science or an oddity of literature. A recognition of its true genre may help to clarify Browne's achievement and enable us to appreciate the work on its own terms.

Arranged in seven books made up of varying numbers of chapters, *Pseudodoxia Epidemica* moves from considerations of the sources of human

---

1. For example, Austin Warren's comment, "Without doubt, Browne designed *Vulgar Errors* as a contribution to 'philosophy' and the advancement of learning, a fulfillment of one of Bacon's proposals, not as a piece of literature," in "The Style of Sir Thomas Browne," *Kenyon Review* 13 (1951): 678; and A. Rupert Hall's omission of *Pseudodoxia Epidemica* in his "English Scientific Literature in the Seventeenth Century," published as the second part of *Scientific Literature in Sixteenth & Seventeenth Century England,* Papers delivered . . . at the Sixth Clark Library Seminar (Los Angeles, 1961), with the aside that he "cannot share the usual admiration for Sir Thomas Browne's style" (p. 35).

errors and the methods of refuting them through discussions of various false or at least dubious tenets pertaining to minerals and gems, plants, animals, and man to errors perpetrated in pictures and in geographical and historical writings to a mixture of problems associated with both secular and scriptural history. Indeed, Browne's catholic range of interests includes embryology as well as philology, and mineralogy as well as cartography (compare *P*, 33).

Moreover, a bewildering variety of treatments parallels the work's enormous range of subjects. Some topics receive only a single paragraph each in conglomerate chapters of "sundry" or "divers" considerations, while others are accorded whole chapters, some of considerable length. In addition, within these smaller units, Browne's attitude toward his subjects ranges at whim from the extremes of the methodical, the sober, and even the dryly pedantic to the wistful, the playful, and the intentionally humorous. Finally, within many of the work's chapters, there is a tendency to wander off the announced topic at the slightest provocation, frequently never to return. It is no wonder that in varying degrees most students of Browne have shared Norman Endicott's affectionate bemusement when faced with such a discussion as "Of the Picture of Adam and Eve with Navels" (*K*, 2:345–47): "it is perhaps worth noting that a chapter which begins with a scholastic inquiry ends with personal observations on tadpoles and the maggots of flies."[2]

What needs to be recognized, however, is that *Pseudodoxia Epidemica* is—to use what must be Browne's most often quoted metaphor—a great amphibian: a contribution to science and scholarship in the form of a collection of personal essays. When the work is so recognized, its apparently eccentric principles of selectivity, its great variety in the treatment of its subjects, its author's constant presence, and its digressiveness and lack of summarizing conclusions in the individual chapters can be seen in context as accepted characteristics of an existing genre.[3] Most significantly, the identification of *Pseudodoxia Epidemica* as a collection of personal essays enables us both to appreciate the book as an imaginative modification of the early familiar essay form and to see its affinity with Browne's other works; and it suggests as well that the book may have been a pivotal contribution toward the development of the scientific essay of the Restoration and beyond.

Although its full implications have hitherto gone unnoted, Browne's

2. *The Prose of Sir Thomas Browne,* ed. Norman J. Endicott (New York, 1967), p. 567, n. 5.

3. Although *Pseudodoxia Epidemica* has never been identified as a collection of personal essays—with all the implications that placing it within that generic tradition entails—several recent critics have noticed the general "essayistic" nature of the book, for example, Leonard Nathanson, *The Strategy of Truth: A Study of Sir Thomas Browne* (Chicago, 1967), pp. 6–8; Rosalie Colie, *The Resources of Kind: Genre-Theory in the Renaissance* (Berkeley, 1973), pp. 86–87; and Laurence Stapleton, *The Elected Circle: Studies in the Art of Prose* (Princeton, 1973), pp. 49–52.

preface "To the Reader" (*K*, 2:3–6) actually betrays the amphibious nature of his book. An apologia of eight paragraphs appended to the first edition of *Pseudodoxia Epidemica* and augmented and emended only slightly as the collection progressed from edition to edition, "To the Reader" is a disingenuous, often witty exercise in the rhetoric of indirection. It has in common with many prefaces—and notably those appended to early collections of essays from Montaigne's onward—a surface modesty that in fact celebrates what it ostensibly apologizes for. In the passages defining the book's scientific and scholarly purpose, Browne wishes, he says, to provide a "service unto our Country, and therein especially unto its ingenuous Gentry" and thus has "endeavoured a long and serious *Adviso;* proposing not only a large and copious List" of probably erroneous tenets in various fields of human knowledge, but also "attempting their decisions." Woven among these statements are passages that intimate genre as well as purpose. Although he never uses the word *essay* itself, what Browne celebrates obliquely in his preface is the essayistic nature of the book that it introduces.

Contrasting the contents of *Pseudodoxia Epidemica* with the work of "Philologers and Critical Discoursers," he refers to his own offerings as "our narrower explorations"; and four times in "To the Reader" he uses a form of the word *attempt* to categorize his efforts, playing on the fact that "attempt" is a primary English equivalent of the French word *essai*. In seeming to apologize for the lack of a "regular and constant stile," Browne shares in the fiction of nearly all early essayists, beginning with Montaigne himself, that what he is presenting is hasty and spontaneous, free of the rhetorical contaminations of revision and polish. His tools and touchstones, "experience and reason," are those of the essayist as well as of the scientist and scholar. His protest that "we are not Magisterial in opinions, nor have we Dictator-like obtruded our conceptions; but in the humility of Enquiries or disquisitions, have only proposed them unto more ocular discerners" is a version of the early essayists' concern that their work be regarded as tentative and noncontroversial. And his tongue-in-cheek admission of "lapses" and "digressions" in his book, taken together with his mock trepidation at having "to wander in the America and untravelled parts of Truth," constitutes not an apology at all but a confession of its author's insatiable curiosity. Moreover, the admission concurrently recognizes two elements of their genre that were important to early essayists: freedom in choice of specific subject matter and freedom to be digressive. Thus "To the Reader" acknowledges the essayistic qualities of the book that it introduces, in effect cataloging all of the important external characteristics of the early essay.

Preeminently, however, the early essay—whatever its ostensible subject matter—is a genre of self. As Montaigne, in his own "Au Lecteur," observes, "Ainsi, lecteur, je suis moy-mesmes la matiere de mon livre," concluding with aggressive but false disparagement, "ce n'est pas raison que tu employes ton loisir en un subject si frivole et si vain."[4] Similarly, when Browne

4. Montaigne, *Essais*, ed. Maurice Rat, 2 vols. (Paris, 1962), 1:1: "Thus, reader, I am myself the matter of my book; you would be unreasonable to spend your leisure

seems to "crave exceeding pardon in the audacity of the Attempt" collected as *Pseudodoxia Epidemica,* protesting that such a compilation deserves "the conjunction of many heads" and should have "fallen into the endeavours of some cooperating advancers" of learning, he actually calls attention to the accomplishments of his "solitary," individualized consciousness. And with a wit equal to Montaigne's, he seems to denigrate those accomplishments by portraying himself as a puny little David of inquiry, "often constrained to stand alone against the strength of opinion, and to meet the Goliah and Giant of Authority, with contemptible pibbles, and feeble arguments, drawn from the scrip and slender stock of our selves." Lying behind the humor, however, is ill-concealed pride. One smiles at Browne's selection of these archetypically unequal contestants as a metaphor for his own efforts, but one does not forget who won the mismatched duel in the valley of Elah. Moreover, a pun identifying genre underlies the specific allusion to David's "scrip," the wallet in which the shepherd lad carried the five smooth stones onto the battlefield (see I Samuel 17:40 AV; and *OED,* "scrip," *sb.* 1). In the seventeenth century, the word *scrip* denoted as well a small scrap of paper with writing on it (*OED, sb.* 3); and by modifying "scrip" with "of our selves," Browne playfully metamorphoses David's bag of ammunition into his own form of weaponry: a collection of personal essays.

II

The last important form of prose expression created by Renaissance humanists, the essay was given its name and its essential characteristics by Montaigne in the last third of the sixteenth century. Wishing to explore at leisure various aspects of human nature and human behavior, Montaigne developed a brief, informal musing that was free in choice of subject matter, fragmentary in scope, tentative in approach, skeptical in attitude, associative in organization, noncontroversial in tone, and reflective in style. Calling up materials from history, philosophy, and belles lettres, the Montaigne essay subjects received truths to personal observation, experience, and reason in a kinetic form that emphasizes its processes as much as its content. In his own words, Montaigne sought to portray not "l'estre" but "passage," not being but passing.[5] And, although he carefully constructed and subsequently revised his essays, he did so with the constant goal of achieving a sense of spontaneity and immediacy.

English writers were quick to adopt the new genre and by 1640 had published more than twenty distinct collections of their own, many of them

---

on so frivolous and vain a subject" (Donald Frame, trans., *The Complete Essays of Montaigne* [Stanford, 1965], p. 2).

5. "Du Repentir," *Essais,* ed. Maurice Rat, 2:222. Of the several fine studies of Montaigne published recently, Margaret McGowan's *Montaigne's Deceits: The Art of Persuasion in the "Essais"* (London, 1974) contains the fullest analysis of his genre.

running to multiple, often revised editions.[6] A few early English essayists, notable among them Sir William Cornwallis the younger, followed Montaigne's model rather closely; but others made modifications in the form. Under the influence of Bacon, many began to categorize areas of subject matter under such heads as "civil," "political," "moral," and "theological," a process that increasingly suggested the applicability of the form to a broader range of concerns than those handled by Montaigne; and Bacon himself in the final augmented revision of his own collection (1625) added essays on domestic architecture and landscape gardening. At the same time, writers such as Joseph Hall and Owen Felltham turned the form to overtly didactic uses, capping essays with vows and resolves designed to better the conduct of both writer and reader. By the 1640s, then, the way had been prepared for someone experimentally minded and sensitive to the nuances of genre to turn the essay form to the treatment of scholarly and scientific subjects with the goal of reaching conclusions of value to the advancement of learning. This Thomas Browne did in *Pseudodoxia Epidemica*.

Most of the chapters of *Pseudodoxia Epidemica* are, in fact, individual essays, musings on axiomatically stated tenets. Even the composite chapters in Books II, III, V, VI, and VII recall one of the major sources of the essay genre, the jottings of the commonplace book. The chapter that opens Book III, "Of the Elephant" (*K*, 2:157–61), is representative of most of the fuller pieces that make up Browne's collection. Its subject is a pair of interconnected tenets reported of this "Animal of the vastest dimension and longest duration": that "it hath no joints" in its legs and that it is thereby "unable to lie down." With a thoroughness approaching the pedantic, Browne lists several ancient writers who have repeated these errors; and he takes up their refutations successively, first subjecting them to reason, then to "the obvious relations of history," and finally to "experience, whereof not many years past, we have had the advantage in England, by an Elephant shewn in many parts thereof, not only in the posture of standing, but kneeling and lying down." From the first sentence, Browne's overall point of view is clear, as he refers to the two tenets as one "absurdity . . . seconded with another." But his attitude toward specifics is mercurial, by turns scholarly, coldly logical, and humorous as well as scornful. Chastising those who have repeated what was "an old and gray-headed error, even in the days of Aristotle," he moves through a rational application of the Stagirite's principle of "Animals' locomotion" to the sardonic judgment that the idea of motion in a creature without joints is as fantastical as the expectation of "a Race from Hercules his pillars" or the hope "to behold the effects of Orpheus his Harp, when Trees found joints, and danced after his Musick." Browne next offers another cool application of logic based on Galen's argument that "station" (in other words, standing) is itself a form of

6. For their understanding and practice of the form, see my study "Not Being, But Passing: Defining the Early English Essay," *Studies in the Literary Imagination* 10:2 (1977): 17–27.

motion, then moves nervously to the whimsical judgment that a good part of Tantalus's punishment must have consisted in his having to stand perpetually, then onward to a gleeful catalog of historical accounts of elephants dancing on tightropes and even genuflecting to popes. He next proceeds to speculate on the reason for the existence of the two errors in the first place, ending that musing with what appears to be a summation of all that has come before: "If therefore any shall affirm the joints of Elephants are differently framed from most of other quadrupedes, and more obscurely and grosly almost then any, he doth herein no injury unto truth. But if *à dicto secundum quid ad dictum simpliciter,* he affirmeth also they have no articulations at all, he incurs the controulment of reason, and cannot avoid the contradiction also of sense."

Significantly, however, although the specific topic of this chapter may have reached a conclusion, the essay is not over. The mind musing on the elephant still has a stock of "Other concernments" relating to the great beast. In fact, the chapter continues for another page, considering in turn the animal's use in hunting, the question of whether its tusks are teeth or horns, the position of its genitals, and whether or not it can be taught to speak and write, finally ceasing on that last curious point. In the essay's final paragraph, moreover, the skeptical scientist who had earlier demanded logic and empirical evidence does "not conceive impossible" various testimonies that elephants have written and spoken. He only wonders why more has not been done to teach them human communication, since "The Serpent that spake unto Eve, the Dogs and Cats that usually speak unto Witches, might afford some encouragement."[7]

This chapter "Of the Elephant" contains examples of all of the features of *Pseudodoxia Epidemica* that readers approaching the book only as a scientific and scholarly work have found problematic: inconsistency in tone; digressiveness; an authorial presence so individualized that it seems at times eccentric; and, in the final passages especially, a tentativeness that appears at odds with Browne's didactic purpose and his insistence on reason and experience.

What these readers have overlooked or discounted, however, is the fact that *Pseudodoxia Epidemica* is an avocational book, not a professional one. Browne's vocation was medicine, his specialty urinalysis. But in "To the Reader" he specifically emphasizes that the chapters following the preface were "composed by snatches of time, as medical vacations, and the fruitless importunity of Uroscopy would permit us"; and he deliberately excludes

7. Compare the "Heare-say newes" reported in Ben Jonson's *Timber:* "That an *Elephant,* [1]630. came hither Ambassadour from the great *Mogull,* (who could both write and reade) and was every day allow'd twelve cast of bread, twenty Quarts of *Canary Sack;* besides Nuts and Almonds the Citizens wives sent him. That hee had a *Spanish* Boy to his Interpreter, and his chiefe *negotiation* was, to conferre or practise with *Archy* [Armstrong], the principall foole of *State,* about stealing hence *Windsor Castle,* and carrying it away on his back if he can" (*Ben Jonson,* ed. C. H. Herford and Percy and Evelyn Simpson, 11 vols. [Oxford, 1925–1952], 8:573).

from his book all "but two or three" of the many possible "vulgar Errors in Physick" that he could have considered professionally (*K*, 2:4, 5). In nearly all of the fields represented in *Pseudodoxia Epidemica,* Browne was talented and well read to be sure, but an amateur. Writing as a determined amateur, he has an advantage over the professional: he may wander at will through any and all subjects that interest him. But as a "lover" and not a "professor" of his subjects, he is wise to exercise caution, especially in "the America and untravelled parts of Truth." Inevitably raising more questions than he can answer with certitude, he must at times be tentative. Browne is scrupulous in this regard. In the first of the two essays on the loadstone (*K*, 2:88–100), for example, he makes many assertions; but he also uses the qualifier "probable" twice, modifies one other statement with "may be," and introduces yet another with "it is not improbable." Significantly, the genre of the personal essay allows Browne both to be bold in choosing subjects and to be cautious in drawing conclusions, for its joys reside not only in discovering the information that it presents but also in following the progress of a questing, discriminating mind as it muses on concerns of interest to it, even when some of its conclusions must perforce remain tentative.

Browne's topics are intrinsically less personal than those traditionally associated with the early essay; but it is the felt presence of an individual mind thinking on a subject, not the subject itself, that makes an essay personal. And Browne's presence as an individual is felt strongly on every page of *Pseudodoxia Epidemica.* His persona throughout the book is not that of an egotist or of a master writing to pupils, however, but rather that of an intelligent and interesting companion. He achieves the essayist's goals of intimacy and immediacy by a brilliant manipulation of pronouns. The word *I* does not occur until the seventh paragraph of the first essay (*K*, 2:20) and is sparingly employed thereafter, usually to discriminate between Browne's opinions or conclusions and those of others or to underline the care or effort that he has personally taken with experiments and investigations. The most commonly used personal pronoun in the book is *we;* and it is not the mock-humble "we" of "To the Reader" but an invitational plural that bonds reader to writer in a joint quest for truth.

Consequently, we participate with Browne as, in each essay, he sets himself a task, reasons the problem through, and, when he can, conducts experiments. We look on as he confirms by personal dissection his reasoned position that a horse must have a gall bladder and as he carries out "the strictest experiment I could ever make" in refuting the axiom that a pot filled with ashes will "contain as much water as it would without them" (*K*, 2:162, 128). We share his obvious frustration at his lack of success in testing whether or not "young Vipers force their way through the bowels of their Dame": "As for the experiment, although we have thrice attempted it, it hath not well succeeded; for though we fed them with Milk, Bran, Cheese &c. the females always died before the young ones were mature for this eruption" (*K*, 2:207, 208). When Browne cannot get specimens, we concur in his use of the next best evidence, the observations of other eyewitnesses who have proved themselves trustworthy. Thus we smile and nod approval when, in lion-free Norwich, he disputes the tenet that a "Lion be . . . afraid of a Cock" by reporting that "In our time in the Court of the Prince of Bavaria, one of the Lions leaped down into a Neighbour's yard, where nothing regarding the crowing or noise of the Cocks, he eat them up with many other Hens" (*K*, 2:259). With subjects that admit of neither specimens nor eyewitness accounts—such as the basilisk, the phoenix, and Adam and Eve—we content ourselves, as Browne must, with his own careful reasoning. And we share his complex emotions of wistful reluctance yet rational determination in the exposure of the fabulous.

Casting his explorations in the form of personal essays, Browne can claim another privilege of the genre, the right to allow his thoughts to move associatively as well as logically and to wander down byways at will. As is the case in "Of the Elephant," he usually reserves the bulk of his digressions for the ends of chapters, though certainly not always. For instance, he momentarily interrupts his discussion of the generation of the phoenix when that fabled creature's reputed uniqueness reminds him of the fact that Adam was created single but contained Eve within his flesh, so at the time of his creation "was (as some opinion) an Hermaphrodite" (*K*, 2:196). Nor do the associations at the ends of chapters necessarily have to follow the example in "Of the Elephant" and confine themselves to the creature, material, or other phenomenon that is the subject of the essay proper. Indeed, the associations that are presented as tumbling into an essayist's mind may move his musing far away from its original topic and never bring it back. Thus, as Browne expanded the essay "Of the Picture of Adam and Eve with Navels," the discussion of the nonhuman birth of the first human beings called to his mind the age-old question of whether "the egg was before the Bird," which in turn led to considerations of snake and frog eggs, with the latter reminding him of tadpoles, the metamorphic nature of which suggested the maggots of flies, the essay's terminal subject (*K*, 2:347).

On the point of digressiveness, it is instructive to compare the chapter titles of *Pseudodoxia Epidemica* as set forth in the table of contents with the actual headings of the chapters within the text. Many are identical, but over two dozen are not; and the variations that exist are generically telling. I have referred to the essay analyzed above as "Of the Elephant," and so it is headed in the text. But in the table of contents it is designated as "That an Elephant hath no joints." Harry Levin has recently reemphasized the importance of titles in relation to genres,[8] and that significance is nowhere more revealing than it is in *Pseudodoxia Epidemica,* where it proves to be yet another indication of the amphibious nature of Browne's book. "That an Elephant hath no joints" is specific and delimiting, a title of scholarship or science that effectively admits of no digression. "Of the Elephant" is general and open-ended, the title of a personal essay that, in effect, invites digression. In every

8. "The Title as a Literary Genre," Presidential Address, *Modern Language Review* 72:4 (1977): xxiii–xxxvi.

instance where the table of contents designation of a chapter differs from the title over the piece itself, the heading that accompanies the text is the more general of the two. Significantly, nearly all of the chapters that have identical designations in both places bear a personal essayist's title, a few beginning with "Concerning," an overwhelming number commencing with that preposition ubiquitous in the headings of early essays—"Of."[9]

The "problems" with *Pseudodoxia Epidemica*, then—its fluctuations in tone, its digressiveness, its tentativeness, and its pervasive and individualized authorial presence—actually proclaim the book as a collection of personal essays. Prepared with sensitivity and skill, such a collection can be in its total effect an autobiography in mosaic, its fragments coalescing into a detailed picture of the individual who is its author. Despite its unusual subject matter, *Pseudodoxia Epidemica* is precisely that. As Frank L. Huntley has observed, "There emerges from Browne's *Pseudodoxia Epidemica* the portrait of a man who is memorable for his writing, a man charitable in his opinions because he is wise in anthropology, a man humorous in his intellectual detachment and devout in his religion."[10] Neither private nor confessional, Browne's book, "drawn from the scrip and slender stock of our selves," is nevertheless deeply revealing of his individual consciousness.

As an oblique self-portrait, *Pseudodoxia Epidemica* is as much an expression of the autobiographical impulse as is the earlier *Religio Medici*. In this respect, Joan Webber's remarks on the latter are equally pertinent to the former:

> We observe that the [seventeenth-century] Anglican does not write autobiography directly; rather, he invites the reader to share with him in the investigation of some "subject," like a doctor's religion, or the anatomy of melancholy. The investigation can seem shared because the style is meditative. The writer allows the reader to follow the course of his mind as he contemplates his subject: thus, in a sense, the reader has to write the book himself—and in the process, he and the author become one, yet not one. The investigation can seem shared, too, because it is never finished. Not only does the meditative style itself suggest work-in-progress, but the whole form of the book is left open.[11]

9. See ibid., p. xxv, and my study, "Not Being, But Passing," p. 20.

10. *Sir Thomas Browne: A Biographical and Critical Study* (Ann Arbor, 1962), p. 169. The sentence quoted is only the beginning of Huntley's excellent discussion of "The Man" who is pictured in *Pseudodoxia Epidemica* (pp. 169–72).

11. *The Eloquent "I": Style and Self in Seventeenth-Century Prose* (Madison, 1968), p. 13. The only comment Webber makes about *Pseudodoxia Epidemica* is to concur in Austin Warren's judgment that, of all Browne's works, it is "most concerned" with making "a practical contribution to knowledge" and is therefore written in the lowest of Browne's three styles (p. 151; see Warren, "The Style of Sir Thomas Browne," p. 678); but compare another of Webber's statements about *Religio Medici:* "The discontinuousness of Browne's prose is one cause of difficulty in his interpretation. The paragraphs are independent essays, each with its own number, rather like what Bacon's essays would be if numbered and given a common title" (p. 154).

Certainly this is one's sense of *Pseudodoxia Epidemica,* a work that is kinetic and open-ended, jointly created by writer and reader. More didactic than *Religio Medici, Hydriotaphia,* and *The Garden of Cyrus,* and as a consequence written in a simpler style than they, *Pseudodoxia Epidemica* nevertheless reflects the same autobiographical urge that prompted Browne's earliest and latest publications. If *Religio Medici* is "pre-eminently the work of a young man"[12] and *Hydriotaphia* and *The Garden of Cyrus* are an aging man's musings on death and eternity, then *Pseudodoxia Epidemica* may rightfully be seen as the great autobiographical expression of his middle years.

III

Pseudodoxia Epidemica is not merely a fresh contribution to an established genre, however. It modifies the tradition it adopts, and that modification may represent a crucial step in the development of a new and important genre, the "experimental" or scientific essay of the Restoration. While always reserving the right to digress at will, Browne introduces a structure into the chapters of *Pseudodoxia Epidemica* more formulaic than that generally found in early familiar essays. He abandons as well the essayists' artfully contrived "random" ordering of topics in favor of a more systematic organization of individual pieces into books that treat single categories of subject matter. While keeping as satisfactory to his purposes the genre's tools of reason and experience, he applies them more actively and deliberately than his predecessors had done. Most importantly, when he can get specimens, he turns the essayist's experience into the scientist's experiment.

Since the appearance fifty years ago of R. F. Jones's pioneering study "Science and English Prose Style in the Third Quarter of the Seventeenth Century,"[13] Browne's relationship to Restoration scientific writing has been seen largely in the context of the Royal Society's condemnation of ornate style. Indeed, the society's early determination, as stated by Thomas Sprat, to remove "the amplifications, digressions, and swellings of style" from investigative reporting in favor of "Mathematical plainness" and "the language of Artizans, Countrymen, and Merchants" may have constituted a reaction specifically against Browne, even though his scientific work— *Pseudodoxia Epidemica*—is written in relatively simple prose.[14] Although the Royal Society rejected the *manner* or style of Browne's writing, its members may nevertheless owe their most popular *form* of discourse to the Norwich physician's application of the personal essay to experimental inquiry in the 1640s.

Among the appreciative early readers of *Pseudodoxia Epidemica* was the young Robert Boyle, who was to become one of the most influential

12. Webber, *The Eloquent "I,"* p. 149.
13. "Science and English Prose Style in the Third Quarter of the Seventeenth Century," *Publications of the Modern Language Association* 45 (1930): 977–1009.
14. *History of the Royal Society* (London, 1667), p. 113.

scientists of the Restoration. His admiration for "the learned D' *Brown*" as a "faithful and candid . . . Naturalist" is stated in the first published of Boyle's many scientific works, *Certain Physiological Essays* (1661), a collection introduced by "A Proemial Essay, . . . with some considerations touching Experimental *Essays* in General. . . ."[15] Although this introductory essay does not mention Browne by name, a careful reading of it suggests that it is a response to the kind of discourse Boyle discovered in the chapters of *Pseudodoxia Epidemica* that relate experimentation. Discussing his choice of "that form of Writing which (in imitation of the French) we call Essaies," Boyle confesses that his "first Designe" had been a "Continuation" of Bacon's *Sylva Sylvarum,* but that he had "declin'd" Bacon's "succinct way of Writing" in favor of "a more free and uncircumscrib'd way of discoursing." Positioned between the statement of Baconian design and the rejection of Baconian terseness is an injunction to the experimentally minded to busy themselves in "the Detection of some Applauded Error." The inspiration for such scientific housecleaning is ultimately also Baconian,[16] but Boyle's immediate model may well have been the "free and uncircumscrib'd" experimental essays of *Pseudodoxia Epidemica.*

Significantly, the generic profile in Boyle's "Proemial Essay" agrees with Browne's practice in every important point save one; and Boyle's determination to avoid "Exotick Words and Terms borrow'd from other Languages" seems a direct response to Browne's use of "expressions beyond meer English apprehensions" ("To the Reader," *K,* 2:4). Complaining that previous inquirers into natural phenomena have been "forbidden by Custome to publish their Thoughts and Observations unless they be numerous enough to swell into a System," Boyle advocates the writing of "Books of Essayes," for the latter need not be "clogg'd with tedious Repetitions of what others have said already," and the writer has "for the most part the Liberty to leave off when he pleases." He argues that investigators should be tentative in their conclusions and that they should not indulge in "wrangling" with others; and he states that he himself has "endeavour'd to write rather in a Philosophical than a Rhetorical strain, as desiring that my Expressions should be rather clear and significant, than curiously adorn'd." In his own essays, Boyle is as digressive, as tentative, and as inconsistent in tone as is Browne, though he is more exclusively committed to experiment and presents a less interesting persona.

Directly through his own numerous writings and indirectly through the considerable influence that he exerted within the infant Royal Society, Boyle popularized among his fellow natural philosophers the use of the

15. *Certain Physiological Essays, Written at Distant Times, and on Several Occasions* (London, 1661). Boyle's assessment of Browne occurs in "Essay II. Of the Unsucceeding Experiments," p. 98; subsequent quotations of "A Proemial Essay" are taken from pp. 5, 7, 9, 10, 11, 14, 15, and 26.

16. See the "calendar of popular errors" in Bacon, *Works,* ed. James Spedding et al., 15 vols. (Boston, 1860–1865), 6:233.

genre that he found in *Pseudodoxia Epidemica*. In short order, Boyle's colleagues took up the essay form, first in fact, and then in name as well. For the first year and a half of its existence, the *Philosophical Transactions* of the Royal Society, begun in 1665 under the editorship of Boyle's friend Henry Oldenburg, published "Accounts," "Observations," "Enquiries," and "Considerations," many of which are in effect personal essays on scientific subjects. Then in the issue of 6 August 1666 appeared *"An Essay of* Dr. John Wallis, *exhibiting his* Hypothesis *about the* Flux and Reflux of the Sea"; and in "A Preface *To the* Third Year *of these* Tracts," dated 11 March 1666/7, Oldenburg referred to the contributions of the preceding two years collectively as "Essays."[17] The scientists of the Restoration went much further than Browne in rigidifying the form, and they tended toward positive approaches rather than the negative ones of *Pseudodoxia Epidemica*. As time wore on, of course, they gradually removed the "personal" aspects of the form altogether and created the impersonally presented, tightly structured essay that was to dominate scientific writing for the next three centuries. As unlikely as it might seem on first thought, Browne's highly personal wanderings in "the America and untravelled parts of Truth" probably made a crucial contribution to the development of this new form.

Pseudodoxia Epidemica will probably never attract quite the same level of interest as *Religio Medici, Hydriotaphia*, or even *The Garden of Cyrus*. Yet it is an important achievement. As a collection of personal essays devoted to the advancement of knowledge, it represents a significant modification in the early essay tradition, and it may also have been influential in the development of the scientific essay. Thus, it deserves appreciative recognition by literary historians and by historians of science. Its greatest importance, however, resides in its function as an autobiography in mosaic, an achievement created of the same thread as Browne's other works. A great amphibian, *Pseudodoxia Epidemica* is also a unified expression of Sir Thomas Browne's integrated consciousness.[18]

17. *Philosophical Transactions* 1 (1666): 263–81; 2 (1667):410.
18. I have benefited from stimulating conversations with Emanuel C. Hertzler, Professor of Biology and Associate Dean of Academic Affairs at the University of Michigan–Dearborn. As always, my greatest debt is to my friend and collaborator, Claude J. Summers.

Thomas Browne
Naturalist

A Special Contribution by Marie Boas Hall

When Thomas Browne was admitted Bachelor of Arts at Oxford in 1626, the new science of the seventeenth century was only beginning. Of Galileo's epoch-making work, only his telescopic discoveries of 1610 were known outside Italy; Francis Bacon was shortly to die in disgrace, his claims for a new method in science largely still unregarded; Descartes was still working on his method of reasoning rightly and finding truth in science, which he was not to publish for ten years; and Harvey's *De motu cordis* was not to appear for another two years. No wonder then that the medical thought that Browne was to encounter four years later when he toured southern France and Italy was very like that Harvey had encountered thirty years earlier. Browne's education was essentially that of the humanist medical world of the sixteenth century: a firm grounding in classical languages and literature and theology, a thorough reading of Aristotle, a good introduction to astronomy, botany, anatomy, medicine, and zoology, all both literary and practical. But he was to develop interests that, later, gave him a place on the edge of the scientific world of mid-seventeenth-century London, notably the world of the College of Physicians (of which he was elected honorary fellow in 1664) and the Royal Society, with a number of whose members (younger than he) he corresponded.

In many ways, Browne conformed to the style of the English virtuoso, who moved easily between the literary and scientific worlds of Restoration London, accepted by both, though ridiculed at the end of the century. Walter Houghton rightly categorized the virtuoso as a late Renaissance type,[1] learned, literary, communicative, differentiating little between ancient and modern learning though conscious of progress, voraciously interested in facts, which he equated with knowledge and which he gathered

---

1. Walter E. Houghton, "The English Virtuoso in the Seventeenth Century," *Journal of the History of Ideas* 3 (1942): 51–73, 190–219. Curiously, Houghton thought that Browne did not quite qualify, because he was too complex.

indifferently from "authorities" and from observation. The virtuoso was a great collector of both facts and opinions, at his most interesting to us when these touch on the world of nature or the relics of the remote past, but he himself did not distinguish one subject from another—all equally absorbed him. Browne was just such a man, who in his interests as well as chronologically lies between Robert Burton, who would never be classed as a scientist, although his *Anatomy of Melancholy* (1621) contains many references to the natural philosophy of his day, and John Aubrey or John Evelyn, both original fellows of the Royal Society (1663). Aubrey was closer in his interests to Burton than to Browne, since Aubrey, although he was a fellow of the Royal Society, would never now be classed as a scientist, for his natural history was an account of antiquities, personalities, customs, and human relics, not an account of natural organisms. Evelyn, with whom Browne corresponded, was closer to his interests but, partly because he collected information on trees, orchards, gardens, and plants, partly because he was concerned with the organization of science, partly because he was an influential courtier and active in the affairs of the Royal Society, usually is classed among scientists.[2]

In what category should Browne be placed? As I shall try to show, he is best seen as a naturalist, a pure natural historian, a serious collector of every sort of fact. Some of those facts pertain to the natural world; hence one may see him as a naturalist. He was in truth a commentator upon the world rather than an original contributor to an understanding of it.[3] Ironically, he demonstrates the truth of Bacon's contention that the importance of natural history was that anyone (however unpracticed in scientific investigation) could contribute to that universal natural history of our world that Bacon took to be a necessary preliminary to our understanding of it—ironically because Browne was not interested in Bacon's dream of the imminent discovery of truth about nature by the application of the experimental method, much as he valued observed fact.

If we view Browne as a naturalist, collecting information about facts, objects, and living beings, we detect a uniformity in his published and unpublished writings that they otherwise lack, for his published writings seem at first sight very different from his private ones. This difference lessens, and almost disappears, if we discount the difference in style. In his letters and miscellaneous works, Browne used a style no less plain and, as the age said, "unvarnished" than did any younger scientific contemporary, in

2. Thus there is an article on Evelyn in the *Dictionary of Scientific Biography*, though none on either Aubrey or Browne.

3. I cannot agree with Gordon K. Chalmers, "Sir Thomas Browne, True Scientist," *Osiris* 2 (1936):28–79; he compares Browne's work with that of Boyle, although he says Browne "was a popularizer, not a discoverer" (p. 89) and believes him a true Baconian because his attitude to scientific method was similar to Bacon's. Nearer to the truth I believe is Arno Löffler, *Sir Thomas Browne als virtuoso* (Nuremberg, 1972), but his survey of Browne's work is narrow, and he is not particularly interested in Browne as a naturalist.

great contrast to the "baroque" style of his published writings—a difference not determined by time, for he used both styles concurrently throughout most of his life. To understand his thought it is necessary to look beneath his style (which clearly was no more natural to him than it appears to us) to the content and purpose of his work. And there he appears uniformly as a collector. Consider *Hydriotaphia,* which is mainly devoted to all the facts he could discover about burial customs; or *The Garden of Cyrus,* a collection of quincunxes or everything to do with the number five, whether found in nature or created by man—and which incidentally contains much of botanical interest. The collecting aspect is emphasized by the subtitle of *Pseudodoxia Epidemica: Enquiries into very many Received Tenents, and commonly Presumed Truths,* in itself a much more exact description than that of the work's running title, for these are not "Vulgar Errors" in the true sense, being found in books, not among the unlettered. *Pseudodoxia Epidemica* is in fact a natural history of learned error.

As for the major works, so for the minor ones, many of them only published posthumously (*K,* vol. 3), most indeed never intended for publication at all. These are also natural histories, or notes for natural histories, their facts drawn more from observation than from books, and many of them belonging to the last twenty years of Browne's life. The observations from books were in part drawn up as preliminaries to various editions of *Pseudodoxia Epidemica,* as, for example, the "Observations upon several Plants mention'd in Scripture." The personal observations were more often drawn up in answer to queries from individuals or for incorporation into the works of others. There is an essay "of Garlands and . . . Garland-Plants" written for John Evelyn; lists of local birds, fishes, and plants, many for John Ray, for inclusion in his own plant catalogs, in his *Collection of English Words* (1673), and in his editions of Francis Willughby's *Ornithologiae* (1676) and *Historia piscium* (1686); and other lists for a projected late edition of Christopher Merret's *Pinax* (first published in 1666). There are essays on hawks, on languages, on books, on artificial hills; "Miscellaneous Observations and Notes" on thunderstorms, echoes, angels, spectacles, medals, battles, anatomy, natural history, motion; and facts about Norfolk, like *Repertorium,* a guidebook to Norwich Cathedral. There must have been many more notes and letters, for no one could have written *Pseudodoxia Epidemica* without preliminary notes, and traces of other activities survive, like the reference to Browne's novel beehive in Samuel Hartlib's *The Reformed Common-wealth of Bees* (1655).

But in notes and letters, as in *Pseudodoxia Epidemica,* Browne retained his humanist belief that wisdom lay largely in books. His great work resembles Burton's earlier *Anatomy of Melancholy,* at least insofar as it is bookish and relies on literary sources, although it differs in displaying more interest in nature and natural history than Burton could summon. Browne was clearly a voracious reader and like any humanist reveled in proving it by the number of authors he could name (a quantity that increased in successive editions).

His prime and favorite source in *Pseudodoxia Epidemica* was the Bible, along with the Church Fathers and later commentators. Second come the ancients: historians, geographers, philosophers, natural philosophers, medical writers, botanists. Throughout his long life, Browne clearly retained the humanist belief that the ancients were unsurpassed. Although he did not insist often upon their authority, he clearly felt it strongly; so he remarked in the dedication of *The Garden of Cyrus,* "the Ancients knew the late Anatomicall discoveries" (*P,* 319). He respected Aristotle above all as the world's leading zoologist of the Mediterranean region, citing him more frequently than any other author in spite of his own reading of Guillaume Rondelet, the sixteenth-century writer on fishes; and this position he maintained in later years, writing to his son Edward in 1675, "you do well to looke upon your Aristotle *de Animal.* upon all occasion" (*K,* 4:57). As a medical man he had read the ancients, Hippocrates and Galen, of whom he generally approved more than he did the contemporary writers, although he was familiar with the sixteenth-century anatomists and with a few of the newer iatrochemical writers like Paracelsus and Oswald Croll (he seldom mentions J. B. Van Helmont or his followers). So too he had read both Dioscorides, and sixteenth-century herbalists like Pietro Andrea Gregorio Mattioli and Jean Bauhin. Of modern writers on natural history his favorite was clearly Ulisse Aldrovandi (1522–1605), for there are references to most of the works (some posthumously published) of this prolific naturalist of Bologna who left systematic studies on birds, insects, shellfish, fish, mammals, reptiles, and trees, and who possessed an unrivaled collection of specimens that Browne had possibly seen (it still exists in the Bologna University Library). He had read many sixteenth-century writers on natural magic, including Cardan (physician, astrologer, and mathematician) and G. B. della Porta. There is little about astronomy in his works, but there are a few incidental references to Copernicus, with whose doctrine he was naturally familiar, though he appears to regard its probable truth as a subject for debate by astronomers (*K,* 2:424, 520, 542; and *P,* 160). More surprising are three references to Galileo for his astronomical discoveries, his theory of tides, and his law of falling bodies (*K,* 2:309, 520; 3:434), showing that he knew both Galileo's *Sidereus nuncius* of 1610 and his *Dialogue Concerning the Two Chief Systems of the World* (1632 in Italian, 1635 in Latin, 1661 in English).

Although most of *Pseudodoxia Epidemica* is concerned with errors arising from the Bible or from living matter, there is some discussion of physical nature, notably in Book II, where Chapters 2, 3, and 4 deal with magnetism and electricity. Naturally the chief emphasis is upon errors associated with these two physical forces, and here William Gilbert's *De magnete* (1600) is the principal authority, cited again and again for his experiments and for his views on magnetic variation. Although Browne knew other learned books on magnetism, like Niccolo Cabeo's *Philosophia magnetica* (1629), he clearly did not know of Henry Gellibrand's discovery in 1634 of the decrease in magnetic variation in London since Gilbert's time, which refuted Gilbert's view of the constancy of magnetism and hence of its use in navigation.[4] Browne refers at length to the discussion on magnetism (based largely on Gilbert and Cabeo) in Kenelm Digby's *Two Treatises* of 1644—he had of course been in touch with that eccentric philosopher since 1643, when Digby's *Observations upon Religio Medici* had appeared. There are also two references to the views of Descartes on magnetism, in both cases to his theory of the mechanism of magnetic attraction (*K,* 2:90); in the first Browne refuses to choose between Descartes's theory and Digby's, while in the second he quotes Descartes's words as authority for the truth of the existence of magnetic attraction, or rather that "the Loadstone draweth Iron" (*K,* 2:101). (In each case the reference is to Descartes's *Principia philosophiae* of 1644.) In the second edition of *Pseudodoxia Epidemica,* though not in the first, there are numerous references to Athanasius Kircher's views, presumably taken from his *Magnes sive de arte magnetica* (1641, 1643). On the whole Browne regarded it as a matter of indifference which explanation was preferred, provided only that it was a rational one, for he was content to have probable hypotheses without concern for their absolute truth.

It is of some interest to examine Browne's reactions to the chief medical innovations of his day, notably anatomical discovery, chemical medicine and physiology, and the discovery of the circulation of the blood. With the first, as already noted, he was certainly familiar, although he did not regard sixteenth-century anatomy as innovative but rather as derived directly from antiquity (thinking, presumably, of Galen's excellent anatomical teachings). With the second he was certainly familiar, since he mentioned Paracelsus several times and had read his follower Croll, but he does not seem to have been sufficiently interested in the attempt by the "chemical physicians" to replace the traditional pharmacopoeia with chemical remedies to comment upon it—he was too convinced a humanist to be tempted to accept the new remedies. More surprising is his lack of interest in Harvey's great discovery of the circulation of the blood. There are no references to Harvey in the first or second editions of *Pseudodoxia Epidemica;* in subsequent editions there are references to his *De generatione* (1651) (*K,* 2:270, 304) as there are references in letters to Browne's son and to Henry Power (*K,* 6:68, 294), always deferential. The one reference to *De motu cordis* is in Browne's letter of advice to the young Henry Power (circa 1646) where he urges, "be sure you make yourself master of Dr Harvey's piece *De Circul. Sang.;* which discovery I prefer to that of Columbus" (*K,* 4:255)—not Christopher Columbus, but the Paduan anatomist Realdus Columbus who taught pulmonary, or lesser, circulation. Browne's relative neglect of Harvey's discovery is explicable only by his extreme humanism, which led him to state that the circulation of the blood had been known to Hippocrates (*P,* 319). And

4. I am indebted to S. P. Pumfrey for pointing this out, and for commenting upon Browne's ideas on magnetism.

it must be noted that before recommending Harvey's book to Power, Browne had insisted that "Galen and Hippocrates must be [held] as fathers and fountains of the faculty" (*K*, 4:255). As the years went by and Power developed wider interests than practical medicine, to be expressed especially in microscopic researches (published in his *Experimental Philosophy* in 1664), his correspondence with Browne turned more to natural history. In one of his few surviving letters to Power (of 1659), Browne, discussing generation in plants, not only refers to Harvey's work but with a touch of pride also makes a modest claim for originality on his own part, for having observed that the whole plant can be traced in the seed "as I instance in beanes & peas, & have long agoe observed in Ashkeys, almonds, Abricots, pistachios before I read any hint thereof in Regius or discription in Dr Highmore" (*K*, 4:268).[5] (The doctrine of preformation was popular in the seventeenth and eighteenth centuries among many learned men.)

In his slight correspondence with Evelyn and more sustained correspondence with Merret, Browne appears as a natural historian par excellence. Here he was able to display his collecting interest to advantage, providing his correspondents with lists of species—plants, birds, shellfish, fish—for them to organize, each individual well characterized and observed, and all related to those in published authorities where possible, for he was generously concerned to insure that the published accounts of his correspondents might be as complete as possible. Similarly, he supplied John Aubrey with biographical details on request.

Browne thus had a community of interest with several members of the Royal Society, and here it might be as well to dispose of the story, for which there is no foundation whatsoever, that he wished to be elected a fellow but was blackballed on account of his elaborate prose style. This is pure invention: nowhere, in any surviving document, is there any indication that he had such aspirations, nor was he ever put up for membership. He twice corresponded with Henry Oldenburg, the active secretary of the society. On the first occasion (1663–1664), he sent an account of the natural history of Iceland, which he derived from "a Native of Island, who comes yearly to England" and with whom he had a long acquaintance (*K*, 3:346). (This, submitted through Sir Samuel Tuke, is in as plain a style as anyone could wish, consisting of a series of flat statements.) It was warmly received, and Oldenburg promptly wrote expressing the society's thanks and asking for more, but Browne did not respond directly.[6] In 1669, when Edward Browne was traveling in Central Europe and observing the mines of that

5. Henricus Regius (Henri le Roy) was a physician and early teacher of Cartesian doctrine in Holland; the reference is probably to his *Fundamenta physices* (1646 and many other editions), which contains a very full account of Cartesian physiology. Nathaniel Highmore's views are contained in his *History of Generation* (1651); like Browne he was a country physician.

6. See A. R. and M. B. Hall, eds., *The Correspondence of Henry Oldenburg*, vol. 12 (London, 1981), letter 304 bis dated circa 27 January 1663/64; it was not published by Keynes.

region, he sent back accounts for the society to his father, who acted as postal agent (*K,* 4:363–69), but the correspondence ceased upon Edward's return.[7]

Edward later turned these letters into two books (1673 and 1677); like any fond parent his father offered him much good advice. Some of this advice was literary, concerned with problems of organizing his material; some was humanistic, with recommendations about references to authorities, ancient and modern, linguistic and geographical. Where content is concerned, Browne is perhaps further in interest from the Royal Society than his son, especially when Browne advised Edward that "for the mines you need not be so particular as to give the full account of preparing the metalls in this narration, butt how you went in, how deep & what you observed &c.; do as you think fitt" (*K,* 4:55). Perhaps the fact that Edward, and not his father, was elected to the Royal Society need not seem strange.

In general, the members of the Royal Society looked benevolently upon Browne. Besides those like Aubrey, Evelyn, Merret, and Ray, who valued him as a collector of facts, there are traces of a general esteem for his keen interest in natural history. As already noted, his information about Iceland was welcomed, though he apparently supplied no more. So too were the "curiosities" he sent for the society's repository in 1668, consisting of "a great Bone petrifyed, a whole Egg in an Egge," and a sealed bottle from which the wine had evaporated, as Oldenburg told Robert Boyle.[8] Five years later Oldenburg wrote to Marcello Malpighi in Bologna about several English works that he intended to send to him, including "what our famous Browne and Sharrock (the two men, that is to say, to whom Mr Grew referred in his little book) published about plants a few years ago."[9] Boyle himself referred to Browne respectfully on the one occasion on which he mentioned him at all in his published works, namely in *Certain Physiological Essays* (published in 1661, although written earlier). Here he called him a "faithful and candid Naturalist," stating that in repeating a certain chemical experiment, he could not consistently achieve the results that he had "been inform'd that the learned Dr. *Brown* somewhere delivers," although he was on the whole willing to believe in Browne's results.[10]

Insofar as the Royal Society's concern was with natural history, its fellows agreed with Boyle's estimate of Browne. But it must be remembered that natural history was only a part of the society's concern, and of its Baconian-

7. See Hall and Hall, *Correspondence of Henry Oldenburg,* vols. 6 and 7 (Madison, 1968 and 1969), 6:568, 7:105, 157, 298, respectively. For Oldenburg's cordial replies, see 7:8, 153.

8. Letter of 3 March 1667/68; Hall and Hall, *Correspondence of Henry Oldenburg,* vol. 4 (Madison, 1967), p. 224.

9. Letter of 18 February 1672/73; Hall and Hall, *Correspondence of Henry Oldenburg,* vol. 9 (Madison, 1973), p. 473. Grew in his *Anatomy of Vegetables Begun* did not refer to Browne by name, although he seems to have intended to do so along with Richard Sharrock, whose name is cited.

10. *Certain Physiological Essays,* 2d ed. (London, 1669), pp. 107–8.

ism. The society genuinely professed a firm Baconianism of one sort, having a deep conviction in the necessity for a universal natural history and a proper suspicion of hypotheses not based upon empirical evidence. But this by no means excluded an equally firm conviction in the importance of both mathematical and theoretical science of a kind that interested Thomas Browne not at all. To be sure, Merret, Evelyn, and Ray were honored and esteemed members of the society. But so were, for example, John Wallis, Viscount Brouncker, Robert Boyle, Robert Hooke, and, among younger men, John Flamsteed and Isaac Newton. Although all of these men were firm believers in experiment, and almost all rejected a priori hypotheses, all were concerned not with the collection of facts but with experiment as a clue to and proof of general laws of nature. Browne, on the other hand, was interested in fact, not theory; was concerned with natural history, not theoretical natural philosophy; and there is no indication of any awareness on his part of what the leading members of the Royal Society were doing to advance knowledge of the natural world beyond mere fact gathering. Browne never mentions most of these names. Nor does he discuss the microscopic discoveries of the 1660s, being apparently unaware of the work by Nehemiah Grew or Marcello Malpighi. He mentioned Hooke's *Micrographia* once, advising his son Edward to read Hooke's observations on hair and skin (*K*, 4:74) but not anything on plant or animal anatomy. Of course, little microscopic work had been done when Browne published the first edition of *Pseudodoxia Epidemica*.

Browne seems indeed to have had little or no interest in the methodological discussions about science of the seventeenth century. He clearly read little by Francis Bacon, and neither the *Advancement of Learning* nor the *Novum Organum* was cited anywhere by him. He was apparently not interested in Bacon's views on the potentialities of science, nor for all the similarity of some of his interests (like his beehive) had he any real intellectual sympathy with such professed Baconian "projectors" as those encouraged by Samuel Hartlib, who was always seeking practical improvements. If Browne was aware of the debate between "Cartesian" and "Baconian" natural philosophers, he ignored it. For him hypotheses were but probable at best; for "as in Astronomy those hypotheses though never so strange are best esteemed which best do salve apparencies; so surely in Philosophy those principles (though seeming monstrous) may with advantage be embraced, which best confirm experiment, and afford the readiest reason of observation" (*K*, 2:90). Not for him the long debates of the age as to which hypotheses, theories, or principles were *true;* nor, one feels, did he care overmuch for a discussion of precisely how one determines the "fit" of observations to physical principles. His was, in effect, a purely commonsense approach, a judgment rather than a scientific investigation, a weighing of the probable rather than a search for the absolute. This leaves him outside all philosophical debate, most scientific debate, and most medical debate. Just as he read Descartes but only remarked on his explanations of magnetism (as he did also with Kenelm Digby's *Two Treatises*), so he recounted some of Paracelsus's remarks about natural phenomena but never commented on his physiological or chemical views. Although he enjoyed Athanasius Kircher's remarks on magnetism, again he said nothing of his mystic views. Browne seems to have ignored contemporary mystic Helmontianism, just as he did contemporary mechanism. Nor had he anything to say about debates over medical doctrine, being happily content to remain a medical humanist, while adopting some newer remedies. In the end it was fact that Browne found fascinating, not theory, unless the theory was simply explanative of known fact. Once again, his was the mind of the collector, not of the synthesizer, and he was well content to gather facts for others like Ray or Merret to make use of, without wishing to offer any original conclusions himself.

To recapitulate, it must be emphasized that Browne's interests were shared by many members of the Royal Society, even when the interests of the latter were wider than those of Browne. His account of a thunderstorm at Norwich in 1665 (*K, 3:239*) or that of a "darke thick Miste" seen in 1674 (*K, 3:240*) is very like many accounts of such phenomena published at the time in the *Philosophical Transactions,* but with the subtle difference that Browne was as much interested in language as in observation, and easily widened his comments from immediate observation to theological considerations. (For example, no sooner has he described the mist he had seen A.D. 1674, than he discusses the first mist after Creation as described in Genesis, and also the mists observable, he claims, in animal corpses.) In this he differs both from the fellows of the Royal Society and from the country gentlemen, apothecaries, and clergymen who wrote to the society through its secretary over the years, more or less persistently, imparting information on natural history of the most various kinds, which was welcome to the society, although not central to its interests. If these men are rightly regarded as virtuosos, then so too is Browne, remembering that it was only at the end of his long life that this term acquired any pejorative connotation.

The term *virtuoso* is, however, for us a purely historical one, and of uncertain meaning. A better term is *natural historian,* and perhaps better still *naturalist,* which was indeed the seventeenth century's preferred term, and which so well fits Thomas Browne. For throughout his life he had a truly passionate interest in nature, preferably that open to his own observation. Scripture to him was incomplete without a characterization of the natural phenomena, animals, and plants mentioned in it. Even advice in *Christian Morals* led its author directly to reflections upon the natural world, and *Religio Medici* is filled with references to the opinions and experiments of astronomers, chemists, and natural philosophers. For Browne, literary, religious, ethical, human, and theological themes were inextricably mixed with natural phenomena. Inevitably, then, he had no sympathy whatsoever for the mechanical, coldly rational attitude of the new science of the seventeenth century, which firmly divorced theology and natural philosophy, and appeared to separate man from nature. To Browne, man was the measure of all things. It was with the eye of a humanist that he viewed both knowledge of nature and knowledge of books, and he reveled in both kinds of knowledge, which he enjoyed collecting for its own sake.